DOLLS' HOUSE DETAILS

DOLLS' HOUSE DETAILS

Over 500 craft projects in 1/12 scale

Kath Dalmeny

David & Charles

For my father, who has always said that the
Dalmeny name should be in print

ACKNOWLEDGEMENTS

I would like to thank the following people for their contributions to the creation of this book.

My friend and partner Joe Short, for constant love and support, expert stair-making, and for remaining calm through thick and thin.

The marvellous Doreen and Sue at Katy Sue Dolls (see Dolls in the Suppliers list on page 172), who were so good-humoured and understanding about last-minute requests. Special thanks, too, to Joyce Davison for creating the beautiful knitwear. The splendid Joanna Westbrook at Heritage Dolls (see Dolls in the Suppliers list on page 172), who never said no to anything, and responded so promptly on every occasion. The amazing Diane Harfield, lover of Tolkien and maker of trees (see Trees and Foliage in the Suppliers list on page 172). And Tony Wilson, for kindly assisting in tree delivery. Jane Newman and Carole Hilbert (see Furniture in the Suppliers list on page 172), whose beautiful furniture brought such style to the photographs, and Margaret Davies (see Dolls in the Suppliers list on page 172), who trusted me with her special dolls.

Lin Clements and Maggie Aldred, for expertly pulling everything together and crafting a heap of notes and diagrams into a book.

Frances Kelly for providing the impetus and expertise to get things done, Jenny Rodwell, for all the sympathetic phone calls and Liz and Martha Smith, for their shared love of all things small. Jane, Simon and Nicole, for their expert advice and professional contributions to the pottery.

My grandfather, Keith Venner, for making the dolls' house which started all this off.

SCRABBLE® is a registered trademark of
J. W. Spear & Sons PLC, Leicester LE3 2WT, England

A DAVID & CHARLES BOOK

First published in the UK in 2000
First published in paperback 2002

ISBN 0 7153 1367 3

Photography by Jon Stewart and Alan Duns
Styling by Kath Dalmeny and Joe Short
Book design by Maggie Aldred
Printed in Spain by Edelvives
for David & Charles
Brunel House   Newton Abbot   Devon

Contents

INTRODUCTION	6
MAKING THE DETAILS	8
TOYS AND GAMES	12
The Edwardian Nursery	14
Board Games and Jigsaws	21
Outdoor Games	24
Bar Games	27
WINING AND DINING	30
A Georgian Banquet	32
An Edwardian Picnic	35
Fast Food	39
A Tudor Meal	42
IN THE KITCHEN	46
The Manor House Kitchen	48
In the Larder	51
Baking Days	57
Kitchen Utensils and Equipment	61
LEISURE ACTIVITIES	64
Sports Equipment	66
The Music Enthusiast	70
The Carpenter's Workshop	74
The Sewing Room	79
THE DECORATOR	84
Home Improvements	86
Dolls' House DIY	89
Flooring	93
Curtains, Blinds and Textiles	99
THE COLLECTOR	102
The Victorian Explorer	104
Grandpa's Clock Collection	108
Grandma's Ornaments	114
Collector's Items	117
FLOWERS AND PLANTS	120
The Flower Seller	122
An Autumn Wedding	127
Topiary	130
In the Conservatory	133
THE ARTIST'S WORKSHOP	138
The Parisian Artist	140
The Eighteenth-century Musician	143
The Illustrator's Studio	146
The Potter's Studio	150
CELEBRATIONS	154
A 1950s Birthday Party	156
Christmas Eve	159
A Garden Party Barbecue	163
Hallowe'en Trick or Treat	167
Suppliers	172
Index	173

INTRODUCTION

When the front of a dolls' house swings open, there is a thrill of pleasure as the wonderful miniature contents are revealed. Each dolls' house or miniature shop is a unique collection of treasured objects, reflecting the life, tastes and interests of its proud owner. There is endless fascination in the arrangement and re-arrangement of the miniature pieces. And what fun it is to find just the right object to make a scene complete – a tiny teddy bear sitting on a patchwork quilt, a laden fruit stand brightening up a bare sideboard, or a birthday cake and decorations bringing celebration to the heart of the house.

Dolls' House Details is a book brimming with suggestions, instructions and templates for hundreds of projects to make as special finishing touches for your own dolls' house. The book focuses on all the details of everyday life – the pots, pans, food, toys, games, tools, flowers, clocks and ornaments to be found in every busy home. But it also takes a look at more unusual objects to bring character to your miniature scenes – such as all the bread, cakes and equipment needed for a baking day, as pictured here. There are exciting fireworks for an autumn evening, a darts board for the wall of a bar, a drawing board for an artist's studio, even a bottle of Champagne to make a 1/12th-scale party go with a real swing!

All of the projects in the book are 1/12th-scale – one inch to one foot – which is a standard scale for most dolls' house collectors. The projects have been designed to use the most basic and widely available of materials, to ensure that you will get the most from the designs. Scraps of cardboard, wood strip and coloured writing papers feature in many of the projects. Sometimes these are transformed into other household materials such as copper, brass and tin, with the addition of paint and varnish. Ready-made mouldings are also used, to give pieces a professional decorative finish.

Maybe you're decorating a Georgian manor, seeking out objects to grace a Tudor hall, kitting out a twentieth-century apartment, designing a Victorian town house, or adding the finishing touches to an Edwardian nursery. Whatever the period or style of your collection, there will be something in this book to brighten up a dull corner, to add colour, realism or a touch of humour to a room set-up, and to bring character to your dolls' house.

MAKING THE DETAILS

All of the dolls' house details in this book have clear descriptions of what is needed and exactly how each piece is made. Some of the projects share similar techniques, such as the use of templates, and these are briefly described at the start of each section in Working Notes. There are some techniques and working practices that are common to all the projects and these are described in more detail here.

This chapter also includes the use of the kinds of tools and materials you will already have around the house or may have stored for many years knowing they would come in useful one day.

PREPARING THE WORK SPACE

The ideal situation is to have a dedicated work space on which you can lay out your tools and materials, readily to hand. Attention to the following points should pay dividends.

• Use a cutting mat to protect the work surface.

• Keep a waste bin near at hand so that you can easily sweep trimmings from the work top and keep your work space clear. Otherwise, you may find yourself spending a lot of time searching amongst sawdust and paper clippings for a dropped bead or component.

• Tool boxes with small compartments are very useful for sorting and storing small items. Glass screw-top jars are useful for larger collections of objects, since the contents are visible through the side. Large plastic ice-cream tubs are good containers for scraps of felt, offcuts of wood, or pens and pencils.

• Good lighting is essential, with a lamp that you can position over your work being the most useful.

• You may spend a long time bent over a tiny project, so make sure you are using a comfortable chair that supports your lower back.

• Take regular breaks to give your eyes a chance to focus on something more than a foot away from your face. If you need extra magnification to work on small projects, invest in a free-standing magnifying glass, available from craft catalogues.

SAFETY

Whatever material you are using, and especially when working with glues, bake-to-harden clays and paints, always start by reading the manufacturer's instructions for guidance on how the material should be used.

• Store solvents, spray cans (such as spray glue and spray paint) and knives beyond the reach of children.

• Take extra care when using a scalpel, or when using a sharp knife or chisel to whittle objects. Always make the cutting strokes away from your hands and body. Change or sharpen the blade frequently and remember that blunt blades can slip more easily.

• If you choose to use real foodstuffs – herbs, seeds, grasses, etc – to put into the dolls' house kitchen, make sure that they are sealed in varnish, that they are not poisonous, or that any child playing with the dolls' house understands that they are not for consumption.

SCALING TIPS

The projects in this book are all designed for a $1/12$th scale collection, that is, every foot in length of the full-size item is represented in the miniature item by one inch. If you are re-creating an object in miniature take one measurement, such as the height, from the original. Divide that by twelve, and you will get the height your object should appear in $1/12$th scale.

USING A PHOTOCOPIER TO REDUCE DESIGNS: Some of the projects mention the use of a photocopier to reduce printed items to a smaller scale. It is sometimes difficult to guess the exact percentage to use. With a pocket calculator and a simple equation you can work this out in the following way:

• Choose one measurement of the original design, such as the height or width, then work out how big you would like that measurement to be in the final design.

• On a calculator, type in the following equation: (Desired size) ÷ (original size) x 100. This will give you a percentage.

• Now simply put the original design on the photocopier and type in this percentage from your calculation, and copy.

Although photocopiers are very useful for reducing designs or text, most cannot reduce to less than 50% of the original in one go, so you may have to reduce several times. For example, the newspaper on page 29 was reduced to $1/12$th scale by placing the paper in a photocopier and reducing it to 54% of its original size. This new copy was then placed in the photocopier and further reduced to 54%. This procedure was repeated four times to reach a $1/12$th scale reproduction.

It is a good idea when you're calculating the size of your miniature object to make a rough guess at the finished size before making your accurate calculation. Then if your calculation and your guess differ wildly, you can look for problems with your measurements before cutting materials.

USING THE TEMPLATES

Full-size templates are provided throughout the book. To use them trace or photocopy them onto paper and cut them out. Then draw round the templates on the material described and cut out using an appropriate tool. Some of the templates can be photocopied directly onto thin card, ready for scoring and gluing. For these templates, the folding lines are marked outside the edge of the template, so they won't show up on a finished piece. Dotted lines show the position of folds unless otherwise stated. When scoring fold lines on card or cardboard, place a metal ruler along the dotted line and run a knife gently along the line, cutting only a little way into the card or cardboard – don't go all the way through.

The projects and templates can be photo-

Some of the tools and materials you may find useful when making dolls' house details

copied and reproduced for private use. It is, however, illegal to use them for commercial purposes without the written consent (license) of the author.

CUTTING TOOLS

Keep some scissors exclusively for paper and some exclusively for fabric projects and thread because paper quickly blunts sharp scissors, making them useless for fabric. A craft knife with multiple blades is useful for paper and card projects. For very fine cutting, a scalpel is the best tool, as it has a very sharp flexible blade. For thicker materials, use a Stanley knife. A small-toothed saw is useful for cutting lengths of wood strip. When scoring or cutting materials in a straight line with a knife, cut against the side of a metal ruler.

GLUES AND GLUING

PVA glue, sold as wood and paper glue, is suitable for most projects in this book. Super Glue (the trade name for an instant, impact adhesive) is sometimes used for larger projects. Epoxy glue is also appropriate for wood projects.

Leave newly glued objects to dry thoroughly before proceeding to the next stage. With Super Glue or thin PVA glue on paper this may take only a minute or so. For wooden projects, leave for at least twenty minutes. Paperclips, bulldog clips, clamps or a vice are useful to hold pieces together whilst drying. A gadget called 'Helping Hands' is invaluable – a heavy base with two adjustable arms holding crocodile clips (see photograph page 9).

When gluing a number of small pieces together, draw out a gluing grid on a piece of paper. This might be just a few parallel lines to aid measurement, or it might be a sketch of the finished object. Assemble your pieces using the lines on the gluing grid as guides. Some gluing guides like this are provided within the book and are reproduced actual size.

PAINTS AND PAINTING

Acrylic paint is used widely throughout the projects when a paint finish is required as it is suitable for colouring wood and for paper projects. Once dry, acrylics can be varnished for a shiny finish. When using acrylic paint on polymer clay or shiny objects, add a little PVA glue to the paint as this will help it stick to the surface without affecting the colour.

Metallic paints are excellent for adding decorative details, or for painting onto card shapes to mimic brass, copper, silver or gold. Dedicate one of your paint brushes to metallic paint, as it will soon become very dirty. Always wash brushes directly after use.

USING WOOD

The projects in this book have been designed to use thicknesses of wood strip and simple mouldings available in DIY stores, for the minimum of cutting and sanding. For the smallest shaped objects, balsa wood is useful as it is very easy to cut. For specialist woods refer to Suppliers on page 172. Dowel, kebab sticks, cocktail sticks, small twigs and pine needles are used in many of the projects.

DRILLING HOLES IN WOOD: When drilling holes in a small piece of wood make the holes before cutting out the piece, as this will help prevent splitting. Tape the wood to a larger piece of scrap wood to hold it secure whilst drilling, and to protect your work surface. Neaten cut edges with fine sandpaper.

CARVING WOOD: Some projects need to be whittled into points or domes, such as the cricket bat on page 68. To do this, hold the wood or stick firmly and using a sharp knife, shave off layers of wood to start the shaping. Turn the piece in your hand between cuts to keep the shaping even, gradually cutting away the wood until the desired shape is achieved. For safety, always make cutting strokes outwards, away from your hands and body.

USING CARD, CARDBOARD
AND PAPER

It is a good idea to keep a collection of different colours and weights (thicknesses) of card,

TIP

Experiment with different paint effects, for example, a tiny piece of sponge dipped in paint is useful for making a realistic shade of colour across the tops of polymer clay loaves and pies.

cardboard and paper. Cardboard from cereal packets and card from greetings cards can be covered with a commercial paper, such as brick-effect, wood-effect, leather-effect, or silver, for use in the projects. Coloured writing papers are good for small boxes, plant leaves and flowers, and for books and music.

Good quality writing paper is the ideal weight for paper projects, such as those featured In the Conservatory (page 133). It folds cleanly, has even colour and tone, and keeps its shape even when there are tiny points or curls in the piece. It is a good idea to wash your hands before making a paper project as grease marks show up clearly on absorbent surfaces.

FOLDING PAPER OR CARD: To fold paper or card neatly score it first. Hold a metal ruler along the fold line (indicated on templates by a dotted line) and run a knife or blade of a pair of scissors gently along the line. Take care *not* to go all the way through the card or paper.

CUTTING PAPER: When cutting small paper shapes, hold the paper down on a clean cutting surface. Put your finger on the shape, close to the cutting line. Use a sharp scalpel and a smooth, confident stroke to cut away the excess paper. For the smallest of cuts, especially on internal curves or where the paper edge tends to crumple, you can stab the point of the knife into the paper at intervals around the curve. Treat yourself to a new blade quite frequently – this will make a real difference in keeping your shapes neat.

USING POLYMER CLAY

Small details and particularly food projects throughout the book are made from polymer clay, which is widely available under the brand names of Fimo, Sculpey, Premo and Formello. Fimo and Sculpey were used in this book. Fimo is more sculptural and a little harder to work than Sculpey, which is more malleable and available in a larger colour range. Air-drying clay can also be used for modelling, although it

is more difficult to form into small details.

To use polymer clay, roll a lump between your hands to soften it up ready for working. When modelling is finished, the pieces should be baked to harden following the manufacturer's instructions. In projects where an item is prepared on a wooden board or on cardboard, you can bake the whole project on its board as long as the piece doesn't contain other materials such as glue or paint.

DECORATING AND COLOURING POLYMER CLAY: Many items made from polymer clay can be made to look much more like the real thing if a little time is taken to decorate the surface of the clay. This can be done in various ways – see Surface Decoration of Polymer Clay Items on page 151. Experiment with different tools and materials for creating textures and shapes in clay, for example, the point of a knife or cocktail stick is good for a stippled texture.

You could use raw clay colours for your pieces but if you prefer a finished look then choose a coloured clay. Finished models can be painted – put PVA glue into the paint to help it stick to the surface. To mimic a glaze or to make a piece look wet, finish with varnish.

WIRE

Flexible craft wire is excellent for creating small metal objects such as tongs, hanging baskets and bird cages. Small lengths of wire can be cut from a paperclip with pliers.

BEADS, BUTTONS AND EARRING FITTINGS

Look out for beads and buttons that remind you of miniature vases, pots, plates, bowls, balls, ornaments, etc. These can be painted or, with simple additions, transformed into a household object.

READY-MADE COMPONENTS

Some dolls' house catalogues feature miniature brass lock plates, key plates, hinges, castors, etc, which can add a really professional finish to your project – see Suppliers on page 172.

TIP

Textiles are a rich source of texture, colour and style for a room and some of the projects use fabrics to great effect. Look out for scraps of lightweight fabrics with small floral or repeat patterns that will suit $^1/_{12}$th scale. Sections cut from fabrics with larger patterns are also appropriate.

TOYS AND GAMES

This chapter features a wide range of fun toys and games – from simple classics that could be found in almost any nursery to popular, more modern board games. The projects are perennial favourites and are very versatile, as most of them have a long history and so would be equally at home in other settings such as Victorian and contemporary scenes.

The Edwardian Nursery

The toys in this nursery are simple classics which have stood the test of time, such as a pull-along train, sailing boat, rag doll, rocking horse and, of course, a teddy bear. Traditional toys like these are very effective at creating the atmosphere of a child's room and small toys could also be used in other room settings to indicate the, often-untidy, presence of children in the dolls' house family.

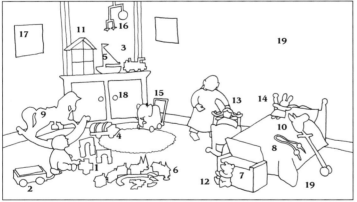

PROJECTS KEY

1 building blocks
2 pull-along building blocks box
3 pull-along train
4 lorry
5 sailing boat
6 tiny houses, trees and road
7 toy chest
8 skipping rope
9 rocking horse
10 hobby horse
11 dolls' house
12 teddy bear
13 rag doll
14 rag doll rabbit
15 elephant on wheels
16 mobile
17 pictures (see pages 118–119)
18 door knobs (see page 87)
19 wallpaper and carpet
   (see page 87)

WORKING NOTES: Many of the toys are made from pieces of pine dowel or pine strip. Wooden kebab sticks are used for making narrow poles and handles. For gluing wood use PVA wood glue (also useful for the card projects), Super Glue or other contact adhesive. For a stained wood appearance use a commercial wood stain, or colour the wood with a felt-tip pen. For an opaque finish use acrylic paint. You can seal and finish the colour with any clear varnish, although it's best to use an oil-based varnish on top of water-based paints to avoid smudging.

In projects for which templates are provided, trace or photocopy the template onto paper, cut it out, draw around it on the material described and then cut it out using an appropriate tool. Dotted lines on templates show fold lines, except for the mobile where it indicates that the hanging thread can be of variable length.

PULL-ALONG BUILDING BLOCKS BOX AND BLOCKS

BOX: The box is made from $^3/_{16}$in thick pine strip. For a box to fit twelve $^5/_{16}$in cubes cut the following from the pine strip: two sides $1^9/_{16}$in x $^3/_{16}$in; two ends $1^1/_{16}$in x $^3/_{16}$in and one base $1^9/_{16}$in x $1^3/_{16}$in. Shave the sides and end pieces to $^1/_{16}$in thick. Glue the pieces together as shown in the diagram and then glue on four circular wooden beads as wheels. The pull-along fitting is the loop of a dressmaker's skirt fastener glued to the base. Attach thread and a bead pull to finish.

BLOCKS: The building blocks are colourful wooden beads, some strewn on the floor, others stuck together as constructions. The arches are offcuts of $^3/_{16}$in thick pine strip x $1^3/_{16}$ x $^7/_{16}$in. Cut out a semicircle using a coping saw and neaten with a sharp knife. Finish with paint and varnish.

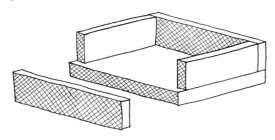

Pull-along building blocks box assembly

PULL-ALONG TRAIN

The train is made from the following pieces: the base is a rectangle of pine strip $^3/_{16}$in thick x $^1/_2$in wide x $1^3/_4$in; the boiler is a 1in length of 10mm diameter dowel; the six wheels are $^3/_{16}$in lengths of 10mm diameter dowel; the cab is a $^5/_8$in length of $^1/_2$in square-section pine strip. For a shaped cab, make two parallel cuts $^5/_{16}$in deep in the back of the cab piece. Carve out the wood between the cuts using a craft knife. Alternatively you could simply paint this detail onto the side of the cab.

Glue the pieces together as shown in the diagram. With a bradawl make a hole in the top of the boiler and glue in a $^5/_{16}$in length of kebab stick. The boiler dome is made from the end of

a piece of 5mm diameter dowel carved into a dome shape. Cut the dome off $^3/_{16}$in in length and glue in place. If you prefer not to carve, glue a dried yellow split pea on top of the boiler instead. The pull-along fitting is the loop of a dressmaker's skirt fastener glued to the base. Attach thread and a bead pull to finish.

Pull-along train assembly

LORRY

BASE: The base is $^1/_8$in thick pine strip, $1^3/_{16}$in x $1^3/_{16}$in. Cut a quarter-circle length of pine into two pieces $1^3/_{16}$in long. Glue the pine strip and the pine quarter-section pieces together as shown in the diagram below, and glue a cardboard rectangle to the underside of the lorry to strengthen the join. Add a tiny strip of wood along the front of the cab for a bumper. Finish by painting and then varnishing.

WHEELS: These are flat, circular wooden beads glued to the side of the lorry. Alternatively you could use 1in axles made from kebab sticks. Push the beads onto the ends of the axles and paint, then glue the lorry on top. The load can be anything you like – this one is twig 'logs', held in place by lengths of chain cut from a toy necklace and painted black.

TIP

Some of the building blocks are made from wooden beads. For a perfect finish you may prefer to fill the bead holes with air-drying clay and when dry paint it to match.

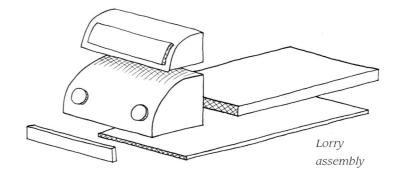

Lorry assembly

SAILING BOAT

BOAT: Take a 1³/₈in length of ⁵/₈in square-section pine strip for the hull and using a sharp knife, and leaving one edge of the strip flat, whittle it into a point at one end and a shallow curve at the other (use the photograph on page 12 as a guide). Use a bradawl to make a hole for the mast. Cut a 1³/₄in length of kebab stick, glue it into the hole and leave to dry. Add a 1¹/₁₆in length of kebab stick as a boom, gluing the end near the bottom of the mast. It won't be very secure until the sail is in place, so lay the boat to one side for the moment.

SAIL: Using the sail template, cut a sail from fine fabric – the dotted line shows where to fold and sew a hem. For very fine fabrics such as muslin use two layers of muslin with an extra line of stitching around the edge to prevent fraying. Attach thread to each corner of the sail and bind to the mast or boom (see photograph on page 12), then secure the ends with glue. Cut the flag from a tiny triangle of coloured paper and glue to the top of the mast.

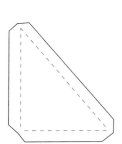

Sailing boat sail template

TINY HOUSES, TREES AND ROAD

HOUSE: The body of each house is made from ³/₁₆in thick pine strip x ⁵/₈in x ⁵/₁₆in. The roof is a triangular wedge of pine strip ⁵/₈in long, stuck on top of the house body. The chimney is a tiny scrap of pine strip with the bottom trimmed into an angle and glued in place. Draw on doors and windows with a pencil, then paint the details.

TREES: Use a wooden bead with a ⁵/₁₆in diameter for the base of a pine tree and push a tiny length of kebab stick into the bead's hole for the trunk. The tops of the trees are ⁹/₁₆in lengths of 10mm diameter dowel, carved into a point. Use a bradawl to make a hole in the base of the tree, put glue in the hole then push in the end of the kebab-stick trunk. Finish with paint and varnish.

ROAD: Photocopy the road sections templates given here onto thin card, colour them with acrylic paints and then carefully cut them out.

Road sections templates

TOY CHEST

Cut the following pieces of ³/₁₆in thick pine strip: one base 1³/₁₆in x 2in; one front and one back 1in x 2in each; two sides 1³/₁₆in x 1³/₁₆in and one lid 1³/₁₆in x 2in. Use sandpaper to round off one long edge of the lid. If you want to stain the box it is easiest to do so now before assembly. Glue all the pieces together except the lid. If you want to paint the chest, it is easiest to do so now before attaching the lid.

Place the toy chest lid in position on top of the box with the sanded edge facing downwards. This is the hinge edge. The hinges are made from two dressmaking pins pushed in through the sides of the box and into the edge of the lid. Use a hammer to lightly tap the hinges into place.

SKIPPING ROPE

The rope is a length of thin string with the ends glued inside two spherical wooden beads. The handles are ⁵/₈in lengths of kebab stick, rounded at each end with sandpaper, then glued and pushed into the beads.

ROCKING HORSE

Using the rocking horse templates on page 17 and ³/₁₆in thick wood, cut the following with a coping saw or electric jig-saw: two of each leg shape, two rockers, one rocker plate and one body. The body can either be made by cutting three pieces from the ³/₁₆in thick wood (gluing them together before sanding) or from one piece of ¹/₂in thick wood. Using sandpaper, smooth off all cut edges of the pieces. Where cutting has been inaccurate, make pieces match up by clamping them together in a vice and sanding them at the same time.

Use Super Glue to stick the legs to the body and leave to dry. Stick the rockers to the insides of the hoofs, and the rocker plate to the middle of rockers. Using the ear template cut two ears from card and glue them to the head.

This horse was painted light grey, the dapple marks being printed with the end of a tubular bead dipped into white and dark grey paint. When the paint is dry, finish with varnish. If you use an attractive wood such as walnut, simply finish with fine sandpaper and then varnish.

Use the saddle template to cut a leather saddle and glue it in place. Use a bradawl or drill to make a tail hole in the rear of the horse. Cut about eighteen 2³/₄in strands of yarn for a tail. Bind them together at one end with thread and dip the end in PVA glue. When nearly dry, mould into a narrow clump, push into the tail hole and leave to dry. With thread, bind the loose ends of the tail together and stick the bundle to the insides of the runners (to hold it in a neat shape), trimming off the excess.

Make the bridle from lengths of satin ribbon ¹/₁₆in wide, gluing them to the horse's face. The bit rings are cut from a toy necklace and glued to the ends of a ribbon rein. Make stirrups from bent paper-clips and hang them in place on lengths of ribbon. Glue on black glass-bead eyes and finish by gluing lengths of yarn across the neck and head for a mane.

HOBBY HORSE

Begin by gluing two flat, circular wooden beads to the end of a 3⁵/₈in length of kebab stick. Trim a second piece of kebab stick to 1⁵/₁₆in long, thinning it down and gluing it as a crossbar to the longer stick.

Using the head and ear templates cut two head and two ear pieces from brown felt. Match up the head pieces and stitch around the edge, leaving the neck open and then fill with a little toy stuffing. Using coloured yarn, make stitches over the seam along the back and top of the head. Fold each ear piece in half and sew the bottom edge to the head. Using black thread sew on two black beads as eyes and make a few stitches for nostrils. Glue a length of the ribbon around the nose and

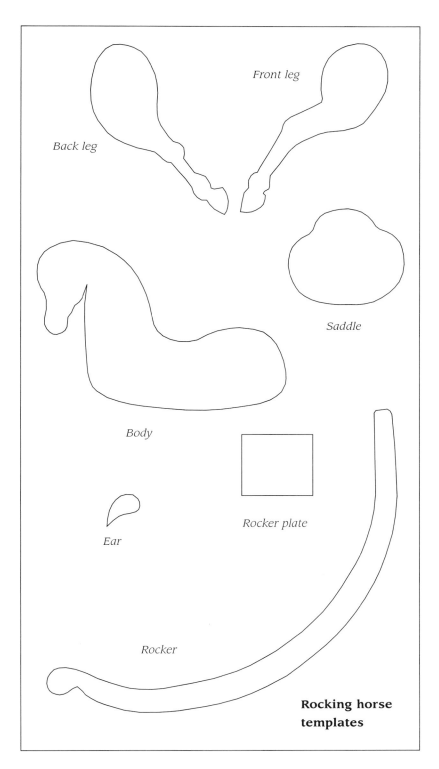

Back leg

Front leg

Saddle

Body

Ear

Rocker plate

Rocker

Rocking horse templates

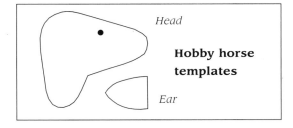

Head

Hobby horse templates

Ear

another piece around the back of the head. Glue two rings cut from a toy necklace to the end of a 3⁵/₈in piece of ribbon for a rein and glue the rings to each side of the horse's head. To finish, put glue on the end of the long stick and push it up inside the hobby horse's head.

DOLLS' HOUSE

Using the card parts templates given below, cut the pieces from 1/8in thick card. Glue them together using the diagram, right, as a guide. Photocopy the interior, central interior wall, exterior, roof and floor templates onto thin card, colour them with water-colour paints or pencil crayons and cut them out. Glue the interior wall pieces together, back to back.

Fold up the side walls and floor of the interior piece and glue it inside the cardboard shell. With tiny dabs of glue, position the interior wall in the centre of the house, slots facing outwards. Push the floor pieces into the house, matching up the slots on the interior wall with the slots in the floor pieces. Hold them in place with tiny dabs of glue. Cover the front and sides of the house with the exterior piece, and the roof with the roof piece.

Tiny furniture can be made from polymer

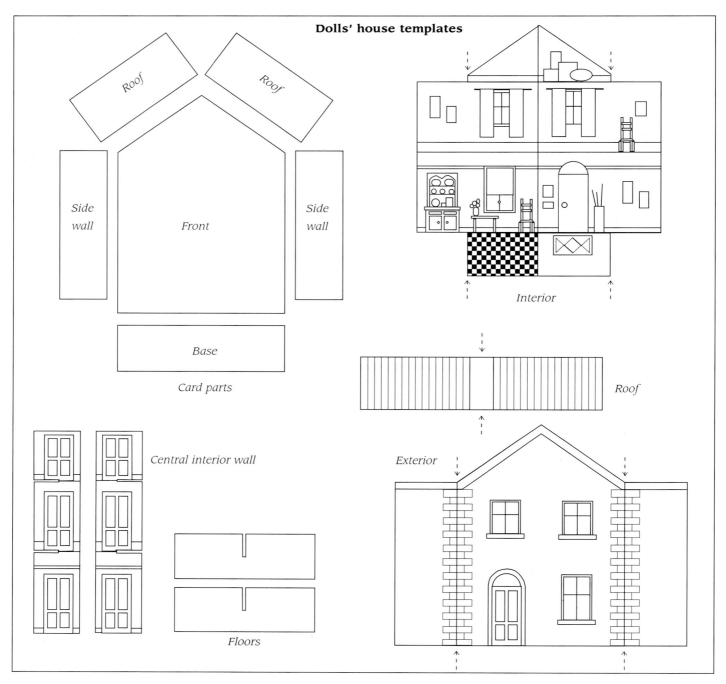

Dolls' house templates

Roof

Roof

Side wall

Front

Side wall

Base

Card parts

Central interior wall

Floors

Interior

Roof

Exterior

Assembling the card parts of the dolls' house

clay or from tiny offcuts of wood coloured with felt-tip pens. Bake the clay according to the manufacturer's instructions.

TEDDY BEAR

Using the teddy bear templates provided here, cut one body, two arms, two legs and two ears from brown felt. Make up each piece in the same way: fold it in half and sew around the edge, enclosing stuffing (leave the ears unstuffed). Sew the limbs and ears in place on the bear's body, then use black thread to sew a nose, mouth and eyes.

RAG DOLL

RAG DOLL: Using the four rag doll templates cut one head, two arms and two legs from flesh-coloured felt, and one body from coloured felt. Make up each piece the same: fold it in half and sew around the edge, enclosing stuffing. Sew the finished pieces together, then use black thread to sew on eyes and a mouth.

SKIRT: To make a skirt, hem the edges of a piece of cotton (2in x 1in with $^1/_8$in hems) and join the narrow edges together to form a tube.

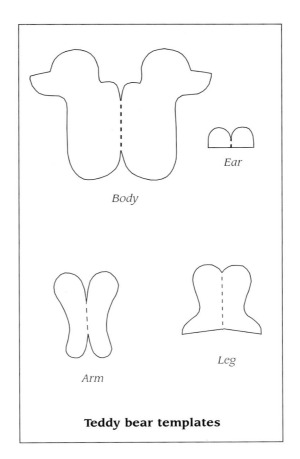

Teddy bear templates

Gather the long top edge with tiny stitches and attach the skirt to the body with a few stitches.
HAIR: To make the hair for the doll, sew the middles of six 2in lengths of yarn to the top of the head. Make plaits on either side and bind the ends with thread.

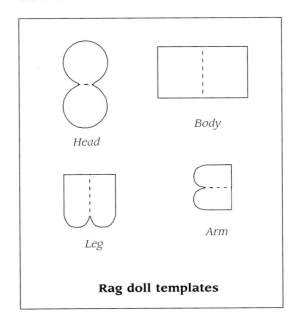

Rag doll templates

RAG DOLL RABBIT

Make the rabbit following the rag doll instructions on page 19, using brown felt for limbs and head. Instead of hair, cut two ears in brown felt from the ear template provided here and sew them in place.

Rag doll rabbit ear template

ELEPHANT ON WHEELS

ELEPHANT: Using the elephant templates below cut two body pieces, four legs and two ears from grey felt, and two tusks from white felt. Sew the body pieces together, enclosing stuffing. Fold each leg piece in half, sew around three sides and fill with stuffing, then sew the opening to the elephant. Fold each tusk in half, sew along the edge and sew into position. Sew on the ears and add black bead eyes.

The back cloth is a rectangle of coloured felt, 1^{11}/16in x ^{13}/16in. Decorate it with stitching in metallic thread and then glue in place.

TROLLEY: Use a 11^{3}/16in x ^{11}/16in piece of ^{3}/16in

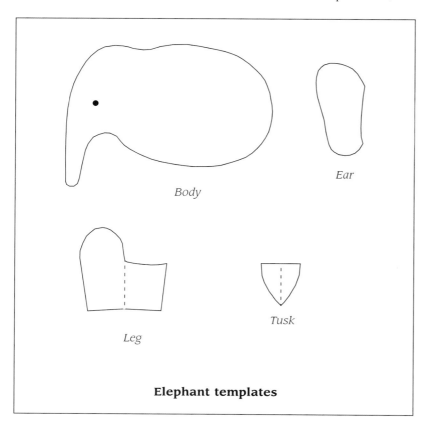

Body

Ear

Leg

Tusk

Elephant templates

thick pine strip for the trolley, painting and varnishing it. For wheels, paint flat, circular wooden beads silver and glue them to the trolley. Bend a piece of wire into a handle with extra at each end, and glue these ends to the underside of the trolley. Glue the elephant to the trolley.

MOBILE

Trace or photocopy the sun and seagulls templates onto white paper and cut them out. Colour the sun yellow on both sides using a felt-tip pen. Cut two crossbar strips from a kebab stick, trimmed to about ^{1}/16in thick – one 1in long, the other ^{13}/16in long. Cut strings of fine cord or button thread using the mobile layout diagram as a guide.

The mobile is a very delicate project and should therefore be glued together into a fixed position. On a piece of card, draw out the mobile layout in pencil, using the diagram as a guide. Lay out the crossbars and paper pieces on top of the drawing and put tiny dabs of glue on the sticks and each paper piece. Place lengths of cord into position, including a long hanging cord. Allow the glue to dry with the mobile lying flat, then gently lift it off to hang in the dolls' house.

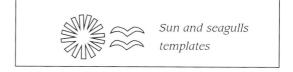

Sun and seagulls templates

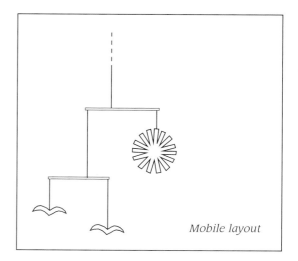

Mobile layout

Board Games and Jigsaws

Your dolls are sure to enjoy a quiet night in with friends, gathered around board games and a jigsaw. Some children's games have been played for centuries – backgammon may date from 3,000BC. Draughts and games like it are also very old, played in the days of the Egyptian Pharaohs. Manufactured games and jigsaws were originally educational tools in the seventeenth century and continue to evolve. Scrabble® was developed in 1931 as Criss Cross, based on crossword puzzles and anagrams.

PROJECTS KEY

1 backgammon
2 Scrabble®
3 snakes & ladders
4 draughts (checkers)
5 jigsaw
6 chess

WORKING NOTES: The board games and jigsaw are all made using the same basic techniques and simple materials, including variously coloured cardboard and paper, felt-tip pens or pencil crayons for colouring, a scalpel and metal ruler and polymer clay for making counters and dice (follow the manufacturer's instructions for baking). Detailed patterns are provided for copying or, ideally, photocopying onto paper. Colour them using the photograph on page 21 or your own full-size version of the game as a guide. Cards and other accessories can also be copied from the patterns provided. It's best to glue all these tiny pieces in place on the board to prevent them getting lost.

Follow these basic instructions for making Scrabble®, snakes & ladders, draughts (checkers) and chess. Cut a 2in square of card and paint it a dark colour or cover it with coloured textured paper – leather or vinyl-effect paper will give an authentic finish. Photocopy the particular board template onto paper (templates and card/paper colours accompany relevant project below). Colour details with felt-tip pens and glue it to the front of the board.

DICE

For games that need dice, cut tiny cubes approximately 3/16in square from wood and draw on spots with a very sharp pencil. For black dice, paint the wood black and add tiny spots in white paint.

BACKGAMMON

Start by cutting a 1⁵/8in x 2in rectangle of card. Photocopy the backgammon template onto cream paper and colour the triangles (see photograph on page 21). Cut out the rectangle

and glue it to the card. Frame with pine strips 3/16in wide x 1/16in thick. Before gluing them in place, stain the strips, the edges and the underside of the card board dark brown using wood stain or felt-tip pen. Make counters from light and dark brown polymer clay and bake. Make dice and a doubling cube, with numbers instead of spots, as described above.

SCRABBLE®

Photocopy the Scrabble board template onto mid green paper. Colour in the details as shown in the picture below. Photocopy the letters grid template onto cream card. With a metal ruler and a scalpel, use the cutting grid to help you cut out accurate squares. Glue the letters to the board as words. Glue other letters to counter stands made from 7/8in strips of grey cardboard, folded in half lengthways to stand up, with a tiny strip added along the front as a letter ledge.

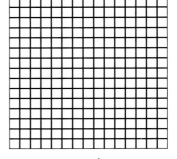

Scrabble board template

Letters grid template

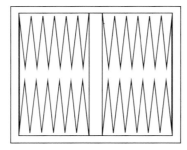

Backgammon board template

SNAKES & LADDERS

Photocopy the snakes & ladders board template onto pale green paper and colour in the details as shown in the photograph on page 21. Make counters from circles of green and red polymer clay and then bake. Make dice as described above.

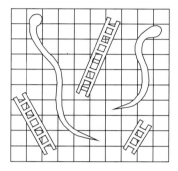

Snakes & ladders board template

DRAUGHTS (CHECKERS)

Photocopy the draughts (checkers) board template onto red paper. Roll out red polymer clay to ¹/₁₆in thick and using the narrow end of a pen tube as a 'pastry cutter', cut out twenty-four counters. When baked, paint twelve black.

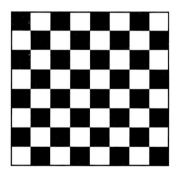

Draughts (Checkers) board template

JIGSAW

Photocopy the jigsaw template onto a Christmas card picture or a picture from a magazine by placing the template on the photocopier glass and feeding the picture through the machine. It will take a little experimentation to get the positioning right, so use rough copies of pictures for first attempts. Alternatively you could copy the design onto the picture with a fine pen (such as Rotring). Glue the puzzle onto card and cut it out around the outer edge. With a very fine scalpel, cut out a few pieces to strew around the jig-saw. If you have a second copy of the picture, you could make a jigsaw box from card and glue the picture to the top.

Jigsaw template

CHESS

Photocopy the draughts board template onto white card.

WHITE PIECES: Roll a sausage shape of white polymer clay, ¹/₁₆in thick and cut eight ⁵/₁₆in lengths. With the point of a cocktail stick, make marks in the sides and tops of the pieces to distinguish them, using a life-size set as a guide.

From the same sausage shape, cut eight ¹/₄in lengths for pawns. Roll tiny blobs of polymer clay and press them on top of the pawns. Bake to harden following the manufacturer's instructions.

BLACK PIECES: Make the pieces from black polymer clay. Or if you can't find black make a set in white and once hardened paint with black acrylic, with a little PVA in the glue to help it stick to the surface.

Outdoor Games

*T*he outdoor games featured in this scene are often associated with the affluent classes. Croquet, famed as the pursuit of ladies and gentlemen on the lawns of country houses, originated in the early thirteenth century as a French game called paille-maille *(pall mall), so it would be appropriate for dolls' houses of many centuries. Another ancient game, quoits, also entertained passengers on cruise-ships in the early twentieth century – the sailors twisting lengths of rope into the quoit loops. Because it is portable, boule would be a perfect choice for an outdoor scene such as a picnic in the park or a beach outing.*

PROJECTS KEY

1 croquet
2 croquet box
3 boule
4 skittles
5 quoits
6 bowl of strawberries
7 Champagne (see page 56)
8 tumblers (see page 165)
9 sandwiches (see page 38)
10 pigeon (see page 38)

WORKING NOTES: To use templates, trace or photocopy the template onto paper, cut it out, draw around it on the material described and cut it out using an appropriate tool. Dotted lines on templates show fold lines.

When drilling a hole in a small piece of wood, hold it firmly in a vice, or tape it to a larger waste piece of wood to keep it steady. Some of the handles in these projects need to be whittled into points or domes. Hold the stick firmly in one hand and using a sharp knife, shave off layers of wood to start the shaping. Turn the stick in your hand between cuts to keep the shaping even. Gradually cut away the wood until the desired shape is achieved. For safety, always make cutting strokes outwards, away from your hands and body. Always ensure the blade is sharp.

Objects made of polymer clay should be baked to harden following the manufacturer's instructions. PVA wood glue is suitable for all of the projects in this section.

CROQUET

CROQUET BALLS: These are made from $^3/8$in spherical wooden beads in green, yellow, red, blue and black. Fill the holes with air-drying clay and when dry, colour to match using acrylic paint.

CROQUET MALLET: Cut a 1in length of 10mm diameter dowel and use fine sandpaper to neaten the ends. With a 5mm drill bit, make a $^1/4$in deep hole midway in the side of the dowel. Cut a $2^3/4$in length of 5mm diameter dowel for the handle and whittle one end into a slight point. Put glue into the hole in the mallet head and push in the pointed end of the handle. With acrylic paint, make a coloured stripe around the top of the handle – one mallet to match each ball.

HOOPS: Each hoop is a $2^1/2$in length of plastic-coated wire, bent into shape. Make six for a British croquet set; nine for an American set.

SMALL MALLET: Cut a $^1/2$in length of 5mm diameter dowel for the head, and a $^3/4$in length of kebab stick for the handle. Assemble as for the croquet mallet above.

FINISHING POST: Cut a $1^5/8$in length of 5mm diameter dowel. Whittle one end into a point and the other into a dome. With acrylic paint, make stripes of green, yellow, red, blue and black (see photograph below).

CROQUET BOX

BOX: Cut the following pieces out of thick card: two sides each $3^1/2$in x $1^1/4$in; two ends each $1^1/4$in x $1^1/4$in and one base $1^3/8$in x $3^1/2$in. Glue the pieces together in a box shape, using brown paper tape to cover and strengthen joins. Moisten the glued side of the tape with water, position it on the box and smooth into place.

LID: Cut the following pieces out of thick card: one lid top $3^1/2$in x $1^3/8$in and one underside $1^1/4$in x $3^1/4$in. Glue the pieces together, then cover with brown paper tape (available from art shops).

Draw planks and wood-grain details with a pencil on the box and lid and finish with matt varnish. Alternatively you could cover the whole box with wood-effect paper.

HANDLES: Make two holes in each end of the box about $^3/4$in apart. For each handle, thread a $2^1/2$in length of string through the holes. Inside the box, tie each string end into a knot and trim off any excess.

BOULE

BOX AND LID: Using the box and lid templates, cut a box and lid from card. Cover both sides of the pieces with wood-effect paper, or draw in wood details using a pencil. Fold up each piece and glue the tabs in position.

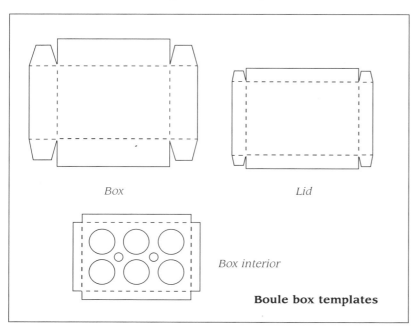

Box *Lid*

Box interior

Boule box templates

Cut two pieces of wood-effect paper each 1in x ¹/₄in. Hold the lid on top of the boule box and glue one piece of the paper to make a hinge between the pieces, then allow to dry. Open the box and glue the second piece of paper across the inside of the hinge. Glue on a lock plate (available from specialist dolls' house mail-order catalogues – see Suppliers on page 172).

Using the box interior template, cut an interior piece from blue card. Cut out the holes with a scalpel, then fold down the sides and put the piece inside the box.

BALLS: The box will hold six stainless steel ball-bearings (available from bicycle and motorbike shops), 8mm diameter, or you could make six balls of polymer clay, baked to harden and painted silver.

JACKS: Make two tiny balls from white polymer clay and bake to harden.

SKITTLES

Mould ten skittles and a ball from coloured polymer clay, then bake to harden following the manufacturer's instructions.

QUOITS

POST: Cut a 1in square of ¹/₄in thick wood for the base. Drill a 5mm diameter hole through the centre. Cut a 1¹/₂in length of 5mm diameter dowel and whittle one end into a slight point, then glue it into the base.

QUOITS: Cut a 5in length of string. Holding one end in each hand, twist the string clockwise until it begins to knot in the centre. Bring the string ends together and, without letting go, smooth the folded string together so that it becomes a single twisted strand. Still not letting go, put glue on the free ends and clip together until dry. Coil the twisted string into a circle and add more glue to join the ends, again clipping together until dry.

BOWL OF STRAWBERRIES

Shape tiny blobs of red polymer clay into strawberries and add green polymer clay leaves. Bake to harden then pile into a bowl (see bowls page 151).

Bar Games

The projects featured in this scene are classic games played in pubs and inns across the world. Dominoes are found in many different cultures, dating back to twelfth-century China. Darts was originally designed as training for archers in the Middle Ages. Cards are also a perennial favourite: the explorer Marco Polo may have introduced a Chinese cards game into Europe in the thirteenth century.

PROJECTS KEY

1 darts board and darts
2 card table
3 cards
4 pool cue and stand
5 pool balls, triangle and chalk
6 dominoes
7 solitaire
8 ashtray and cigar
9 newspaper
10 tankard (see page 44)
11 chess (see page 23)
12 backgammon (see page 22)
13 pictures (see pages 118–119)
14 grate (see pages 44–45)
15 pots (see page 151)
16 dried plants (see page 125)
17 carpet (see page 87)
18 furniture (see Suppliers, page 172)

WORKING NOTES: To use templates, trace or photocopy the template onto paper, cut it out, draw around it on the material described and cut it out using an appropriate tool.

When framing a piece of cardboard or wood, cut four pieces the same lengths as the sides of the piece. Shape the ends of each piece into a 45-degree angle and then glue the frame pieces in place. PVA glue is suitable for all the project in this section, unless otherwise stated. You can colour wooden projects using commercial wood stain, paint, or felt-tip pen. For projects in which polymer clay is used, bake the finished models to harden, following the manufacturer's instructions.

DARTS BOARD AND DARTS

BOARD: Photocopy the darts board template onto paper, glue it to cardboard then cut it out. With red and green felt-tip pens, colour the details (see photograph). Glue the darts board in the centre of a 2in square cut from a cork table-mat. Frame the cork with 1/8in thick strips of balsa wood, glued on.

SCOREBOARDS: Cut two scoreboards from sheets of 1/8in thick balsa each 1 1/8in x 2 1/8in. Frame with 1/8in thick strips of balsa, glued on. Cut rectangles of green card to fit inside each frame and glue them in place, then use white acrylic paint to add the scoring details. The chalk sticks are made from tiny sausages of white polymer clay, baked to harden.

DARTS: With pliers, cut a 3/8in length from a dressmaker's pin. Cover the cut end with a blob of polymer clay and mould into flight shapes. Bake to harden with the pin in place. Make holes in the darts board with a large needle, then gently glue a dart into each hole.

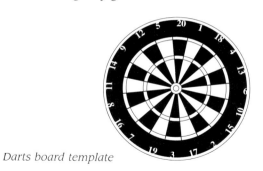

Darts board template

CARD TABLE

Cut a 2 1/4in square table top from 1/4in thick pine strip. Frame with pine strip 1/8in thick x 1/4in wide. Using the leg and crossbar templates, cut four legs from 1/8in thick pine strip, and two crossbars. Glue the legs together in pairs, with the tops and bases parallel. When dry, glue the legs to the table and add the crossbars, then paint or stain the wood. Cut a 2 1/4in square of green felt and glue it to the table top.

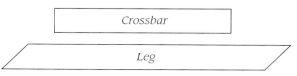

Crossbar

Leg

Card table templates

CARDS

Photocopy the cards template onto thin card, including the cutting grid. Use a red felt-tip pen to colour the details of the hearts and diamonds cards. With a metal ruler and a scalpel, use the cutting grid to cut accurate rectangles.

Lay out the cards in a game set-up, and glue each one in place on the table. For any card that is placed face down, add a rectangle of plain colour to the back with a felt-tip pen.

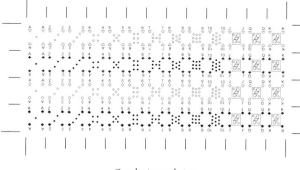

Cards templates

POOL CUE AND STAND

CUE: Cut a 4 1/2in length of kebab stick and with fine sandpaper, round off the handle and taper the other end. Use acrylic paint to colour the handle and to make a blue chalky tip. Add a stripe of black to edge each coloured area, and then a stripe of gold to finish (see photograph).

STAND: The base is a flat, circular wooden bead 1¹/2in in diameter. Cut a 3in length of kebab stick and glue it into the centre of the bead. The top of the stand is a second wooden bead, 1¹/4in in diameter. With a sharp knife, cut eight notches in the edge of the bead and then glue the bead near the top of the kebab stick. Paint the cue stand with acrylic paint. The cue clips are eight 'eyes' from dressmaker's hooks and eyes. Stick them on top of each notch with Super Glue.

POOL BALLS, TRIANGLE AND CHALK

BALLS: Roll sixteen balls of polymer clay – one in black, one in white and two in each of the following colours – yellow, red, green, purple, orange, pink and blue. Once baked, use acrylic paint to make the spot and number details, using a life-size set as a guide.

TRIANGLE: Assemble the pool balls (without the white cue ball) into a triangle. Measure the length of one of the sides of the triangle, then add ¹/8in. Cut three pieces of ³/16in thick pine strip to this length, slightly bevel the ends, then glue them together as shown in the diagram. Paint the triangle brown.

CHALK: Cut a cube of pale blue polymer clay and make a dent in the top. Bake to harden, then glue a strip of white paper around the chalk.

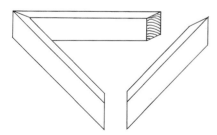

Assembly of pool triangle

DOMINOES

Cut thirty-six rectangles from black card each ¹/4in x ¹/8in. Use white acrylic paint and a very fine brush to paint spots on each, using a life-size set as a guide.

To make the box use the templates to cut

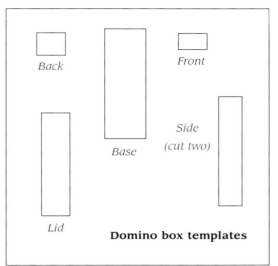

Back   Front

Base   Side (cut two)

Lid   **Domino box templates**

box pieces from ¹/16in thick balsa wood. Glue the pieces together as shown in the diagram.

SOLITARE

Photocopy or trace the solitaire board top template onto paper, glue it to thick card and then cut it out. Use a bradawl or sharp nail to make holes in the card in the positions marked.

Use the base template to cut a base piece from thick card. Glue the top board and base pieces together and then paint them brown. Glue a tiny bead in each hole (except the central one).

ASHTRAY AND CIGAR

The ashtray is made from brown polymer clay. The cigar is a short length of incense (joss) stick cut to size. The end is painted black, with glowing end details added in scarlet paint.

NEWSPAPER

The newspaper is reproduced by reducing the front page of a newspaper on a photocopier to its smallest setting and then reducing the small copy further until it is 2³/4in wide. Specifically this means putting the newspaper in a photocopier and reducing it to 54% of its original size. Then place this new copy on the photocopier and reduce it to 54%. Do this four times to reach a ¹/12th scale reproduction. Cut out the page and some extra blank pages and fold them together into a newspaper.

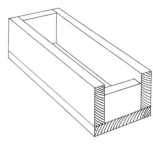

Assembly of dominoes box

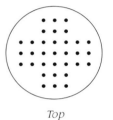

Top

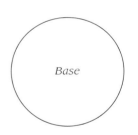

Base

Solitare board templates

WINING AND DINING

Food is a focal part of the life of a house – whether it be a formal banquet, fast-food snacks, or an evening meal by the fireside. In this chapter, a Georgian couple prepare for a sumptuous banquet, two Tudor huntsmen relax by the fireside with homely foodstuffs, while an Edwardian couple enjoy a picnic in the park. Bringing the food theme right up to date, there are hot-dogs, fish and chips and take-out pizzas – perfect for a night in front of the television.

A Georgian Banquet

The silverware in this banquet scene has been created very simply, using beads, buttons and craft wire – developed into a co-ordinated set by the addition of silver metallic paint. In Georgian times, ladies and gentlemen of the upper classes enjoyed the opportunity to entertain their guests in style, laying out the table with extravagant tableware. In houses of the nineteenth and twentieth centuries, these pieces would be family heirlooms – perhaps displayed in a cabinet to be brought out for use only on the most important occasions. For more highly decorative metallic plates, take a look at pages 117 and 118–119.

PROJECTS KEY

1 plates
2 place mats
3 cutlery
4 bowls
5 napkins
6 goblets
7 candlesticks and snuffer
8 place names
9 covered serving dish
10 fruit stand
11 cooked vegetables
12 oval serving dish
13 cheese
14 serving trolley
15 plant stand
16 basket design floor (see page 98)
17 fruit (see page 38)
18 plants (see page 135–136)
19 roast turkey (see page 50)
20 pictures (see pages 118–119)
21 dolls (see Suppliers, page 172)

WORKING NOTES: Many of the projects in this section are made from beads, buttons and jewellery fittings. When glued together and finished with metallic paint (such as Humbrol enamel), they can mimic metal items very effectively. Look out for oddments of chain, unusual beads, little bells and electrical components that bear some resemblance to other household objects. When using metallic paint, always wash your brush well soon after use, following the manufacturer's instructions.

Objects made of polymer clay should be baked to harden following the manufacturer's instructions.

To use templates, trace or photocopy the template onto paper, cut it out, draw around it on the material described and cut it out using an appropriate tool. PVA glue is suitable for all the projects.

PLATES

The plates are made from buttons, with small circles of cardboard glued over the holes. Paint the plates silver.

PLACE MATS

To make one place mat, cut a rectangle of fine cotton fabric 2¹/₂in x 1¹/₄in. Fold a ¹/₄in hem under around each side and sew around the edge to hold in place. Press flat with an iron.

CUTLERY

Copy the cutlery templates onto paper and glue to the back of silver card. Cut out the shapes and paint the backs silver. Slightly curve the heads of the forks and spoons.

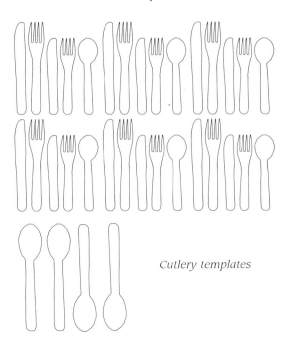

Cutlery templates

BOWLS

See page 151 for general instructions on making pots and bowls. Model bowls from polymer clay and when hardened paint them silver.

NAPKINS

Cut a small square of fine cotton fabric. Roll it up and push it through a small circular silver bead or earring fitting.

GOBLETS

The base of each goblet is a flat bead. Push a short dressmaker's pin up through the central hole and glue two beads onto the pin, as shown in the diagram. Glue a bell-shaped earring fitting on top. Once dry, drip more glue into the goblet to cover the end of the pin.

CANDLESTICKS AND SNUFFER

CANDLESTICK: The base of each candlestick is a flat bead. Push a short dressmaker's pin up through the central hole. Glue a bell-shaped earring fitting on top, with the pin poking up into the middle of the bell. Once dry, push a birthday-cake candle onto the pin.

SNUFFER: Glue a bell-shaped earring fitting to the end of a piece of craft wire. Bend the wire into a handle and glue a small silver bead on the end.

PLACE NAMES

Copy the place name templates onto thin card and cut them out. Fold each card in half and with a fine pen, write the names of the guests.

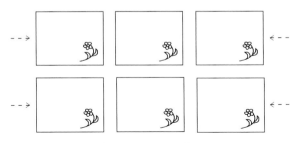

Place name templates

COVERED SERVING DISH

LID: The domed lid of the serving dish is made from one of the plastic components of a pendant light fitting. (Half of a plastic egg, e.g. a Kinder egg, would also be suitable.) Glue a bell-shaped earring fitting on top. Bend a piece of wire into a handle shape and glue the ends inside the earring fitting. Paint the cover silver.

PLATE RIM: Draw round the lid on cardboard. Draw another circle, about ¹/₄in bigger all round and cut out the shape.

PLATE BASE: Cut a second circle of cardboard, slightly larger than the inner circle of the rim and glue to the bottom of the rim piece. Paint the whole plate silver.

Making the goblet stem

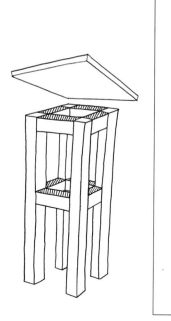

PLANT STAND

Using the three plant stand templates, cut the following from ⅛in thick wood – four legs, eight struts and one top. Glue them together as shown in the diagram. Use wood stain to colour the stand if desired (the same colour as used for the serving trolley below).

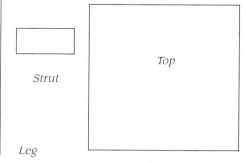

Strut

Top

Leg

Plant stand assembly

Plant stand templates

COOKED VEGETABLES

The vegetables shown are all made from polymer clay. For each type of vegetable, start by pressing a large blob of polymer clay into your chosen bowl, shaping it into a shallow mound. Individual vegetables are then made and piled on top of the mound. Remove the finished piece from its bowl to bake.

CARROTS: Roll out thin sausages of orange polymer clay and cut into slices.

SPROUTS: Roll balls of dark green and mark a cross on each with a knife.

PEAS: Roll out tiny balls of bright green.

SNOW PEAS: Press out a thin layer of green and use a knife to cut pod shapes.

OVAL SERVING DISH

Using the oval dish templates, cut rim and base pieces from cardboard. Cut them out, glue them together and when dry paint silver.

Oval serving dish templates

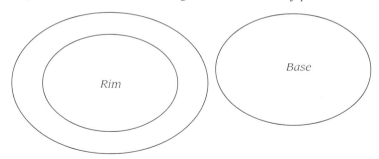

Rim

Base

FRUIT STAND

The fruit stand is made of two four-holed buttons – the top button slightly larger than the base button. Cut four 1¼in lengths of kebab stick and glue them into the holes in the base button, then glue the other ends into the top button. Paint the fruit stand silver.

CHEESE

The cheeses are all made from polymer clay and the following gives a guide to the colours and shapes.

EDAM: A wedge of bright yellow polymer clay, with a thin red rind.

GOAT'S CHEESE: A flattened ball of white, with a green herb leaf added on top.

BRIE: A wedge of pale yellow, with a white rind.

EMMENTAL: A wedge of yellow, with holes made with a cocktail stick.

CHEDDAR AND RED LEICESTER: Lumps of yellow or orange.

SERVING TROLLEY

UPRIGHTS: Cut four 2¾in lengths from ¼in square wood and use sandpaper to round the tops.

SHELVES: Cut two 3in x 1½in rectangles from ⅛in thick wood then cut a ⅛in square from each corner, as shown in the diagram. Glue the shelves and uprights together, with the uprights pushed into the corner notches in the shelves. Allow to dry thoroughly. Glue lengths of kebab stick along the edge of the shelves.

CASTORS: Push a 1/12th scale castor (available from dolls' house suppliers – see page 172) up into the base of each upright, or glue on four spherical beads to mimic wheels.

Use wood stain to colour the serving trolley, if desired, the same shade as the plant stand.

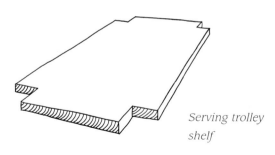

Serving trolley shelf

An Edwardian Picnic

*P*icnics have always been popular, whether they take place on a beach, in the park or simply in the dolls' house garden. It is also a setting ideally suited to a room box. Line the box with grass-effect paper (available from model and architec-

tural shops – see Suppliers, page 172) and with blue paper for the sky, then set to work on a spread to suit your chosen period. If you haven't got an outdoor setting, these objects could appear in the kitchen, with someone preparing the basket of goodies for a summer's outing or even in a child's bedroom at a play tea party. Take a look at Baking Days (page 57) for party food if you want a picnic for a special occasion.

PROJECTS KEY

1 kite
2 plates
3 picnic hamper
4 picnic blanket
5 pies, pasties
   and sausage rolls
6 fruit
7 buns, biscuits (cookies),
   shortbread and sandwiches
8 jug and cups
9 ginger beer
10 pigeons
11 railings (see page 88)
12 tree (see Suppliers, page 172)

WORKING NOTES: Polymer clay is an ideal medium for food projects (see page 11 for using polymer clay). The finished models should be baked following the manufacturer's instructions. If you are painting details onto the polymer clay models, add a little PVA glue to the paint as this will help it to stick to the surface, without affecting the colour. PVA glue is suitable for all of the projects in this section.

To use templates, trace or photocopy the template onto paper, cut it out, draw around it on the material described and cut it out using an appropriate tool. Grey dotted lines show the line of sewing.

KITE

KITE: Using the kite template, cut a kite shape from cotton fabric. Roll a hem along each edge and sew in position. The grey dotted line on the template shows the finished size and shape of the kite. If you prefer to use felt, cut out the template along the grey dotted line and draw round it on the felt.

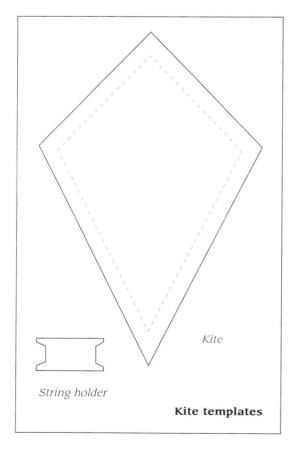

Kite

String holder

Kite templates

Cut one 2in and one 3in length of kebab stick. Cut shallow notches in the ends, then use thread to bind the sticks into a cross. Stitch the notched ends of the sticks to the fabric, using the notches to trap the thread. Tie a length of string to the centre of the kite.

STRING HOLDER: Using the template, cut a string holder from card. Wrap the loose end of the string around the holder, securing with glue.

Sew a 4in long string tail to the bottom of the kite. Cut a rectangle of coloured cotton fabric, 3/4in x 1/2in, then tie it in the centre with thread to form a bow shape and use the remaining thread to tie it to the string. Add more fabric bows in the same way.

PLATES

Cut a 1in diameter circle from thin card. With a coloured pen draw a decorative line around the edge. Glue food to the plates.

PICNIC HAMPER

Using the templates (top right), cut hamper basket pieces from card: one base, two short sides, two long sides, one lid, two long lid sides and two short lid sides. Lay each piece of card onto the back of some calico or fine canvas. Draw round the card pieces leaving a 1/2in margin and cut out the fabric.

Now cover each card piece as follows. Attach a piece of thread to one edge of the fabric. Stitch the thread as a lace to pull the fabric edges together, enclosing the card as shown in the diagram. Sew the fabric-covered pieces together as shown in the diagram, to make up the basket shape. Sew the hinge between the basket and lid in the same way.

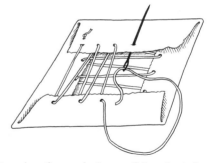

Covering the card pieces of the picnic hamper

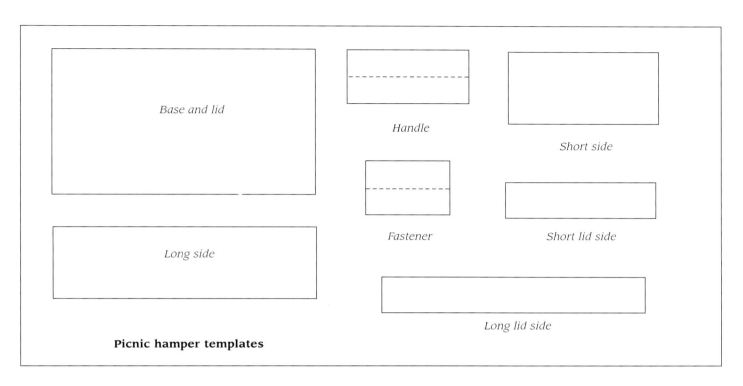

Base and lid

Handle

Short side

Fastener

Short lid side

Long side

Long lid side

Picnic hamper templates

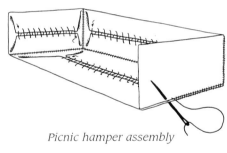

Picnic hamper assembly

Using the same hamper templates, cut the hamper liner pieces from card. Trim off 1/8in from two sides, then cover them with coloured cotton fabric, as described above. Sew the liner pieces into a box, with the fabric facing inwards. Put the liner inside the basket. Sew the top edges of the liner and basket together. Sew the lid liner in position inside the lid.

HANDLE AND FASTENERS: Using the templates, cut a handle and four fastener pieces from fabric. Fold each piece in half and sew around the edges, tucking loose fabric edges inside. Sew the handle and fasteners to the front of the hamper, using the photograph as a guide. Bend wire from a paper-clip into square buckles, and sew to the end of the fastening straps, or use ready-made buckles (see Suppliers, page 172).

PLATE HOLDERS: Make eight plates as described above. Glue them in two piles with pieces of cardboard sandwiched in between each layer. Wrap 1/8in thick ribbon around the plates in a cross and secure the ends with glue, then glue the plate piles inside the hamper lid.

PICNIC BLANKET

Cut out a square of tartan wool fabric, cutting carefully along the lines of weaving. Remove a few woven threads from each edge for a fringe.

The following projects are all modelled from polymer clay. Decorative markings can be made by pressing the point of a knife into the clay. To harden, bake the clay following the manufacturer's instructions.

PIES, PASTIES AND SAUSAGE ROLLS

MEAT PIE IN TIN: Roll a ball of light brown polymer clay and slightly flatten it. Cover one side with darker clay, pinching it out to form a rim. Add leaf shapes to the top of the pie and markings around the edge.

PASTIES: Press out a circle of light brown polymer clay. Fold the circle in half, enclosing a

TOMATOES: Described on page 49.

APPLES: Roll balls of green polymer clay and push in tiny twig stalks.

BUNS, BISCUITS (COOKIES), SHORTBREAD, SANDWICHES

BUNS: Roll balls of brown polymer clay, add white icing, and tiny red blobs as cherries.

BISCUITS: Press out tiny blobs of brown polymer clay, then add decorative markings.

SHORTBREAD: Press out a thick circle of light brown polymer clay. Cut it into wedges and make marks on the top.

SANDWICHES: Press out a layer of light brown polymer clay, then add a filling layer in a different colour and top with another layer of light brown. Cut into triangles.

JUG AND CUPS

Mould a piece of polymer clay around the end of a circular dowel. Poke a pointed kebab stick into the top of the front of the jug and ease it forward to create a spout. With a pencil, draw a handle shape on card. Roll out a tiny sausage of polymer clay, shape and trim it on top of the drawing. Stick the handle to the side of the jug and smooth the join. Bake to harden with the dowel still in place. While still warm, remove the dowel. Make the cups in the same way but without the spout.

PIGEON

Cut a 2in length of pipe cleaner and fold it into feet as shown in the diagram. Using polymer clay, model a pigeon body around the legs and bake to harden with the legs in place. Paint using the photograph above as a guide.

small blob of clay. Make a hole in the pasty and markings around the edge.

SAUSAGE ROLLS: Roll out a sausage of mid brown polymer clay. Wrap the sausage with lighter clay, then use a knife to cut it into short rolls. Add decorative markings.

GINGER BEER

Model a ginger beer bottle from light brown polymer clay, then add a lid from darker clay and bake to harden. Photocopy the label templates onto paper and write on the name of your beer. Cut out the label and, once the bottle is hardened, glue in place. Wrap thread around the label to keep it in shape until dry.

Ginger beer label templates

FRUIT

WATER MELON: Roll a ball of dark pink polymer clay. Cover it with a thin layer of white, then a layer of dark green. Roll out thin sausages of paler green and smooth them as lines on the skin. Cut a slice from the melon. Once baked and hardened, add seeds with black paint.

BANANAS: Roll sausage shapes of yellow polymer clay, with brown stalks. Pinch a few bananas together in a bunch.

GRAPES: Make a cone of purple polymer clay and cover it in tiny blobs. Add a stalk of brown.

ORANGES: Roll balls of orange polymer clay and add tiny blobs of green for stalks.

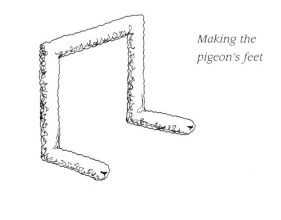

Making the pigeon's feet

Fast Food

*E*ven dolls' house inhabitants enjoy taking an evening off from cooking, and crashing in front of the television with a take-away meal. To accompany the food projects, there's also a TV remote-control unit. Dolls who are too lazy to have made their own food would certainly prefer to eat their meal and flick between TV channels from the comfort of their own armchairs!

PROJECTS KEY

1 pizzas
2 Indian take-away
3 Chinese take-away
4 fish and chips
5 burgers and hot-dogs
6 TV remote-control unit
7 newspaper (see page 29)
8 patchwork cushion (see page 80)

WORKING NOTES: Most of the fast food in the picture is made from polymer clay (see page 11 for using polymer clay). Follow the manufacturer's instructions for baking guidelines. You could also use air-drying children's clay and once dry, paint the food with acrylic paint.

To use templates, trace or photocopy the template onto paper, cut it out, draw around it on the material described and cut it out using an appropriate tool. Dotted lines on templates show fold lines. PVA glue is suitable for all of the projects in this section unless otherwise stated.

PIZZA

PIZZA: Make three circles of polymer clay: a brown base, a red tomato layer and a yellow cheese layer. Form anchovies, salami, tomatoes or peppers from pieces of coloured polymer clay and arrange them on top then bake to harden.

BOX: Using the pizza box template, cut a box from white card. Fold up the box and stick together as shown in the diagram. Photocopy the pizza logo template onto white paper. Cut it out, colour it using red and green felt-tip pens then glue it to the box lid. Draw green and red lines on the sides of the box (see photograph).

MENU: Photocopy the pizza menu templates onto white paper and cut them out. Colour in the details then glue the pieces together back to back and fold into three.

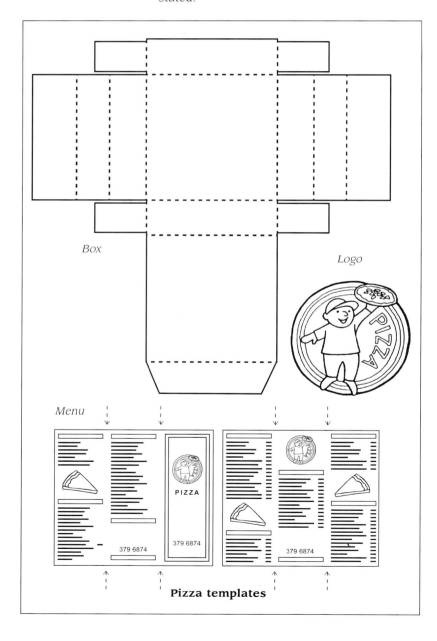

Box

Logo

Menu

Pizza templates

Folding up the pizza box

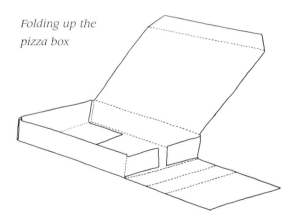

INDIAN TAKE-AWAY

CURRY CONTAINER: Using the template, cut a container mould from thin card. Fold up the sides and tape in place. Press thick silver foil (from a milk-bottle top or foil container) over the outside of the mould then trim away excess leaving a $1/16$in rim. Remove the cardboard, then fold the rim to make a thicker edge. Fill the container with curry-coloured polymer clay, and add lumps as meat and vegetables. Bake the whole container with the polymer clay in it.

LID: Using the template, cut a container lid from white card and paint one side silver.

RICE CONTAINER AND LID: Using the templates, cut a rice container mould and lid from thin card. Make the container and lid as described above. For rice make a heap of trimmings of white, red and yellow sewing thread in the container and drip PVA glue on top. Add more trimmings on top of the glue.

POPADOM: Make twenty or thirty tiny blobs of polymer clay. Press out a lump of light brown polymer clay into a thin circle and drop this circle over the blobs, gently pressing it down without squashing the blobs.

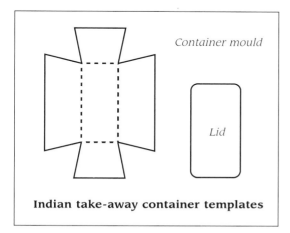

Indian take-away container templates

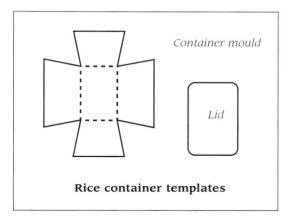

Rice container templates

CHINESE TAKE-AWAY

CONTAINERS: Make the containers using the curry container instructions and templates above.

FOOD: Make the food in a similar way to the curried food above. Make rice as above, using white thread. Roll out a very long thin sausage of polymer clay and arrange it into a container as noodles. Make balls of brown polymer clay for meatballs and bake them in a container. Add chopsticks cut from a kebab stick.

When the polymer clay food is finished, stick a tiny strip of wood into it as a spoon handle.

SWEET AND SOUR SAUCE: Shape white polymer clay round the end of a pen lid to form a pot. Trim the top of the pot with a knife, then remove the pen lid. Fill the pot with red polymer clay and then bake.

SOY SAUCE: Make a small cone of dark brown polymer clay, trim off the top and add a red lid from polymer clay.

MENU: Photocopy the menu templates (right) onto coloured paper and cut them out. Glue the pieces together, back to back, and then fold in half.

FISH AND CHIPS

Cut chip-shaped pieces from pale brown polymer clay. The fish is made from a triangle of orange polymer clay, textured by snipping with the points of a pair of scissors. The pie is a circle of brown polymer clay, with edging texture and central hole made with the end of a knife. For tomato sauce, press out a little red polymer clay and drop it over the chips. Once baked and hard, wrap the food in newspaper which has been reduced on a photocopier to be in keeping with the 1/12th scale (see page 29).

BURGERS AND HOT-DOGS

BURGER: Make a round bread-roll from polymer clay and slice it in half. Form flat circles of red and brown polymer clay, place them on the base and replace the lid. Texture the top of the bun.

BOX: Using the burger box template, cut a box from white card. Fold along the dotted lines and use pieces of white sticky labels to hold the edges together.

HOT-DOG: Make a long bread-roll from polymer clay and slice it down the middle. Add a sausage of brown clay and tiny strips of red and yellow for tomato sauce and mustard. Once baked, hard and cool, place the hot-dog in a tissue napkin.

TV REMOTE-CONTROL UNIT

Form a block of dark brown polymer clay and add red clay buttons and a grey screen, then bake to harden.

Chinese take-away menu template

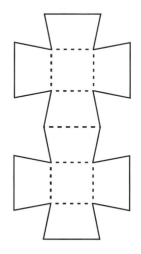

Burger box template

A Tudor Meal

Two Tudor gentlemen have returned from a day out on their estate and are enjoying a quiet meal together, with simple foodstuffs such as bread, cheese, vegetables and sausages, eaten from wooden platters by the light of a glowing fire. Even the dog has a sausage to chew.

The platters and candlesticks featured in this scene would have been made in Tudor times from native woods turned on a foot-operated pole lathe. These miniature 'turned' pieces are re-created simply from wooden buttons and beads, stained with commercial wood stain or a felt-tip pen. This scene is set in the late Tudor period. Remember that if your scene is set before the 1560s, potatoes and tobacco had not been introduced to Europe. These items were brought back from the New World during the second half of the sixteenth century.

PROJECTS KEY

1 wooden platters	8 toasting fork
2 candlesticks	9 knife
3 food	10 clay pipes and
4 leather tankards	tobacco pouch
5 pottery jugs	11 tapers and
6 cider bottles	container
7 fire grate	

WORKING NOTES: In projects for which templates are provided, trace or photocopy the template onto paper, cut it out, draw around it on the material described and then cut it out using an appropriate tool. Dotted lines on templates show fold lines. Many of the items use polymer clay which should be baked to harden, following the manufacturer's instructions.

WOODEN PLATTERS

The platters are wooden buttons stained with wood stain or felt-tip pens to mimic dark wood. If you prefer, you could fill the holes with air-drying clay, then paint to match.

CANDLESTICKS

CANDLESTICKS: These are wooden beads and buttons stuck together. The upright is a decorative tube bead and the base is a button.
CANDLES: White candles can be cut from small birthday-cake candles. For a more authentic beeswax colour, melt batik wax (available from craft shops) following the manufacturer's instructions. Briefly dip the end of a piece of black thread into the wax. Lift it out and allow to cool. Repeat until the desired diameter has been reached. On the final dip, smooth the warm wax with your fingers, then trim to size with a knife.

FOOD

The bread, sausages, cheese, carrots, parsnips, potatoes and apples are all made from polymer clay, baked according to the manufacturer's instructions. For fine detail such as apple pips, or the brown ring on the parsnips, use acrylic paint once the piece has been baked.

For the bread, stipple the clay and once baked and cool paint the surface with brown acrylic paint to mimic a crust.

LEATHER TANKARDS

Using the three tankard templates, cut a body, base and handle piece from thin black leather. Fold the body piece in half and sew together along the straight edges. Cover the bottom hole with the base piece and sew in place around the edge. Using Super Glue, fix the ends of the handle piece in place on the side of the tankard.

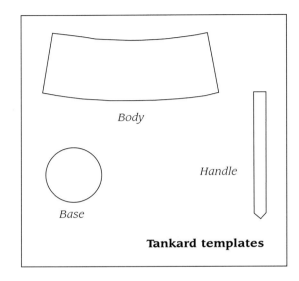

Body

Handle

Base

Tankard templates

POTTERY JUGS AND CIDER BOTTLES

POTTERY JUG: To make a pottery jug, mould a piece of polymer clay around the end of a piece of dowel. Poke a kebab stick into the top of the front of the jug and gently ease it forward to create a spout. Draw a handle shape on card. Roll out a tiny sausage of polymer clay and shape it on top of the drawing. Hold the handle on the side of the jug and smooth the join. With the dowel still in place, bake to harden. Whilst still warm, remove the dowel, allow to cool; then sand to finish.
CIDER BOTTLE: Make the cider bottle and handle following the instructions for the jug, using the picture on page 43 as a shape guide, and omitting the spout. Once baked, use acrylics to paint the bottom section of the bottle pale grey and the top mustard yellow. Finish with varnish. With a scalpel cut a tiny stopper from a wine cork.

FIRE GRATE

Using the fire grate template (top right) cut a grate piece from card. Score and fold it along the dotted lines, then use glue and the tabs to hold it together. Paint the grate black and finish with varnish.

TIP

For some ideas for decorating pottery items, and to see more styles and designs to suit other periods see pages 150–153. For more food projects, such as meat and fruit, see pages 48–50 and page 38.

Fire grate template

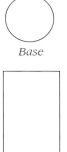

Base

Body

Taper container templates

For the base of the fire, make a lump of red sweet-wrapper foil. Dab it unevenly with black acrylic paint. Pile twigs on top until only tiny glimpses of the foil are visible. Paint the logs nearest the centre of the grate charred black.

TOASTING FORK

Twist a fork shape from thin wire and add a piece of baked polymer clay 'bread' on the end.

KNIFE

Using the knife template, cut a knife shape from thin card. Paint the blade silver and the handle brown.

Knife template

CLAY PIPES AND TOBACCO POUCH

Mould clay pipes from white polymer clay (see photograph on page 43 as a guide) and bake to harden. Cut a rectangle of leather, fold it into a pouch then sew the sides together. Make tobacco with shavings of dark wood.

TAPERS AND CONTAINER

TAPERS: Roll long thin sausages of polymer clay around black thread and bake to harden.

CONTAINERS: Using the templates, cut a body and base from thin black leather. Fold the body piece in half and sew together along the short edges. Cover the bottom hole with the base piece and sew in place.

IN THE KITCHEN

This chapter has all the fruit, vegetables, meats, cakes, pots, pans and equipment you need to make your kitchen complete. There is a busy manor house kitchen scene, and a small dolls' house room transformed into a packed larder. A mother and daughter on baking day prepare a medley of cakes, breads and cookies and there is a section full of utensils and equipment. Many of these projects will suit all periods of dolls' house.

The Manor House Kitchen

The projects in this scene are versatile enough to be included in other room set-ups. The tea towel rack would be useful in a garden shed for hanging a coat, and the overhead rack could hold drying prints in an artist's studio. The meat and vegetables would suit all periods of house, while the bowls, pans and dishes are more suited to scenes from the early nineteenth century onwards. For older houses, you can use the same construction principles, with simpler finishes. Chopping boards, for instance, can be made from thicker pieces of dark wood for seventeenth and eighteenth century houses, and bowls can be made in simple earthenware colours.

PROJECTS KEY

1 overhead hanging rack
2 garlic
3 spice and herb jars
4 eggs in rack and fried egg
5 sliced bread
6 vegetables
7 mixing bowls
8 trug
9 tea towel rack
10 saucepans
11 meat
12 casserole dishes (see page 152)
13 dried herbs (see page 53)
14 cheese (see page 34)
15 plates and bowls (see page 151)
16 goblets (see page 33)
17 cups (see page 152)
18 fruit (see page 38)
19 dried flowers (see page 125)
20 baking tins (see page 60)
21 picture (see pages 118–119)
22 cat (see page 166)
23 utensils (see pages 61–63)
24 cardboard tray (see page 55)
25 washing and cleaning equipment (see pages 61–63)
26 simple kitchen tiles (see page 96)
27 pots (see page 151)
28 decorative tiles (see pages 87–88)
29 dolls and furniture (see Suppliers, page 172)

WORKING NOTES: When drilling a hole in a small piece of wood, hold it firmly in a vice, or tape it to a larger waste piece of wood. Bake polymer clay items following the manufacturer's instructions. When painting polymer clay projects, add a little PVA glue to the acrylic paint to help it stick to the surface. To use templates, trace or photocopy the template onto paper, cut it out, draw around it on the material described and cut it out using an appropriate tool. Dotted lines show the position of folds. PVA glue is suitable for all projects in this section.

Spice and Herb Jars

These are made by gluing cork circles to the top of tubular beads. Cork spots are often available in hardware stores as protective feet for household items, or cut them from a cork table-mat. Photocopy the labels templates onto paper, cut them out and glue to the jars.

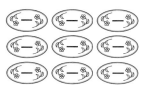

Spice and herb labels templates

Garlic

Make garlic bulbs from white polymer clay, marking lines with a knife, then add a root mark made from brown polymer clay. Fold a 2¹/₄in length of 5mm wide white ribbon in half and glue together, leaving a loop at the top. Glue the garlic bulbs along the ribbon.

Sliced Bread

BREAD BOARD: Cut a 1¹/₄in diameter circle from ¹/₈in thick pine strip.

SLICED LOAF: Make a loaf shape from polymer clay, then use a scalpel to cut some slices. Bake to harden on the bread board.

With a piece of sponge, dab paint onto the loaf to mimic darkened areas. For a brown loaf, use ochre paint on the lower areas. Add burnt umber paint as you move up the loaf and a touch of black on the top. For the cut areas, use white with a little ochre mixed in.

Vegetables

The vegetables are all made from polymer clay. Once complete all the finished models need to be baked to harden, following the manufacturer's instructions.

CARROTS: Use orange polymer clay rolled into a taper and make marks on the sides with a knife. Chop up some carrots. For freshly picked carrots, make a hole in the end and once baked, push a piece of dried grass into the end for leaves. Arrange the whole carrots and chopped up pieces, with a knife, on a chopping board, or pile the pieces into a bowl.

PARSNIPS: Use yellow polymer clay rolled into a taper, marked on the sides with a knife.

PUMPKINS: Use orange polymer clay rolled into a ball and make deep marks on the sides with a knife. Add a green polymer clay stem.

AUBERGINES: Use purple polymer clay rolled into shape, adding green leaves and a stem.

CABBAGE: Use dark green polymer clay rolled into a ball. Press out five or six leaf shapes and put them on the outside of the ball, pinching them together into a stem at the bottom.

CAULIFLOWER: Use cream polymer clay rolled into a ball, then texture the ball with a knife. Press out five green leaf shapes in polymer clay and put them on the outside of the ball, pinching them together into a stem at the bottom.

TOMATOES: Use red polymer clay rolled into small balls. Add green leaves and a stalk.

MUSHROOMS: Roll dark brown polymer clay into a small ball, cut it in half with a scalpel and texture the cut face. Cover the dome with a thin layer of pale brown polymer clay and add a stalk on the dark brown face.

PEPPERS (CAPSICUM): Use red, yellow or green polymer clay rolled into shape. Use a pointed stick to create the dents and shaping and finish by adding a green stem.

POTATOES: Roll balls of brown clay.

Overhead Hanging Rack

Using the hanging rack template, cut two rack ends from ¹/₈in thick pine strip. With a 3mm drill bit, drill holes in the rack ends in the positions marked on the template. Cut four 5in lengths of kebab stick and push the ends into the holes in the rack ends and glue in place. Hang the rack with thin string.

Eggs and Rack

Using the egg rack template, cut an egg rack from coloured card. Score and fold legs along the dotted lines then use a scalpel to cut out the circles. Fold the sides down along the dotted lines. Make eggs from white or pale brown polymer clay.

The fried egg is made of white polymer clay with a tiny blob of yellow for the yoke.

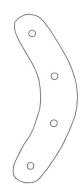

Hanging rack template

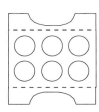

Egg rack template

TEA TOWEL RACK

Using the template, cut a rack piece from ⅛in thick pine strip. Cut five ½in lengths of kebab stick and cut a 45-degree angle on one end of each and then glue them to the rack in the positions marked on the template.

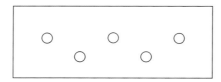

Tea towel rack template

MIXING BOWLS

Model polymer clay over the end of a bit of dowel and trim the rim with a knife. Press decorative marks on the side then bake with the dowel in place. While still warm, remove the dowel.

TRUG

Using the templates, cut one base, two sides, two feet and one handle from ¹⁄₁₆in thick wood. Bevel the long straight edge of each side piece and shave the handle piece thinner until flexible. Glue the pieces together as shown in the diagram. Curve the handle piece and glue its ends to the outer faces of the sides of the trug.

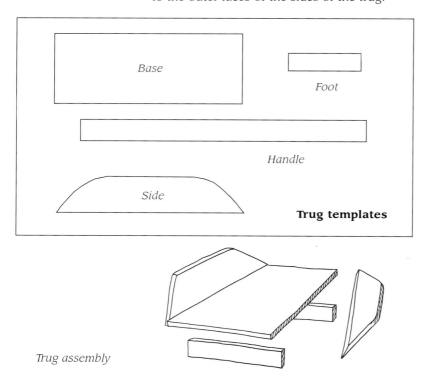

Base

Foot

Handle

Side

Trug templates

Trug assembly

SAUCEPANS

The pans are made from lengths of cardboard and plastic tube – some saved from the inside of rolls of tape, others purchased from a hardware store. Cut a length of tube and use fine sandpaper to smooth the ends. Cut a circle of card for the base and glue it in place. Paint the pan silver. Make handles from polymer clay and bake them separately. Glue the handles in place and paint silver. Fill the saucepans with scraps of coloured polymer clay.

MEAT

TURKEY: Using a cookery book picture as a guide, model a turkey from light brown polymer clay. When baked, dab brown acrylic paint on the upper surfaces with a sponge.

ROASTING TIN: Using the template, cut a roasting tin from cardboard. Score along the dotted lines and fold up the sides and hold the corners together with gummed paper tape. Paint the tray black, then varnish.

BEEF: Roll a thick sausage of dark red polymer clay and texture the ends with a knife. Wrap this red sausage in a sheet of cream polymer clay. Tie thin string around the meat, then bake to harden with the string in place.

SAUSAGES: Roll out sausage shapes in polymer clay and bake. Some can be put on plates, others can be coiled up and hung from the rack.

HAM: Roll a thick sausage of pink polymer clay, tapering it at one end. Add a blob of white on the thick end then wrap the pink in a sheet of cream polymer clay and bake.

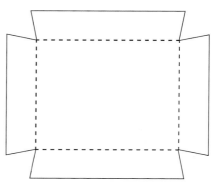

Roasting tin template

In the Larder

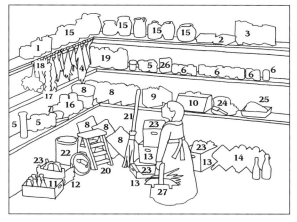

PROJECTS KEY

1 decorative pots
2 biscuit and cracker tins
3 cereal packets
4 dried herbs
5 glass jars
6 tins of food
7 pestle and mortar
8 paper and fabric sacks
9 box of macaroons
10 bread bin
11 milk crate and bottles
12 wooden crate
13 cardboard boxes
(cartons)
14 wine rack, wine
and Champagne
15 clay pots (see page 151)

16 spice and herb jars
(see page 49)
17 garlic (see page 49)
18 sausage (see page 50)
19 cider bottles (see pages
44 and 152)
20 step ladder (see page 91)
21 broom (see page 168)
22 dustbin (see page 63)
23 fruit and vegetables
(see pages 38 and 49)
24 sliced bread (see
page 49)
25 turkey in roasting tin
(see page 50)
26 flour bag (see page 60)
27 trug (see page 50)

A small room of a dolls' house or a cellar area can be transformed into a larder with a few shelves and boxes. It is a good opportunity to make a treasure-trove of colourful food packaging and boxes that might otherwise clutter up the kitchen. Look around at the packets and tins on your own shelves for inspiration.

WORKING NOTES: Some of the templates provided can be photocopied directly onto thin card, ready for scoring and gluing. For these templates, the folding lines are marked outside the edge of the actual template so they won't show up on your finished piece. Dotted lines on templates show fold lines. See page 11 for folding and scoring card. Other templates can be traced or photocopied onto paper, cut out, and drawn around on the material described. Cut out shapes using an appropriate tool.

The templates have been prepared without any text on them. To add words to your projects, such as 'tinned peas' or 'baked beans', cut the words from a magazine recipe or advertisement and glue them in place, or write them on the label using a very fine pen. Alternatively, simply draw black lines to indicate text. Clear acetate can be cut from food packaging.

PVA wood or paper glue is suitable for all of the projects. Clip pieces together with the glue sandwiched between until dry.

DECORATIVE POTS

Glue colourful wooden beads together. The handles are smaller glass or metal beads.

TINS OF FOOD

Make tins by cutting $^9/_{16}$in lengths of 10mm diameter dowel, using sandpaper to smooth the ends. Paint the tins silver. Photocopy the food tin labels templates onto paper and colour with felt-tip pens (see photograph on page 51 as a guide). Cut out the labels and glue them to the tins.

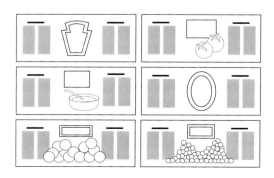

Food tin labels templates

BISCUIT AND CRACKER TINS

Photocopy the base and lid templates onto thin card and colour each tin with a felt-tip pen (see photograph). Score along lines indicated by the folding markers and cut out the shapes. Fold up the shapes and glue the tabs in position.

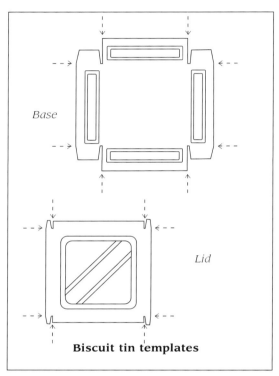

Biscuit tin templates

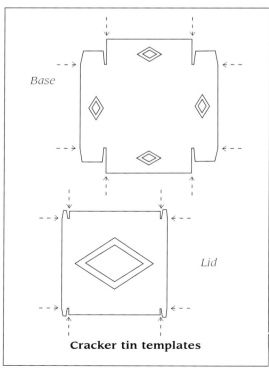

Cracker tin templates

CEREAL PACKETS

Photocopy the cornflakes packet template and the branflakes packet template onto thin card and colour with felt-tip pens (see photograph). Make up the cereal packets following the instructions for the biscuit tin above.

Cornflakes

Branflakes

Cereal packet templates

DRIED HERBS

Cut sprigs of garden plants, grasses and herbs and tie them together in bunches. Hang them in a warm, dry place for a few weeks.

GLASS JARS

The various jars are cut from 10mm diameter clear plastic tube (from model shops – see Suppliers, page 172). A jam jar and spaghetti jar are described here but you could make other jars to contain beads or tiny blobs of polymer clay.

JAM JAR: Fill a short plastic tube with red polymer clay, but don't bake to harden. Cut a ³/₄in diameter circle of fine cotton fabric and stick it

to the top of the tube. When dry, wrap coloured thread around the fabric and tube and tie the ends together.

SPAGHETTI JAR: Glue a circle of clear acetate to the end of a long plastic tube, then fill the jar with lengths of dried grass. Glue a circle of cork cut from a table-mat to the top as a lid.

PESTLE AND MORTAR

PESTLE: Model a stick shape from polymer clay and bake to harden. Once cool, paint the handle brown.

MORTAR: Mould a piece of polymer clay around the end of a circular dowel. Poke a cocktail stick into the top of the front of the bowl and ease it forward to create a spout. Bake to harden with the dowel in place. While still warm, remove the dowel.

BOX OF MACAROONS

BOX: Photocopy the macaroon box base and lid templates onto coloured card, painting the details on the box. Score along the lines indi-

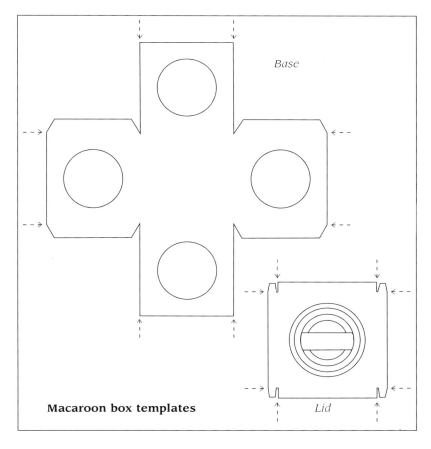

Base

Lid

Macaroon box templates

cated by the folding markers. Cut out the box and lid shapes, then, using a scalpel, cut out the circles on the box. Cut 1in squares of clear plastic and glue them inside the box to cover the holes. Fold up the box and lid and glue the tabs in position.

MACAROONS: Crumple up small squares of tissue paper to fill the box. Leave a few pieces flat and make macaroons from brown polymer clay, speckled with white on top.

BREAD BIN

Using the bread bin templates, cut one back, one base, one lid, one top and two sides from 1/8in thick wood. Glue the pieces together (except the lid) as shown in the diagram. Glue a strip of fabric to one long edge of the lid to act as a hinge. Glue the other half of the hinge to the underside of the top of the bread bin. Glue a small circle of wood to the lid for a handle. You could stain or varnish the piece to finish.

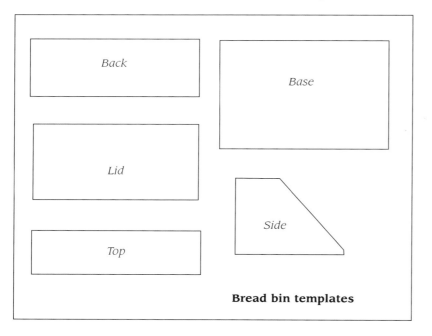

Back

Base

Lid

Side

Top

Bread bin templates

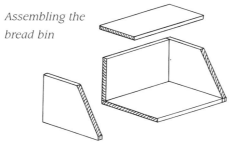

Assembling the bread bin

WOODEN CRATE

Using the wooden crate templates, cut a base piece from 1/8in thick wood, and two long slats and two short slats from 1/16in thick wood. Cut four narrow sticks 7/8in long, for uprights.

To construct the first side, glue the ends of two long slats to one of the uprights. Glue the other ends of the slats to another upright. Repeat for the second side. Glue the side pieces to the base, then glue on the short slats on either end.

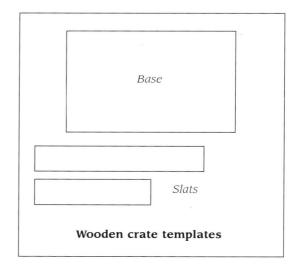

Base

Slats

Wooden crate templates

MILK CRATE AND BOTTLES

CRATE: Photocopy the milk crate and inner grid templates onto coloured card. Score along the lines indicated by the folding markers and cut out the shapes. Fold up the milk crate and glue the tabs in position. Slot the inner grid pieces together and put them into the crate.

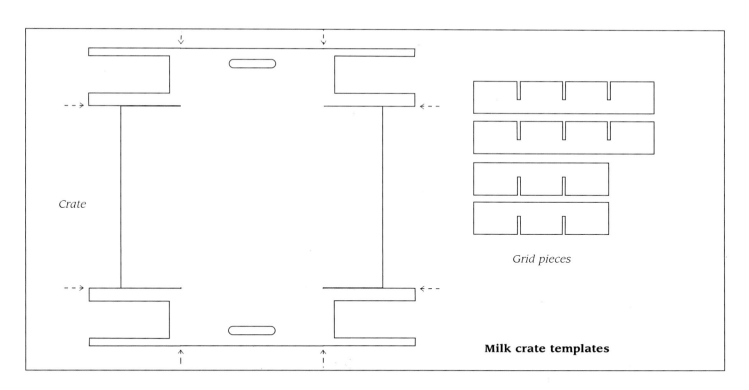

Milk crate templates

BOTTLES: Model milk bottles from white polymer clay, making sure they'll fit into the crate. Once baked and hard, paint the lids silver.

CARDBOARD BOXES (CARTONS)

TALL BOX: Using the tall box template, cut a box from cardboard. Score along the dotted lines and fold into shape, gluing the tabs in position.

SHALLOW TRAY: Using the shallow tray template, cut a tray from cardboard. Score along the dotted lines and fold into shape, using the diagram as a guide. The narrow section at each end

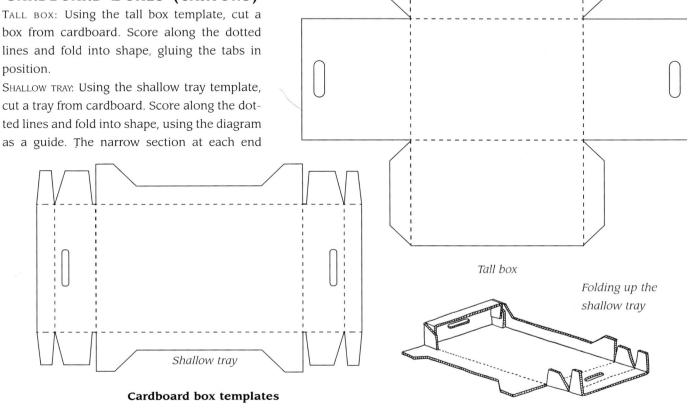

Tall box

Folding up the
shallow tray

Shallow tray

Cardboard box templates

folds over to thicken the handle area (see photograph as a guide). Glue the tabs in position.

Paper and Fabric Sacks

Paper sack: Cut a rectangle of brown paper, fold in half and glue together around three edges. Fill with beans or polymer clay potatoes.

Fabric sack: Cut a rectangle of calico or hessian, fold it in half and sew two edges together. Turn right side out and fill with beans, peas, lentils or seeds. Either hem the top edge, or roll it down and secure with a few stitches. Sacks can also be sewn shut.

Wine, Rack and Champagne

Wine rack: From 1/8in wide x 1/16in thick wood, cut the following: twelve strips 1 7/8in long; four strips 1 3/8in long; two strips 3/4in long. Glue these pieces together to create two grids, using the gluing grid as a guide.

Cut sixteen 5/8in lengths of kebab stick. Lay

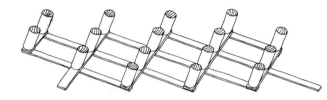

Making the wine rack

one of the wine rack grids on a flat surface and glue the kebab sticks pointing upwards, one from each cross-over in the grid (see diagram). Once dry, put glue on the free ends of the sticks and place the second grid on top. Leave to dry thoroughly.

Wine bottle: Model wine bottles from green polymer clay. Once hardened, paint the lids and necks dark red. Photocopy the wine label templates onto paper and colour them with felt-tip pens. Add text with a fine pen – maybe the name of your favourite wine. Cut out the labels and glue them on to the bottles. Wrap thread around the labels to keep them in shape whilst the glue dries.

Champagne: Follow the instructions for the wine bottle above but cover the lid and neck with gold foil and use the Champagne label template and extra neck label template (as shown in the photograph, bottom left).

Wine rack gluing grid

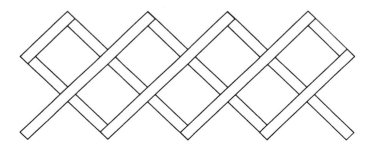

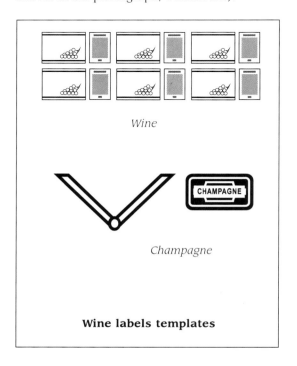

Wine

Champagne

Wine labels templates

Baking Days

Every special occasion on the calendar has a food associated with it, so in this baking days scene there are heart biscuits for Valentine's Day, mince pies and a cake for Christmas, a fabulous tiered wedding cake, and a birthday cake complete with candles and decorations.

PROJECTS KEY

1 bread in baking tins
2 bread plait
3 cookies on pastry board
4 cookies on baking trays and plates
5 wedding cake
6 birthday cake
·7 Christmas food – cake, mince pies, mincemeat
8 pastry
9 flour bag and shaker
10 butter
11 jam tarts in baking tin
12 milk jug
13 bowl of seeds
14 eggs (see page 49)

15 iced buns and short-bread (see page 38)
16 sausage rolls, pasties, and pies (see page 37)
17 utensils (see page 63)
18 casserole dishes (see page 152)
19 tea towel (see page 62)
20 mixing bowls (see page 50)
21 spice jar (see page 49)
22 pictures (see page 119)
23 'doughcraft' ring (see page 115)
24 pots (see page 151)
25 dolls (see Suppliers, page 172)

WORKING NOTES: Polymer clay (see page 11) is an ideal medium for food projects. In projects where it is prepared on cardboard or on a wooden board, you can bake the whole project on its board (as long as the piece doesn't contains other materials, such as glue or paint). Experiment with different tools and materials for creating textures and shapes. The point of a knife or cocktail stick is good for a stippled texture. (See also page 151 for Surface Decoration of Polymer Clay.) A tiny piece of sponge dipped in paint is useful for making a realistic shade of colour across the tops of loaves and pies.

Cardboard makes realistic baking trays once it is painted and varnished. With thick cardboard, score lines before folding – place a metal ruler along the dotted line, then run a knife gently along the line. Don't cut right through.

To use templates, trace or photocopy the template onto paper, cut it out, draw around it on the material described and cut it out using an appropriate tool. Dotted lines show the position of folds. PVA glue is suitable for all the projects.

BREAD IN BAKING TINS

BREAD TIN: Using the template, cut a bread tin from cardboard. Score along the dotted lines and fold up the sides, holding the corners together with gummed paper tape (available from art shops) or strips of paper glued across the joins. Paint the tray black, then varnish.

BASIC LOAF OF BREAD: Push light brown polymer clay into the tin and shape, then remove the polymer clay and bake to harden. With a piece of sponge, dab paint onto the loaf to mimic the sort of loaf required (see below). When dry, glue the loaf into the tin. See also sliced loaf on page 49.

WHITE BREAD: Leave the bottom plain and dab a little brown paint on the top surface.

BROWN BREAD: Start with ochre paint towards the base, moving up into burnt umber, and then add a touch of black on the top.

BURNT LOAF: Make with dark brown polymer clay, and dab black paint onto the top.

TIP

Many of the baked items in this section could appear in a kitchen scene or turn a dining room or parlour into the centre of a celebration. Most of the food featured would particularly suit a picnic setting or a birthday celebration. Take a look at pages 35–38 for picnic ideas. For birthday party decorations and presents, see pages 156–158.

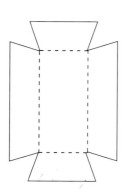

Bread tin template

BREAD PLAIT

Roll out three sausage shapes of polymer clay and join them together at one end. Plait the strands and join the ends together. Bake, then paint as for the brown loaf above.

COOKIES ON PASTRY BOARD

On a small rectangle of wood, roll out a blob of polymer clay on the wood. Using one of the three cookie templates cut around the shape on the clay using the point of a scalpel and removing excess clay. Bake to harden on the wood. Once cool, glue the cookies to the baking tray, plate or board. Place other details on the board, such as a rolling pin (see below) or tiny scraps of red polymer clay as cherries.

Gingerbread man   Heart   Teddy bear

Cookie templates

COOKIES ON BAKING TRAYS AND PLATES

BAKING TRAY: Using the template, cut a baking tray from cardboard. Score along the dotted lines and fold up the sides, holding the corners together with gummed paper tape. Paint the tray black and then varnish.

PLATE: Cut a circle of card approximately 1in in diameter. Draw a line around the edge with a coloured felt-tip.

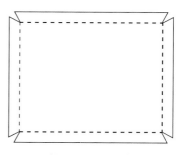

Baking tray template

COOKIES: Roll out a piece of polymer clay on cardboard. Using one of the three cookie templates, cut around the shape on the clay using the point of a scalpel, removing any excess clay. Once hardened, glue the cookies to the baking tray or plate.

WEDDING CAKE

Copy the nine wedding cake templates onto thin white card, cutting out two circles and one edge piece for each tier. Score along all the dotted lines and fold the tabs inwards. If you photocopy the templates, fold the tabs inwards to hide the black lines.

MAKING EACH TIER: Curl the edge piece into a tube, and glue the large tab to the free edge of the tube. Put glue on one set of tabs and stick one of the circles in place. Repeat for the other side. Repeat for all three tiers.

DECORATIONS: Cut three more circles from white card using the small, medium and large circle sizes on the cake templates. Create decorative borders on each circle using coloured polymer clay (see photograph). Bake the decorations on their card, then stick the card circles on top of each cake tier. Find figures for the top of the cake from the very smallest gauge of toy train set, or model some from polymer clay.

COLUMNS: Cut eight ³/₈in lengths of matchstick. Glue four to each underside of the small and medium tiers. Once dry, put more glue on the bases of the sticks and stack the tiers.

DISPLAY BOARD: Using the cake display board template, cut a circle of wood or thick cardboard. Cover it in silver foil (foil from a chocolate bar or aluminium cooking foil are ideal), then glue the cake in place on top.

BUTTER

Cut a rectangular piece of yellow polymer clay (approximately ³/₈in long). Once baked and cool, fold a square of greaseproof paper around the butter for a wrapper. Crease edges firmly, then unfold to display.

MILK JUG

Mould a piece of polymer clay around the end of a circular dowel. Poke a pointed kebab stick into the top of the front of the jug and gently ease it forward to create a spout. Roll out a sausage of polymer clay and join it to the side of the jug as a handle. Fill with white clay 'milk'. Bake to harden with the dowel in place. While still warm, remove the dowel.

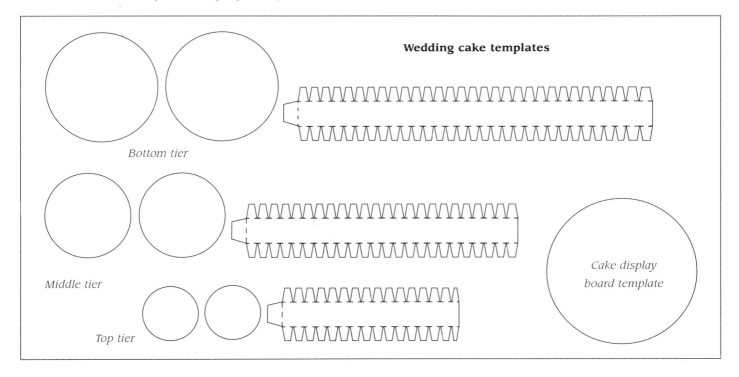

Wedding cake templates

Bottom tier

Middle tier

Top tier

Cake display board template

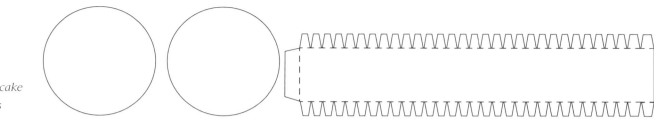

Birthday cake templates

BIRTHDAY CAKE

CAKE: Using pink card and the deeper birthday cake edge template, make a cake shape following the instructions for one of the tiers of the wedding cake on page 59. Glue ribbon around the sides, and make polymer clay shapes or numbers to glue on the top (see photograph).

CANDLES: Cut a tiny length of cocktail stick and sharpen one end. Push the stick through a flattened blob of polymer clay as a candleholder, and bake to harden with the stick in place. Once cool, paint the stick and add a speck of black paint as a wick. Make a hole in the top of the cake with a needle, then push the pointed end of the stick into the hole.

CHRISTMAS FOOD

CAKE: Using white card, make a cake shape following the instructions for the large tier of the wedding cake above (use the bottom tier templates). Cover the edge with Christmas ribbon and glue pre-baked polymer clay shapes of holly berries and leaves on top. Make a display board as above.

MINCE PIES BAKING TIN: Using the templates, cut a baking tray top and eighteen circles from card. Glue six circles to the underside of the baking tray in the positions marked. Glue six more circles on top of the first set, then six more as a final layer. Paint the whole baking tray with silver paint.

MINCE PIES: Cut six circles of brown polymer clay and mark the edges and the centre of each with a knife. Once baked, glue the pie pieces to the flat side of the baking tin.

MINCEMEAT: Roll out thin sausage shapes of dark brown, mid brown and red polymer clay. Using scissors, snip tiny lengths of each colour into a bowl. These can be left unbaked, or baked in a pile.

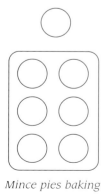

Mince pies baking tin templates

PASTRY

Cut a rectangle of wood for a board (approx. 1in x 1½in). Then roll or press out pale brown polymer clay on the board and bake to harden. Put a pre-baked blob of 'pastry' into a mixing bowl (see pages 50 and 151 for making bowls).

FLOUR BAG AND SHAKER

FLOUR BAG: The flour is a rectangular offcut of wood. For the bag, draw coloured lines on a piece of white paper and wrap it around the wood. The title on the bag shown in the photograph below was cut from a magazine, with the colour of the felt-tip lines on the bag chosen to match.

FLOUR SHAKER: Model the shaker from polymer clay, pushing holes into the top with a nail. Once baked, paint the shaker silver.

JAM TARTS IN BAKING TIN

Make the baking tin and jam tarts as for the mince pies (above), but adding red polymer clay to the centre of each tart.

BOWL OF SEEDS

Fill a small bowl with sesame seeds. See page 151 for making bowls.

Kitchen Utensils and Equipment

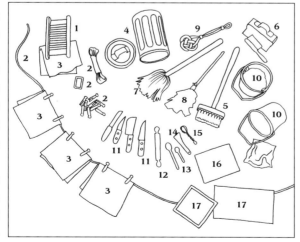

These kitchen utensils and pieces of cleaning equipment would not look out of place in any dolls' house from the beginning of the nineteenth century onwards. They are classic objects found in the sculleries and under-stairs cupboards of all types of abode – from a terraced house to a grand palace. This equipment will make a dolls' house look busy and lived in. They are the perfect props to accompany servant dolls, to make scenes full of interesting activity.

PROJECTS KEY

1 washboard
2 washing line, pegs and soap
3 tea towel
4 dustbin (trash can)
5 broom
6 dustpan and brush
7 mop
8 feather duster
9 carpet beater
10 bucket and floor cloth
11 knives
12 rolling pin
13 wooden spoons
14 wooden spatula
15 wire whisk
16 chopping board
17 tiled pot stand and cork mat

WORKING NOTES: Most of the items are made from card and bits of wood. Old Christmas cards are an ideal thickness for the dustpan and dustbin. A small tenon or coping saw is used for cutting wooden pieces. Use a sharp scalpel for trimming and neatening edges. Use PVA wood glue for sticking wood or paper together. Allow glue to dry thoroughly before moving on to the next stage. Follow the manufacturer's instructions for baking polymer clay.

To use templates, trace or photocopy the template onto paper, cut it out, draw around it on the material described and cut it out using an appropriate tool.

WASHBOARD, WASHING LINE, PEGS AND SOAP

WASHBOARD: Cut twelve lengths of pine strip $1/16$in thick x $7/8$in wide x $1/4$in. Glue these slats together as in the diagram. Cut two lengths of pine strip $1/8$in thick x $7/8$in wide x $3/8$in as cross pieces and glue them to each end of the slat section. If uneven, trim with a scalpel. Cut two lengths of pine strip $1/8$in thick x $1/4$in wide x $1 1/8$in as side pieces. Glue the slat section between the side pieces. Varnish to finish.

WASHING LINE: This is thin string, which can be strung up or bound into a hank for storage.

PEGS: These are tiny sausage shapes of polymer clay – shaped with a head and slit.

SOAP: This is made of green polymer clay.

Washboard slats assembly

DUSTPAN AND BRUSH

DUSTPAN: Using the dustpan and handle templates, cut a dustpan from thin card. Fold up the tabs, curl the back edge of the dustbin over the top and glue to the tabs, as shown in the diagram. Fold the handle along the dotted lines and glue in position. Paint and varnish to finish.

BRUSH: For the handle cut a length of pine strip $1/8$in thick x $3/16$in wide x $1 1/2$in. With a sharp knife, carve it a little thinner in the middle. Use sandpaper to smooth the edges and ends, then paint and varnish. Cut a second piece of pine strip $1/8$in thick x $5/16$in

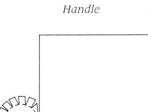

Handle

Dustpan and handle templates

wide x $5/8$in and cut lines into the sides to resemble bristles. Paint black and stick to the end of the handle.

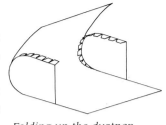

Folding up the dustpan

BROOM

Cut the head from a wooden-handled toothbrush. Cut a $3 1/2$in length of 5mm diameter dowel and use sandpaper to smooth all sawn edges. Use a 5mm drill bit to make a hole in the top of the toothbrush head, then Super Glue the handle in place. Varnish all wooden pieces.

MOP

Cut a 4in length of 5mm diameter dowel and sand the ends smooth. Cut about forty lengths of string and bind them with thread to the end of the stick. Put glue on top of the thread and fold the string down to form the mop head. Using a needle, fray out the ends of the string.

FEATHER DUSTER

With coloured thread, tie feathers to the end of a $2 3/4$in length of kebab stick.

BUCKET AND FLOOR CLOTH

The bucket is a clean single-portion milk container, the top trimmed to a circle, and painted with pewter metallic paint. Make a small hole in each side, near the top. Fold a handle from wire, using the bucket handle template as a guide, and push the ends into the holes. Fill the bucket with 'plastic water' (available from craft catalogues) or PVA glue which dries to look like soapy water. The cloth is a crumpled piece of calico.

Bucket handle template

TEA TOWEL

Hem a $1 3/4$in x 3in piece of white cotton fabric. The red patterns on the tea towels in the photograph are embroidered with sewing thread. The blue patterns are drawn with felt-tip pen.

DUSTBIN (TRASH CAN)

Using the dustbin template, cut a dustbin outer edge piece from thin card. With a scalpel, cut out the oval panels and glue the card to the outside of a plastic camera-film canister.

Using the dustbin handle template, cut a handle from card, fold along the dotted lines and glue onto the canister lid. Paint the lid and bin with pewter metallic enamel paint.

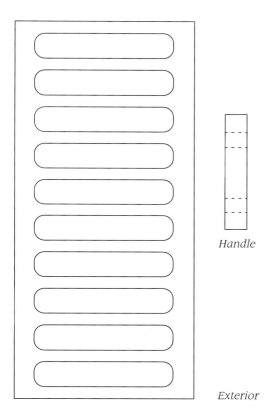

Handle

Exterior

Dustbin (trash can) templates

TILED POT STAND AND CORK MAT

TILED POT STAND: Cut a 1³/8in square of ¹/8in thick pine strip. Stain or colour with a felt-tip pen, then glue four squares cut from dolls' house tile paper on top.

MAT: Cut a rectangle from a cork table-mat.

CARPET BEATER

Bend three lengths of thin basket-maker's cane into the carpet beater shape, using the diagram as a guide. You may need to wet them to make them flexible. Tie thread securely

around the handle and dab PVA glue onto the thread ends to hold them in place.

ROLLING PIN

Cut a 1³/4in length of 5mm diameter dowel. To shape the handles, roll the dowel under a sharp knife to make vertical cuts at each end, without going all the way through. These are stop cuts. With a sharp knife, carve the handles into shape, stopping at the stop cuts.

KNIVES AND CHOPPING BOARD

KNIVES: To make a bread knife, vegetable knife, meat cleaver and large knife, use the templates to cut shapes from silver card. The bread knife's serrated texture is drawn on with a pencil. Cover the handle section with dark polymer clay and bake to harden with the card in place. Paint silver spots on the handle as rivets.

CHOPPING BOARD: Cut a rectangle of pine or balsa strip ¹/8in thick x 1⁵/16in wide x 1³/4in. Smooth the edges with sandpaper then varnish.

WOODEN SPOONS AND SPATULA

WOODEN SPOONS: These can be of various sizes. Cut a length of 5mm diameter dowel and shape the handle by rolling the dowel under a sharp knife, making a vertical cut a little way in from one end, without going all the way through. This is a stop cut. With a sharp knife, carve away wood to form a thin handle, stopping at the stop cut. In the thicker section, carve the back of the spoon into a dome. Use a small scoop chisel to carve a dent in the front face of the dome. Smooth with sandpaper to finish.

WOODEN SPATULA: Using the template, draw the shape on a thin piece of balsa wood. Drill a hole in the handle with a tiny drill bit (1mm or smaller). Cut out the spatula with a scalpel, smooth with sandpaper and varnish to finish.

WIRE WHISK

With thin wire, make a ¹/4in wide loop, then another loop crossing the first. Twist the ends of the wire around to form a handle. Cut off the ends with wire cutters and push them back up into the handle. Pinch with pliers to neaten.

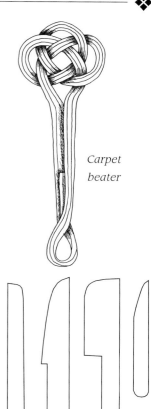

Carpet beater

Knives templates

Spatula template

LEISURE ACTIVITIES

This chapter gives ideas for specialist hobbies for your dolls, covering a wide range of leisure activities – from carpentry to needlecraft, from pop music to soccer, baseball and cricket. Many of the carpentry tools are classics found in workshops from the seventeenth century onwards. The needlework and sports items would suit settings from the late eighteenth century onwards, and bringing the projects up to date, there are instructions for magazines and a record player.

Sports Equipment

Choosing sports equipment for your dolls' house will depend on the period you wish to re-create. Most sports have a long history, evolving from invented forms to the standard versions of today. Hockey has the most ancient heritage – originating with the Romans, Greeks and Aztecs, who all played versions of a similar game. Cricket and tennis can claim roots in the twelfth and thirteenth centuries, although the equipment has changed over time with the invention of new rules and materials. For schoolboys of the nineteenth and twentieth centuries, you may prefer to choose rugby, baseball or soccer, which have all emerged more recently, becoming popular through schools and universities.

PROJECTS KEY

1 sports bag	14 soccer hat and
2 tennis racket	scarf
3 cricket stumps,	15 soccer boots
bails and ball	16 soccer ball
4 cricket pads	17 boomerang
5 cricket bat	18 model biplane
6 rugby ball	19 pin-board,
7 catapult	soccer-card
8 trophy	board, pictures of
9 hockey stick and	sporting heroes
ball	(see page 119)
10 medals and	20 teddy bear (see
certificates	page 19)
11 baseball bat and	21 books (see page
ball	119)
12 baseball	22 dolls (see
magazines	Suppliers, page
13 exercise books	172)
and pencils	

WORKING NOTES: Most of the photos and magazine pictures in this scene were cut from a sporting magazine. If you have access to the Internet, try searching for your chosen sport, or for the name of a particular sporting hero. The pictures reproduced there can be printed out in miniature.

To use templates, trace or photocopy the template onto paper, cut it out, draw around it on the material described and cut it out using an appropriate tool. Grey dotted lines on templates show lines of sewing. Black dotted lines show where to fold the piece. PVA wood glue is suitable for paper, card and wooden projects. When painting polymer clay projects, add a little PVA glue to the paint to help it stick to the surface.

SPORTS BAG

Using the three templates provided, cut two side pieces, one edge strip, and two handles from blue felt. With matching thread, sew the sides and strip together as shown in the diagram. Fold a handle in half along the dotted line, join along the edge, and sew the ends to the bag. Repeat for the second handle. You can also add a fastener to your bag – see the travel bag on page 107.

Edge

Handle

Side

Sports bag templates

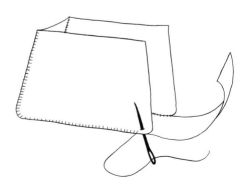

Sewing up the sports bag

TENNIS RACKET

Using the template, cut one string grid racket shape. With a scalpel, cut tiny slits and holes in the positions marked. Using white thread, and holding the threads in position through the slits and the holes in the handle, make the upright lines of the string grid as shown in the diagram. Secure the end of the thread with a dab of glue. Repeat for the horizontal threads, using a needle to weave them in and out of the vertical threads.

Using the tennis racket template, cut two plain racket shapes from card. Glue them to either side of the stringed shape, clipping them together until dry. Cut two $1^5/8$in lengths of 5mm diameter half-round dowel, taper each slightly at one end, then glue them on either side of the racket handle. Paint the racket, then bind the handle with coloured thread.

Stringing the tennis racket

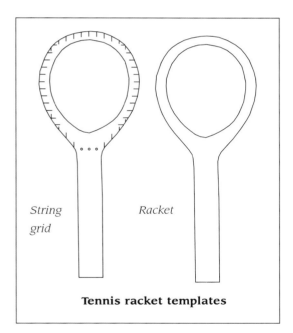

String grid

Racket

Tennis racket templates

CRICKET STUMPS, BAILS AND BALL

STUMPS: Cut three $2^3/4$in lengths of kebab stick and whittle the end of each into a point.

BAILS: Cut two $^1/2$in lengths of kebab stick and carve the ends to be slightly narrower.

BALL: Model a ball from red polymer clay. When hardened, use white acrylic paint to make stitching lines.

Fabric pad

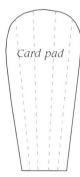

Card pad

**Cricket pad
templates**

Cricket bat template

CRICKET PADS

Using the cricket pad fabric template, cut four fabric shapes (two for each pad) from white cotton fabric. Using the cricket pad card template cut two pad shapes from card. Match up two fabric pieces with the right sides together and sew them along the grey dotted line. Turn the pieces right side out through the hole, fill with a card pad shape, then sew up the hole.

Sew lines through the fabric and card in the positions marked in grey dotted lines on the card template. Sew ribbon tapes to the back of the pads for tying to the doll's leg.

CRICKET BAT

Using the template, cut a cricket bat shape from $1/4$in thick pine strip. With a sharp knife, cut the back of the bat into a wedge shape. Cut a $1^3/4$in handle from 5mm diameter dowel, trimming one end into a point and gluing it into the slot in the bat. When dry, use sandpaper to smooth the join. Bind the handle with coloured thread.

RUGBY BALL

Shape a rugby ball from brown polymer clay and mark the leather panels with a knife before baking (see photograph).

CATAPULT

Find a small fork-shaped twig (about $3/4$in long), remove the bark and trim to size. Slightly split the end of the two twigs at the top of the fork. Cut an elastic band in half and thread it into a needle. Sew the elastic through an oval scrap of leather. Push the ends of the elastic into the splits in the twig. Hold in position with glue, then trim any loose ends.

TROPHY

With polymer clay, make a cup shape on the end of a piece of dowel. Roll out tiny sausages of polymer clay for handles and press them into place. Extend the cup shape into a stem, then add a base. Bake to harden with the dowel still in place. While still warm, remove the dowel and paint the base black and the trophy silver. Paint a silver plaque on the base.

HOCKEY STICK AND BALL

HOCKEY STICK: Two templates are provided for the hockey stick: the one with the shallow hook is based on an old design popular until the 1950s; modern hockey is played with a smaller hook and is represented in the second template.

Using your chosen template, cut a hockey stick shape from $3/16$in thick pine strip. Cut out the shape using a sharp knife and use sandpaper to smooth the edges of the stick.

BALL: Shape a ball (about $5/16$in diameter) from white polymer clay.

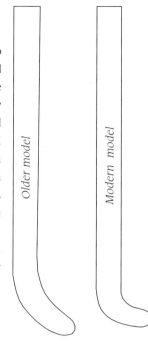

Older model   *Modern model*

**Hockey stick
templates**

MEDALS AND CERTIFICATES

MEDALS: Glue silver and gold sequins to loops of embroidery thread then cover the sequin holes with scraps cut from other sequins.

CERTIFICATES: Photocopy the two certificate templates onto paper and cut them out.

Certificates templates

BASEBALL BAT AND BALL

BAT: Cut a $2^3/4$in length of 5mm diameter dowel. Whittle the bat end into a dome and the handle end into a taper, leaving a small knob on the end. Use sandpaper to smooth the bat, then bind the handle with coloured thread.

BALL: Model a ball from white polymer clay, using a knife to mark the leather piece shapes. Once hardened, the shapes can be painted in team colours.

BASEBALL MAGAZINES

Cut four rectangles of magazine page, twice as wide as the finished baseball magazine (the finished magazine is about $1^1/4$in x 1in). Holding them together, fold them in half. Cut a miniature cover from a sporting magazine and fold it around the pages, either stapling or sewing them together in the centre. If you cannot find a suitable cover picture, use a small sporting picture and add text with a fine pen.

EXERCISE BOOKS AND PENCILS

Make pencils and small exercise books following the instructions for the sketch book and pencils on page 148.

SOCCER HAT AND SCARF

SCARF: Using the smallest knitting needles and two- or three-ply yarn, cast on five or six stitches. Work in stocking stitch (first row plain, second row purl) until you have the desired length. For stripes, work two rows of each colour in turn. Cast off. Sew any loose ends of yarn back into the work.

HAT: Cast on between 12 and 20 stitches (depending on the size of the doll). Work two rows in stocking stitch. Then, knitting two together three or four times evenly across every other row, work until you have only a few stitches left. Break off the yarn, thread the end through the remaining stitches and pull tight. Sew together the side of the hat.

POM-POM: Wind yarn many times around two fingers and tie tightly in the middle with another piece of yarn. Cut the loops and trim the pom-pom to shape then sew to the top of the hat.

SOCCER BOOTS

Shape boots from polymer clay, with blobs on the base for studs. With a needle, make lace holes. Once hardened, sew thread through the holes as laces.

SOCCER BALL

Shape a soccer ball from brown polymer clay. With a piece of cardboard, mark a square on one side of the ball as shown in the diagram.

Marking the soccer ball

Turn the ball around and mark another square. Join up the corners of the squares with four lines then divide each square down the middle into two rectangles (see photograph page 65).

BOOMERANG

Using the template, cut a boomerang shape from $^1/8$in thick wood, using fine sandpaper to smooth the edges.

Boomerang template

MODEL BIPLANE

Cut a $1^1/4$in length of 10mm diameter dowel as the plane body, whittling one end into a blunt point. Using the wing template, cut two wings from $^1/16$in thick wood. Use a needle to make holes in the wings in the positions marked on the template. On one of the wings, make holes in the positions marked by crosses and sew a hanging thread through the holes. Glue the wings to the top and bottom of the body. With white thread and a fine needle, sew cables between the wings, on either side of the plane's body, as shown in the diagram.

Glue two small strips of wood to the front as propeller blades; a tiny triangle of wood to the end of the tail as a fin; and three beads to the base of the plane as wheels – two at the front and one at the end of the tail.

Model biplane wing template

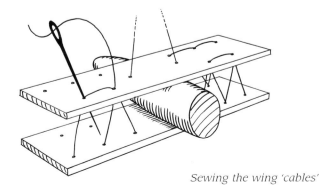

Sewing the wing 'cables'

The Music Enthusiast

Creating a teenage bedroom in a dolls' house can be a real piece of escapism – an opportunity to indulge in nostalgia for a time when music meant everything. In this bedroom, a doll-child of the late '60s or early '70s wears a flowered headband while strumming tunes on her guitar. The record player and records could be adapted to fit other settings. For example, some of the items could be put up for sale in a garage sale, as suggested by the photograph on page 2.

PROJECTS KEY

1 record player
2 records and record sleeves
3 guitar
4 song book
5 posters
6 bedspread
7 flowered headband
8 teddy bear
9 wallpaper (see page 87)
10 stencilled chair (see page 92)
11 carpet (see page 87)

WORKING NOTES: Most of the photos and magazine pictures in this scene were cut from a pop magazine. If you have access to the Internet, try searching for your chosen period or singer. The pictures reproduced there can be printed out in miniature.

If you can't find wood-effect paper (see Suppliers, page 172) for the guitar project, or if you'd like to give the record player a wood-effect finish, cover the piece in brown paper and draw on wood-grain details with a pencil.

To use templates, trace or photocopy the template onto paper, cut it out, draw around it on the material described and cut it out using an appropriate tool. Dotted lines show lines of folds. PVA wood glue is suitable for all of the projects.

RECORD PLAYER

Copy the record player base, lid and inner piece templates onto thin coloured card and score along the lines indicated by the folding markers. Cut out the shapes, fold along the scored lines and glue the tabs in position.

INNER PIECE: Push a drawing pin up through the centre of the turntable and glue in position. Put a small bead and then a record (described below) onto the pin. Use the templates to cut two knobs and a decorative corner piece from silver card. Cut three more knob circles from card and glue them in a pile at the pivot end of the playing arm. Use the template to cut a playing arm from silver card and glue the pivot end on top of the pile. Push the completed inner piece inside the record player base.

HINGE: Cut a rectangle of card $1/4$in x $1 1/8$in and fold it in half lengthways. Hold the lid on top of the base and glue the hinge across the join.

LABEL: Draw a maker's label on a scrap of card and glue it inside the lid.

RECORDS AND RECORD SLEEVES

RECORD: Cut a 1in or $5/8$in diameter circle from black card. Glue a smaller circle of coloured card to the middle, then make a hole in the middle of the record.

RECORD SLEEVE: Copy the record sleeve templates (large or small) given overleaf onto paper and score along the lines indicated by the folding markers. Cut out the sleeve, fold along the score lines and glue the tabs in position. If using the decorated templates, colour the designs with felt-tip pens. To make your own design of sleeve, copy the blank record sleeve template onto paper and make up as above. Glue on a picture cut from a pop magazine, or draw your own design with a fine pen.

TIP

There are lots of different places where you could find pictures to decorate your music enthusiast's bed-room. Take a look on page 118 for notes on picture sources.

TIP

To evoke the preferences of an older doll with a more sedate taste in music, choose record-sleeve pictures of classical musicians, and perhaps include some of the instruments and manuscript music from the section starting on page 143.

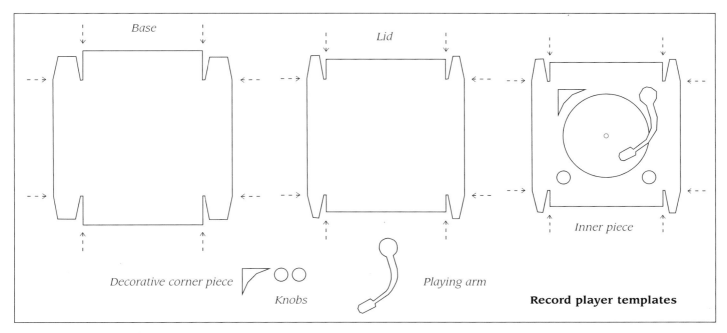

Base

Lid

Inner piece

Decorative corner piece

Knobs

Playing arm

Record player templates

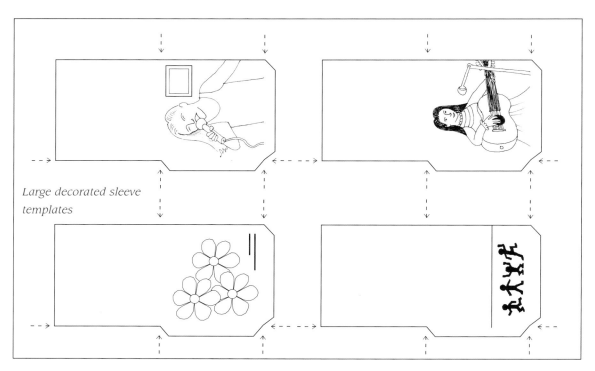

Large decorated sleeve templates

Record sleeve templates

Small blank sleeve

Large blank sleeve

TEDDY BEAR

Using the templates cut the following: a head and body from white felt and four limbs from coloured felt. Make up each piece the same: fold it in half and sew around the edge, enclosing stuffing. Sew the finished pieces together. Cut a muzzle and two ears from red felt and sew them to the bear's head. Use black thread to sew eyes, nose and a mouth.

SONG BOOK

Copy the songbook music template onto paper and cut out. Cut four rectangles of paper the same size, and one rectangle of coloured paper $1/16$in larger around the edge. Holding them together, fold them in half, then either staple or sew the pages together in the centre.

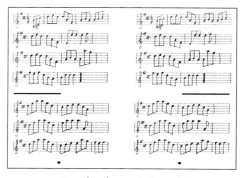

Songbook music template

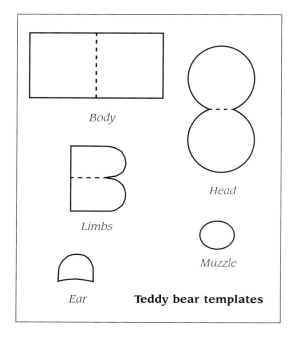

Body

Head

Limbs

Muzzle

Ear   **Teddy bear templates**

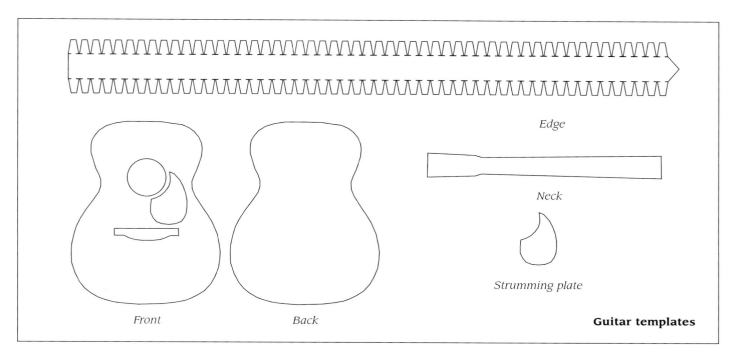

Front   *Back*   *Edge*   *Neck*   *Strumming plate*

Guitar templates

GUITAR

It is important to allow the glue to dry well between each stage of this project. Using the guitar templates, cut the following from card: one front (also cut out the sound hole); one back; one neck; one edge piece. Glue each piece to wood-effect paper and allow to dry, then cut away excess paper. Score along the dotted lines on the edge piece and fold the tabs inwards. Curve into a guitar shape and glue the tabs to the front piece. Paint spots of black and pale brown around the sound hole. Paint a black string plate below the sound hole in the position marked on the template (see photo).

STRUMMING PLATE: Using the template, cut a strumming plate from contrasting wood-effect paper and glue in place next to the sound hole.

NECK: Use a felt-tip pen to colour the neck black, then glue in position on the guitar. Cut a strip of 1/8in thick wood to fit along the back of the neck, but not into the wider strings area. Use sandpaper to smooth the edges of the wood, then glue to the back of the neck.

STRINGS: Use a sharp needle to make holes in the top of the neck, and in the bar on the front, as marked. Sew lines of thread between the holes, using the photograph as a guide.

BACK: Use a felt-tip pen to colour the inside of the back piece black. Glue to the remaining tabs on the edge piece.

HEAD AND TUNING PEGS: Glue a strip of wood to the back of the head of the guitar. Glue six tiny glass beads to the sides.

NOTE: To make a guitar from wood, use the template for the front piece to cut a guitar from 1/4in thick wood. Paint on a sound hole and strumming plate. Make the rest of the guitar following the instructions above. For the strings, cut a black string plate from card and sew the threads through this rather than through the front of the guitar. Glue in position.

POSTERS

Cut small pop images from a pop music magazine and stick them on the wall.

BEDSPREAD

Fray the edges of a rectangle of bright coloured fabric and sew floral ribbon around the edge.

FLOWERED HEADBAND

Cut a strip of felt to fit your doll's head. Copy the flower templates onto paper and cut out. Attach the flowers to the headband with coloured stitches in the centres. Wrap the band around the head and sew the ends together.

Flowers templates

The Carpenter's Workshop

A garden shed or basement room is a good place for a dolls' house carpenter's workshop. There, broken wooden objects can be placed for repairs, or pieces from one of the projects in this book to show work in progress. The hand tools in these projects are suitable for settings from late Victorian days onwards – though modern workshops may have heirloom tools still in use.

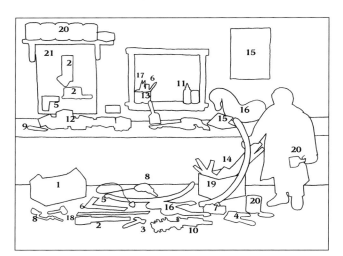

PROJECTS KEY

1 tool box
2 saws
3 hammer
4 chisels
5 right angle and 'L'
6 rulers
7 plane
8 hand and electric drills
9 knife
10 spanners
11 glue
12 boxes of nails and components
13 tins
14 wood offcuts and sawdust
15 rocking horse plans
16 rocking horse project pieces
17 pencils (see page 148)
18 mallet (see page 25)
19 cardboard box (see page 55)
20 paint tins and brush (see page 90)
21 tool board (see Tip page 78)

WORKING NOTES: When drilling holes in small pieces of wood, make the holes before cutting out the piece, to prevent splitting. Tape to a larger piece of scrap wood to hold secure whilst drilling and to protect your work surface. When cutting shaped holes, such as in the saw handles, you can stab the point of a knife into the wood at intervals around the curve, and gently carve away between the stab marks until the shape comes away. Neaten edges with fine sandpaper.

To use templates, trace or photocopy the template onto paper, cut it out, draw around it on the material described and cut it out using an appropriate tool. Dotted lines on templates indicate fold lines. PVA glue is suitable for all the projects in this section.

TOOL BOX

Using the templates, cut the following from 1/8in thick wood – two side pieces, two end pieces and one divider. Using the base template cut a base piece from cardboard. Drill 3mm holes in the end pieces in the positions marked on the template. Glue the pieces together as shown in the diagram. Cut a 2 1/8in length of kebab stick and glue it as a handle, through the holes. Sand and varnish to finish.

SAWS

WOOD AND TENON SAWS: Using the templates, cut blade pieces from cardboard. Cut out the holes and paint the blades silver.

HANDLES: For each handle, use the handle templates to cut two handle shapes from 1/16in thick balsa wood. Glue them together, enclosing the end of the blade. Use sandpaper to smooth cut edges and then paint the handle brown. Glue a tiny strip of black card along the top edge of the tenon-saw blade.

COPING SAW: Cut a 1/2in length of soft wood and sand into a smooth handle. Paint the handle brown. Cut a 1in length from a real coping-saw blade and push the end into the handle. Thread

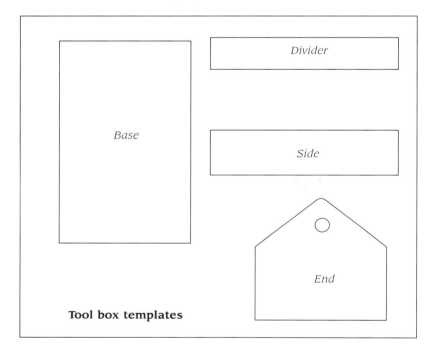

Tool box templates

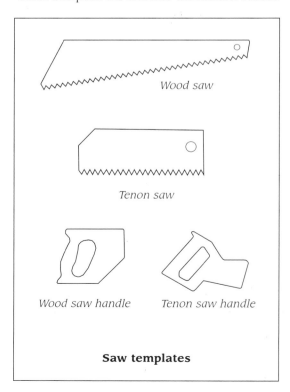

Wood saw

Tenon saw

Wood saw handle *Tenon saw handle*

Saw templates

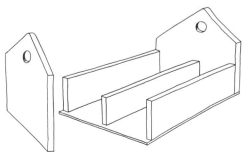

Tool box assembly

a bead over the blade and glue to the handle. Bend a paper-clip into the shape of the top of the saw, with short protruding spikes at each end. Push one spike into the bead. Glue a second bead over the end of the spike and blade, as shown in the diagram.

Coping saw assembly

HAMMER

Model a hammer head from polymer clay and push it onto a length of kebab stick. Bake to harden with the stick in place. Paint the stick brown and the head silver.

CHISELS

Using the two templates, cut chisel shapes from card. With a knife, bevel the ends into blade shapes. Model polymer clay handles onto the card and bake to harden with the card in place. Paint the blades silver.

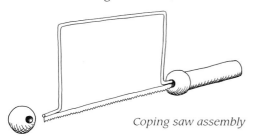

Chisel blades templates

RIGHT ANGLE AND 'L'

RIGHT ANGLE: Cut a $1/4$in x $3/4$in piece from $1/8$in thick wood. Cut a slit in the top and slot in a $1/4$in x $3/4$in piece of card. Paint the card silver and the handle brown. Paint silver screw spots where the pieces join.

'L': Copy the template onto paper and glue it to black card then cut out the shape.

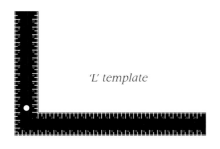

'L' template

RULERS

LONG RULER: Copy the long ruler template onto paper and glue it to card. Cut out the shape and colour it with a yellow felt-tip pen.

SHORT RULER: Cut a 1in length of wood and make the markings with a fine pen.

PLANE

Cut a 1in piece from $1/4$in square wood and paint it brown. Make a blade slot in the base and another on the top. Glue a $1/4$in square of card into the top slot, supported at an angle by a $1/4$in piece of cocktail stick. Glue a bead to the front of the blade. Paint the blade, bead and lower slot silver, and the cocktail stick black.

DRILLS

HAND DRILL: Bend a drill shape from wire using the diagram as a guide. Model handles and a drill chuck from brown polymer clay and bake to harden, with the wire in place. Once cool, paint the drill chuck silver.

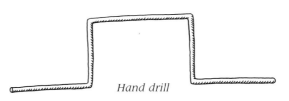

Hand drill

ELECTRIC DRILL: Model a drill from polymer clay. Poke the end of a piece of card into the clay to mimic ventilation grill marks. Push a tiny length of craft wire into the chuck section as a drill bit. Poke a length of cable into the base of the drill. Make a polymer clay plug on the other end of the cable and push tiny lengths of craft wire into the plug. Bake to harden with the cable in place. Once cool, paint the drill chuck silver.

SOCKET: Cut a rectangle of polymer clay and make socket holes. Add a tiny blob as a switch. Once hardened, glue to the wall.

KNIFE

Using the knife blade template, cut a knife shape from card. Model a polymer clay handle onto the card and bake to harden with the card in place. Paint the blade silver.

Long ruler template

Knife blade template

SPANNERS

Copy the spanner templates onto paper and glue them to the back of silver card. Cut them out with a scalpel.

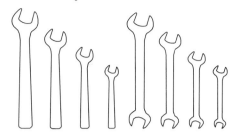

Spanners templates

GLUE

Model a glue bottle from blue polymer clay and the lid from red clay.

TIP

To make a tool board, lay out tools on a rectangle of dark card. Draw round them then paint the shapes in a light colour. Push in small pins on which to hang the tools (see photograph on page 74).

TINS

Cut a piece of card $1\frac{1}{4}$in x $\frac{5}{8}$in, coil it into a tin shape, glue the short edges together and clip together until dry. Glue a circle of card to the base, then paint the tin silver. Using the food tin label templates on page 52, cut labels from paper. Colour the details with a felt-tip pen and glue to the tin.

BOXES OF NAILS AND COMPONENTS

Copy the box base and lid templates onto thin card and score along the lines indicated by the folding markers. Draw stripes on the boxes with a felt-tip pen. Cut out the boxes, fold into shape and glue the tabs in position. Fill the boxes with earring fittings, beads or other small objects, or cut tiny lengths of craft wire to look like nails.

WOOD OFFCUTS AND SAWDUST

Collect lengths of wood, sawdust and other offcuts you have made whilst working and scatter them around the carpenter's workshop or stack them in boxes (see page 55 for boxes).

ROCKING HORSE PLANS

Copy the rocking horse plans and booklet templates onto paper. Colour in the details with felt-tip pens, then fold the booklet piece in half.

ROCKING HORSE PROJECT PIECES

Following the instructions on page 16, cut wooden rocking horse pieces for your carpenter to work on.

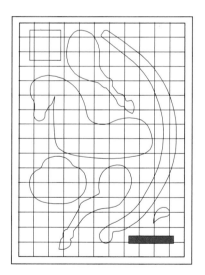

Rocking horse plans template

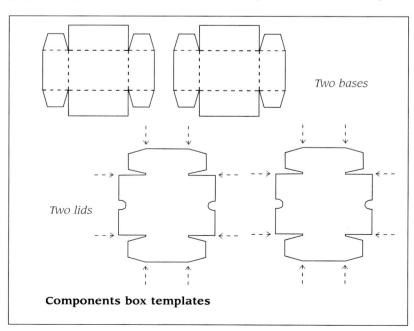

Two bases

Two lids

Components box templates

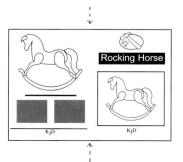

Rocking horse booklet template

The Sewing Room

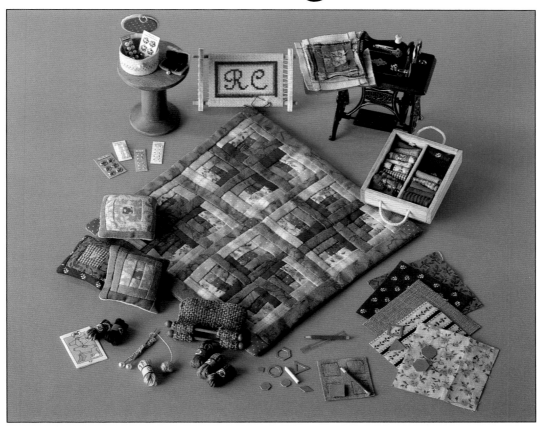

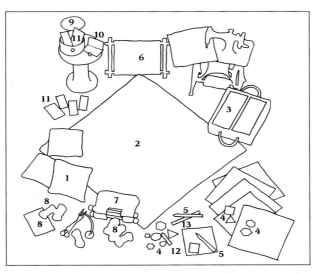

A sewing scene can be an attractive activity in a dolls' house: a grandmother might be darning socks or stitching a sampler to celebrate the birth of a new member of the family. In a Victorian household, servants might be earning a few extra pennies by making patchwork cushions to sell at the market. Perhaps a group of women have gathered during wartime to knit socks for their men-folk away at the front. Whatever your choice of scene, your own needlecraft items can be miniature records of events in your own family history. Ask relations for scraps of fabric from wedding and christening dresses, and from their own treasured fabric collections.

PROJECTS KEY

1 patchwork cushion
2 patchwork bed cover
3 box of fabric samples
4 patchwork templates
5 pencil
6 embroidery frame
7 knitting bag
8 knitting, yarns and pattern
9 sewing basket
10 needle book
11 cards of buttons
12 pastel (see page 148)
13 ruler (see page 149)

WORKING NOTES: When making fabric projects, look out for scraps of lightweight fabrics with small floral or repeat patterns. Sections cut from fabrics with larger patterns are also appropriate. When choosing colours and planning your layout, arrange all the fabrics on a work surface and sort them into tone or colour order. This technique is also useful when choosing colours of embroidery threads that will work well together.

When drilling holes in small pieces of wood, it is best to make the holes before cutting out the piece, to prevent splitting. Tape to a larger piece of scrap wood to hold secure whilst drilling, and to protect your work surface. Neaten cut edges with fine sandpaper. PVA glue is suitable for all the projects.

To use templates, trace or photocopy the template onto paper, cut it out, draw around it on the material described and cut it out using an appropriate tool. Grey dotted lines show lines of sewing.

PATCHWORK CUSHION

The cushion is made from a single 'block' of patchwork. Using the templates A, B, C and D below, cut the following:
one piece A in first fabric;
two piece A and two piece B in second fabric;
two piece B and two piece C in third fabric;
two piece C and two piece D in fourth fabric.

The grey dotted lines show the lines of sewing. FRONT: Match up the square of the first fabric with one piece A of second fabric. With right sides facing, sew together along one edge. Attach the second piece A of the second fabric in the same way. Press the patchwork flat. Sew the two piece B of the second fabric to each side of this piece. Continue adding rectangles in pairs until the cushion front is complete.

BACK: Cut a 2in square from fabric. Match it with the patchwork piece, with right sides facing together, then sew around three edges. Turn the cushion right-side out, and fill with a little stuffing. Push the raw edges of the fabric inside the cushion and sew the edge closed.

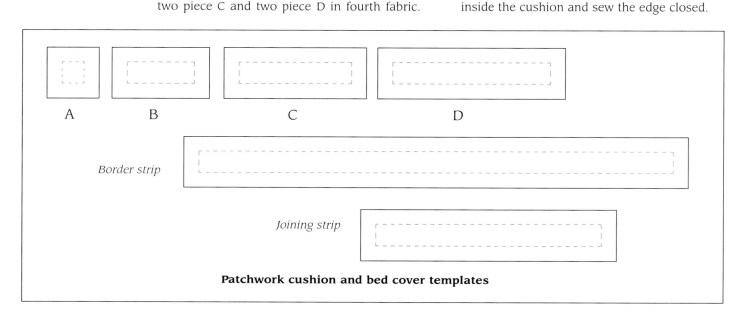

A   B   C   D

Border strip

Joining strip

Patchwork cushion and bed cover templates

PATCHWORK BED COVER

The patchwork bed cover is for a single dolls' house bed (see photograph on page 13). It is built up from sixteen blocks following the instructions for the patchwork cushion (above) and using the same A, B, C and D templates, but it uses nine different fabrics. Each block uses one less row than a cushion block. Use the photograph as a guide for colours and tones, or design your own arrangement of fabrics. Make sixteen blocks, then sew them together in four squares – four blocks to each square.

Choose a border fabric and using the joining strip template, cut four short joining strips from the border fabric and one contrasting central square using template A. Sew the patchwork squares, joining strips and central square together, using the picture as a guide.

Using the border strip templates, cut four long border strips from border fabric, and four corner squares from contrasting fabric using template A. Sew them around the patchwork, using the photograph as a guide.

BACK: Cut a 7in square from backing fabric. Match it with the patchwork piece, with right sides facing together. Sew around three edges. Turn the cover right side out, push the raw edges of the fabric inside the cover and sew the edge closed.

BOX OF FABRIC SAMPLES

Using the templates, cut two side and two end pieces from 1/8in thick wood, and one interior piece from 1/16in thick wood. Drill two holes in each end piece in the positions marked on the template. Cut two 2in lengths of string and push the ends through the holes, tying each in a knot and trimming off any excess.

Using the base template, cut a base piece from cardboard. Glue all the wood and cardboard pieces together in a box shape, with the interior piece running down the middle.

Roll up tiny scraps of fabric to fill the box, arranged in order of colour and tone.

The fabric samples box showing how the wooden pieces fit together

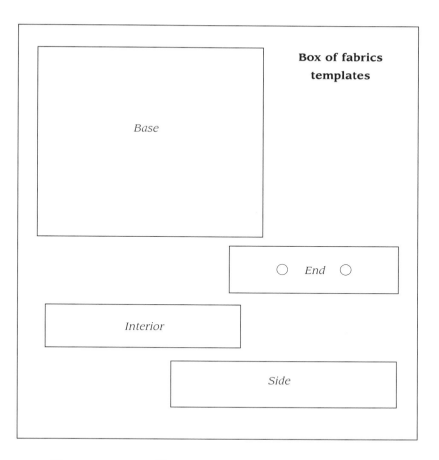

Box of fabrics templates

Base

End

Interior

Side

PATCHWORK TEMPLATES

Copy the patchwork templates onto paper and glue them to the back of silver card. Cut them out with a scalpel.

Patchwork templates

PENCIL

Cut a tiny length of wooden cocktail stick. Paint the stick red, leaving the point plain. Dip the tip in black paint. To add an eraser at the end of the pencil, dip the end in pink paint and add a line of gold.

EMBROIDERY FRAME

FRAME: Using the template, mark out two embroidery frame edge pieces on $^1/_8$in thick wood, ready for cutting. Drill two 3mm holes in each piece in the positions marked on the template, then cut out the edge pieces. Cut two 3in lengths of kebab stick and push the ends through the holes to form the rectangular frame.

Embroidery frame edge template

Cut a 2$^1/_8$in x 2$^5/_8$in piece of embroidery canvas (20-30 holes per inch is ideal). Embroider a floral or letter design of your choice in the middle of the canvas using single strands of embroidery thread.

Glue the top and bottom of the canvas to the kebab sticks, allow to dry, then roll them round to tighten. Secure the kebab sticks in their holes with glue.

Attach white thread to one side of the canvas and make big stitches over the edge of the frame and into the canvas as tightening laces. Repeat on the opposite side.

NEEDLE: Push a tiny length of craft wire through the canvas. Glue a piece of embroidery thread around the end of the wire.

KNITTING BAG

Using the template, cut two knitting bag pieces from hessian, and cut a T shape in each piece as marked. Sew around all cut edges with buttonhole stitch, as shown in the diagram, to prevent fraying. Fold the edges in along the dotted lines and secure with stitches.

Cut two 2$^1/_8$in lengths of cocktail stick. Glue four small wooden beads on the ends, then

TIP

Look in embroidery books and stitching magazines for ideas on designs which can be scaled down and worked in the embroidery frame. Cross stitch designs are particularly adaptable and can be stitched using whole or half cross stitch.

paint the sticks and beads. Fold the top sections of one of the bag pieces over the stick and stitch in place (see photograph on page 79). Repeat for the other bag piece. Match up the two bag pieces with right sides outwards and sew together around three edges between the two crosses marked on the template.

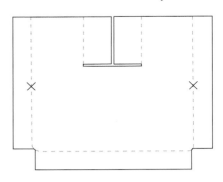

Knitting bag template

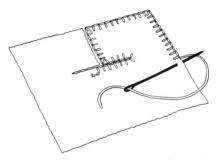

Buttonhole stitching around the edges of the knitting bag

KNITTING, YARNS AND PATTERNS

KNITTING: Using long dressmaker's pins and embroidery thread, work a few lines of knitting. Roll the end of the thread into a ball and secure the end with a dab of glue.

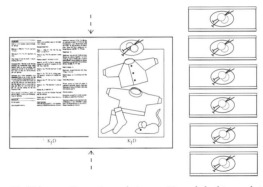

Knitting pattern template   Yarn label templates

YARNS: Wind tiny balls of yarn from embroidery thread, securing the ends with a dab of glue. Copy the yarn label templates onto paper, colour them with felt-tip pens to match the yarns and cut them out. Glue a label around each ball.

KNITTING PATTERN: Copy the knitting pattern template onto paper and colour it with felt-tip pens. Cut it out and fold it in half.

SEWING BASKET

BASE: Using the template, cut a base piece from cardboard. Glue a circle of lining fabric to one side.

SIDE: Cut a $3^1/8$in x $^5/8$in piece of embroidery canvas. Dab a little PVA glue on the edges to prevent fraying. Put glue on the edges of the base piece. Coil the side piece around the base and glue the short edges together, clipping together until dry.

HINGE: Cut a 1in length of ribbon and glue it inside the basket as shown in the diagram.

LINING: Cut two pieces 3in x $^1/2$in – one from card and one from lining fabric. Glue them together, coil into a tube and glue inside the basket.

A needlewoman's side table can be made by gluing a circle of wood to the top of a wooden cotton reel

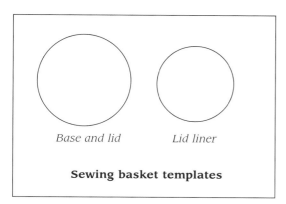

Base and lid   *Lid liner*

Sewing basket templates

Making the hinge on the sewing basket

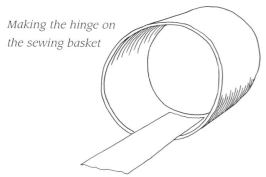

LID: Using the template, cut a lid piece from cardboard. Glue it to a circle of embroidery canvas. Using the lid liner template, cut a lid liner from card and glue it to a circle of lining fabric. Glue the lid and lid liner together, trapping the end of the ribbon between them, and a loop of cotton sticking out of the front of the lid. Clip together until dry.

FASTENER: Sew a bead to the front of the basket.

NEEDLE BOOK

Cut a piece of black felt, $^3/4$in x $^5/8$in and a piece of coloured felt, 1in x $^3/4$in. Sew them together down the middle. Push tiny lengths of wire into the black felt, then sew on a loop of thread and a bead fastener.

CARDS OF BUTTONS

Copy the templates onto thin card. Glue tiny beads or earring fittings on the spots.

Button card templates

THE DECORATOR

This chapter looks at techniques and materials for decorating your dolls' house – from curtain tiebacks and poles to fabrics and decorative tassels. There are designs for doorknobs, key plates and tiles of different periods. There is also a range of flooring – from a simple corduroy covering to complex parquet designs suited to a grand dining room. And there are patterns for paint brushes, paint tins, rollers and a step ladder – the tools of the trade for the DIY enthusiast.

Home Improvements

On display in this DIY store are a range of floor coverings from textured fabrics, a selection of hand-made wallpapers, different designs of curtain poles and tiles, and a choice of door furniture. The projects show how different periods and styles can be evoked by very simple variations in shape, colour and texture. Colourful doorknobs made from wooden beads would look appropriate on a 1950s cabinet or in a child's bedroom. But with the addition of metallic paint, they become the door handles of a Victorian town house. Tiles cut from thick card can be decorated with bright wrapping paper for a modern kitchen, or with a simple design in blue to surround a seventeenth-century fireplace. If you are making a dolls' house DIY scene in progress, in which the dolls are choosing their own décor, then the carpet swatch book, paint charts, wallpaper books and catalogues will be perfect additions to your scene.

PROJECTS KEY

1 floor coverings
2 samples book
3 wallpapers
4 curtain poles
5 door furniture
6 tiles, chart and boxes
7 paint charts
8 fences and railings
9 posters and catalogues
10 tins of paint (see page 90)
11 wood offcuts (see page 78)

WORKING NOTES: When using a ruler and felt-tip pen to draw regular lines on the wallpapers or tiles, wipe the ruler edge with a paper tissue between strokes to avoid smudging. When erasing pencil guidelines and marks, keep the eraser clean by rubbing it frequently on a spare piece of paper.

For projects that use polymer clay, make the model on a piece of plain cardboard, then bake to harden following the manufacturer's instructions. Delicate pieces can be baked on the cardboard and removed once completely cool.

To mimic metal, paint finished models with metallic paint (such as Humbrol enamel). For a wrought-iron effect, paint the piece with black acrylic paint, with a little PVA glue in the paint to help it stick to the surface. Finish with varnish. PVA glue is suitable for all of the projects, unless otherwise stated.

To use templates, trace or photocopy the template onto paper, cut it out, draw around it on the material described and cut it out using an appropriate tool.

FLOOR COVERINGS

The rolls of blue, red, brown and green in the photograph show different textured fabrics useful for floor coverings – the red is velvet, the blue is very fine corduroy, the brown is hessian and the green is felt. Corduroy, velvet and hessian tend to fray, so back your carpet piece with an iron-on fabric backing such as Vilene, following the manufacturer's instructions.

PATTERNED VINYL: Using the templates and instructions in Flooring on pages 94–95, make the pattern from coloured papers, or draw out the design with felt-tip pens.

SAMPLES BOOK

Cut about ten rectangles of coloured felt for carpet samples or ten rectangles of wallpaper samples, and two rectangles of black card. Stack them and hold them together in a clip or vice with the hinge edge protruding. Sew a hinge with silver thread and tie the ends together.

WALLPAPERS

The wallpapers displayed in this scene are created with felt-tip pen or acrylic paint, applied to coloured paper. Tape the base paper to a work surface whilst working.

TWO-COLOUR STRIPED WALLPAPER: Using a ruler and felt-tip pen, draw the bold parallel lines. Using a pencil and very faint marks, make regular positioning marks along the stripes. Draw in the details using the pencil marks to keep the design regular. Gently erase pencil marks.

FLORAL STRIPED WALLPAPER: Draw in the parallel lines as described above. Use a pencil to mark out the long wavy curves of the flowers and foliage. Using a pencil and very faint marks, make regular flower positioning marks along the curves. Paint in the flowers. Join with green stems, then add the leaves. Once dry, gently erase pencil marks.

LARGE FLORAL PAPER: Using a pencil and very faint marks, mark out a grid of squares. Using a fine paint brush, paint small flowers at the corners of the squares. In the centre of each square, paint a circle, and then petals. Once dry, gently erase the pencil marks.

CURTAIN POLES

For a basic pole, cut a kebab stick 1in wider than your window. Note, if you are hanging your curtain on rings, remember to put the rings onto the stick before gluing the end pieces in place. See Curtains, Blinds and Textiles pages 99–101 for hanging curtains.

FLEUR-DE-LIS AND CURLS: Model end pieces from polymer clay. Push onto the ends of the kebab stick and bake to harden with the stick in place. Colour the pieces with metallic paint and once dry, glue pieces together.

WOODEN POLES: Glue beads or buttons on the ends of the kebab stick. Paint the stick to match.

DOOR FURNITURE

The brass-effect door furniture is made from polymer clay. Make the models on cardboard, then bake to harden following the manufacturer's instructions, with the cardboard in place. Once cooled, remove the cardboard and colour the model with brass metallic paint.

DOOR KNOCKERS: Press out polymer clay and, with a knife, draw the oval or decorative plate shape and cut away any excess. Add a knocker, shape the details and draw surface designs with a pointed stick.

DOORKNOBS: Press out polymer clay and, with a knife, draw the round, hexagonal or square plate shape, cutting away any excess. Put a tiny blob of clay in the middle, then a larger handle blob on top. Press down to join the pieces.

HANDLES WITH KEY PLATES: Press out polymer clay and, with a knife, draw the plate shape and cut away any excess. Put a tiny blob of clay near the top. Model a handle and press gently on top of the blob. Support the end of the handle with a blob of clay (remove when hardened). Use a pointed stick to make the keyhole detail.

COLOURED HANDLES: Glue coloured wooden beads onto flat circular wooden beads.

TILES, CHART AND BOXES

TILES: Start by cutting 9/16in squares of thick white card and decorate in the following ways:
• Draw designs with fine pen and colour some areas with pencil crayon.

TIP

If you are displaying your home improvements projects in a miniature shop, coordinate your display racks and boards by using labels of the same coloured card, with a line of paler colour around the edge. In the photograph on pages 84–85, two greens were chosen for the coordinating colour scheme.

Tile chart template

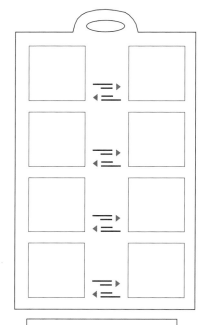

Tile box template

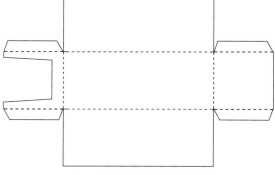

Paint chart templates

• Cut squares from the repeat patterns on wrapping paper and glue in place.

• Paint floral designs.

• Paint the whole tile with a plain colour, then add polka dots in white paint.

In a store, tiles can be displayed in boxes or on a chart. To make a chart, copy the tile chart template onto white card and glue the tiles in place.

TILE BOX: Copy the tile box template onto thin card and score along the dotted lines. Cut out the shape, fold it up and glue the tabs in position. Tiles can then be stacked in the box.

PAINT CHARTS

Copy the two paint chart templates onto thin card and cut them out. Use pencil crayon to colour the samples, pressing lightly at the bottom and more heavily towards the top (see photograph, right).

FENCES AND RAILINGS

GARDEN FENCE: For each panel cut the following: from card, thirteen slats 4in x ^{3}/$_8$in; from ^{1}/$_8$in thick wood, one base 4in x ^{1}/$_2$in; from ^{1}/$_4$in thick wood, one top 4in x ^{1}/$_4$in. Tape the base piece to a work surface and glue the slats in position, one by one, overlapping each piece slightly as shown in the diagram. Glue the top piece in place and leave to dry thoroughly.

POST TOPS: Cut sufficient ^{1}/$_2$in x 5in post pieces from ^{1}/$_4$in thick wood. Glue the posts and fence panels together.

PICKET FENCE: Cut two long ^{1}/$_4$in wide strips of thick white card. Tape them parallel on a work surface, 1in apart. Cut lots of 2^1/$_2$in long, ^{1}/$_4$in wide strips of thick white card and trim one end of each into a point. Glue these uprights to the long strips, ^{1}/$_4$in apart.

RAILINGS: Cut two long poles from 5mm diameter dowel. Tape them parallel on a work surface, about 3in apart. Cut lots of 4^1/$_2$in lengths of kebab stick and use Super Glue to stick them to the long poles, ^{1}/$_4$in apart. Paint black and finish with varnish.

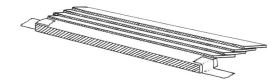

Gluing the fence slats together

POSTERS AND CATALOGUES

POSTERS: Cut interiors pictures from magazines and glue onto white paper. Cut out leaving a border, adding tiny text or logos with a fine pen.

CATALOGUES: Follow the instructions for the baseball magazines on page 69, using pictures cut from an interior decorating magazine.

Dolls' House DIY

When you are in the process of decorating your dolls' house, or if a room is still incomplete, it can be great fun to leave some DIY paraphernalia scattered around the place to make it look as if the . dolls are hard at work. *DIY as a hobby became tremendously popular in the late nineteenth and early twentieth century, with the great rise in home ownership, and people's desire to make their personal mark on their dwellings. This section gives plenty of ideas for all the DIY equipment needed to satisfy this popular hobby.*

PROJECTS KEY

1 paint cloth and sponge
2 paint spill
3 tins of paint
4 paint brushes
5 step ladder
6 plaster, hod and trowel
7 roller and paint tray
8 rolls of wallpaper
9 stencil stippling brush and palette
10 stencils and borders
11 stencilled chair
12 stencil edging
13 cardboard box (see page 55)
14 bucket (see page 62)

WORKING NOTES: The paint brushes, ladder and hod are made from pieces of dowel and pine strip. It's good to have a range of these to hand to create the different shapes required. For a stained wood appearance use a commercial wood stain, or colour the wood with a felt-tip pen. For an opaque finish use acrylic paint. You can seal and finish the colour with any clear varnish, although it's best to use an oil-based varnish on top of water-based paints, to avoid smudging. PVA wood glue is suitable for all of the projects.

To use templates, trace or photocopy the template onto paper, cut it out, draw around it on the material described and cut it out using an appropriate tool.

TINS OF PAINT

Cut $3/4$in lengths from a $5/8$in diameter cardboard tube, using sandpaper to neaten. Glue circles of cardboard to the ends of the tubes, then paint the tins silver.

Copy the paint tin label templates onto paper, colour in the details, and cut them out. Glue to the tins. Fill the tins with coloured paint (such as emulsion) and leave to dry. Or fill with air-drying clay and when dry, paint the top of the clay.

LID: Using the lid top and inner piece templates, cut two circles of cardboard and glue them together. Paint the lid silver, then glue a circle of coloured paper to the top to match the paint inside.

PAINT BRUSHES

Using one of the paint brush templates and a sharp scalpel, cut a paint brush shape from $1/8$in thick wood, smoothing the edges with sandpaper. Score along the grey dotted line on both sides of the brush. Below the line, score deep lines into the wood as bristles. Paint this bristle area black and the handle red, then paint a silver stripe in between.

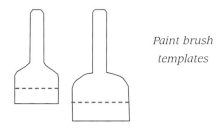

Paint brush templates

PAINT CLOTH AND SPONGE

CLOTH: Spatter a piece of crumpled calico with paint and leave to dry.

SPONGE: Cut a small rectangle from a bathroom or kitchen sponge.

PAINT SPILL

Mix acrylic paint with PVA glue and drip it into a spill shape on a smooth plastic surface (such as the lid of a plastic box). Allow to dry thoroughly, then carefully peel up the spill shape and position in the scene.

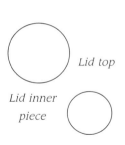

Lid top

Lid inner piece

Paint tin templates

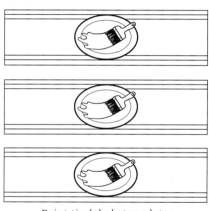

Paint tin labels templates

STEP LADDER

Using the step ladder templates, cut the following from 1/8in thick wood: four legs; six steps; two struts, one top piece; one top step. Glue three small steps between two of the legs, and three small steps between the other two legs as shown in the diagram. Glue these pieces together with the top piece, then glue the top step on top. Push a strut up between the legs on either side and glue in position.

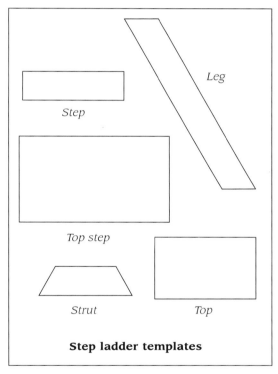

Step — *Leg* — *Top step* — *Strut* — *Top*

Step ladder templates

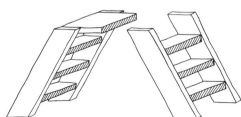

Step ladder assembly

PLASTER, HOD AND TROWEL

HOD AND PLASTER: Using the template, cut a hod handle from 1/8in thick wood, and a 1 1/2in square of wood for the hod plate. Glue them together and paint the hod brown. Add a lump of pre-baked white polymer clay as plaster.

TROWEL: Cut a 1 1/8in x 1/2in trowel plate from

card and paint it silver. Using the trowel template, cut a handle piece from 1/8in thick wood and paint it brown. Glue the pieces together.

Hod handle template   *Trowel handle template*

ROLLER AND PAINT TRAY

ROLLER: Bend a 2 1/2in length of wire into a roller handle using the template as a guide. Wind coloured tape tightly around the handle.

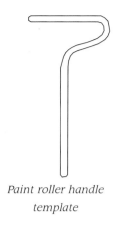

Paint roller handle template

Cut a rectangle of sponge or foam and wrap it around the roller spindle. Glue it in place, and clip the ends together until thoroughly dry.

TRAY: Using the seed tray template on page 136, cut a paint tray piece from card. Score and fold along the dotted lines and glue the tabs in position. The top edge folds out and down to form a rim. Paint and varnish the tray to finish.

ROLLS OF WALLPAPER

Roll up long thin rectangles of wrapping paper or dolls' house wallpaper (see page 87). The bucket (see page 63) has been filled with PVA glue to look like wallpaper paste.

STENCIL STIPPLING BRUSH AND PALETTE

Cut a 1in length of 5mm diameter dowel, whittling one end into a narrow handle and then smoothing the edges with sandpaper. Score a line around the other end to mark the top of the bristles. Below the line, score deep lines into the wood as bristles. Paint this area black with a silver stripe above it.

PALETTE: Cut a rectangle of card and dab on patches of coloured paint.

Stencils templates

STENCILS AND BORDERS

Copy the stencil templates onto thin card. Using a very sharp scalpel, cut out the designs. The card stencils cannot be used with paint, as they become damaged too quickly, but using a very sharp, hard pencil, you can draw through the stencils onto paper or painted wood. Remove the stencil and paint in the shapes using a very fine brush.

STENCILLED CHAIR

For another stencil effect, draw and colour stencil patterns on paper. Glue them to painted furniture. Remember that the paper colour should match the furniture.

STENCIL EDGING

Cut stencils can also be glued directly to furniture to look like moulding. The card colour should match or complement the colour of the furniture.

Flooring

*T*he choice of flooring in a room can really set the tone, indicating the wealth and taste of the dolls who inhabit it. An elegant eighteenth century ballroom demands a wooden parquet floor.

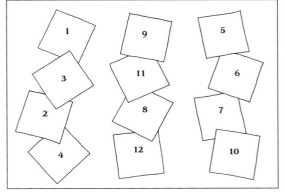

The clean white lines of a conservatory would be beautifully complemented by a colourful tiled floor, and interest and colour can be added to a plain kitchen with a simple tiled floor created with coloured papers. For a modern patio area, choose a crazy-paving design. In this section, ideas for interesting flooring techniques are explored, using the most inexpensive of materials.

PROJECTS KEY

1 hessian squares
2 bamboo matting
3 cork tiles
4 embroidered canvas border
5 crazy paving
6 complex geometric tiles
7 simple kitchen tiles
8 brick tiled border
9 wooden parquet floor
10 complex parquet floor
11 basket design parquet floor
12 parquet border on wooden floor

WORKING NOTES: When constructing floors be accurate and careful at every stage. Take care to make accurate measurements, draw accurate grids and cut shaped tiles with regular shapes. To plan out your floor, cut a piece of cardboard the exact size and shape of your room. Use this as the baseboard upon which to draw gluing grids and to compile your work. For awkward corners, make separate segments of the floor, to match up later. For complex flooring patterns, suggestions have been made for the best order in which to work. PVA glue is suitable for all of the flooring projects. Allow the glue to dry between each stage.

To use templates, trace or photocopy the template onto paper, cut it out, draw around it on the material described and cut it out using an appropriate tool.

HESSIAN SQUARES

Draw out a grid of squares (approximately 1in square or bigger) on your baseboard. Cut squares of fine hessian or canvas fabric and glue them in position using the grid as a guide. Leave under a weight (such as a large book protected by a plastic bag) to dry.

BAMBOO MATTING

Select kebab sticks of a similar colour and tone, using sandpaper to smooth any obvious defects or splinters. Glue lengths of kebab stick next to each other on the baseboard to cover the whole area. This method is best for small areas such as the floor of a conservatory or hallway.

CORK TILES

Draw out a grid of squares (approximately $1/2$in square or bigger) on your baseboard. With a sharp knife, and cutting slowly so as not to drag pieces of cork out of position, cut square cork tiles from a cork table-mat. Cork has natural variations in colour, so sort the tiles into a pleasing design. You may find that if you turn half of the tiles over, you have a different tone that can be alternated across the floor (as in the photograph). Glue the tiles in position using the grid as a guide.

TIP

Once you've mastered the tiling techniques described in this section, try making up your own designs. You could even create a freestyle mosaic floor using pictures of Roman designs as your inspiration, and using tiny fragments of coloured paper.

EMBROIDERED CANVAS BORDER

Cut a piece of embroidery canvas to fit your room. Dab a small amount of PVA glue around the edge to prevent fraying and allow to dry. Use the embroidery grid pattern as a guide to embroider a border around the edge using embroidery stranded cotton (floss) or normal sewing thread. This edging design can also be used for canvas rugs.

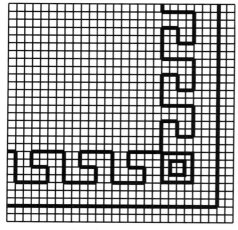

Embroidery grid pattern

CRAZY PAVING

With a dark pen, draw out a crazy paving design onto your baseboard – irregular polygons separated by grouting borders (see photograph as a guide). With a dark pen, trace the pattern onto tracing paper. Glue the tracing paper, pen side down, onto a piece of light grey cardboard. Cut out the cardboard tile shapes and then paint the grouting pattern on the baseboard in dark grey. Glue the light grey tile shapes in position on the baseboard.

COMPLEX GEOMETRIC TILES

The templates and layout stages are on page 95. First paint the baseboard brown. Then trace the large hexagon template onto paper and cut it out. Draw round it on your baseboard. Leaving a $1/16$in border, trace around the hexagon again and again across the board, tessellating the shapes (see stage one diagram). Count the number of hexagons on your board.

Using the small shapes templates, cut tile pieces from coloured card. Cut six border pieces, six shallow triangles, six tall triangles, and one small hexagon for each of the large hexagons on your baseboard.

Glue the border pieces in place on the baseboard, lining up with the edges of the large hexagon shapes (see stage two diagram).

Glue the shallow triangle pieces in place on the baseboard, leaving a small border with the border pieces (see stage three diagram).

Glue the tall triangles in place on the baseboard (see stage four diagram).

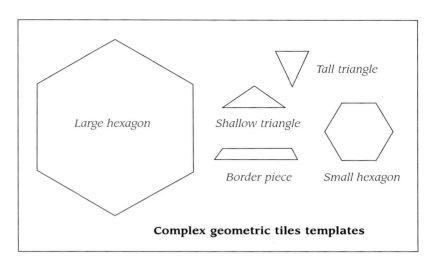

Complex geometric tiles templates

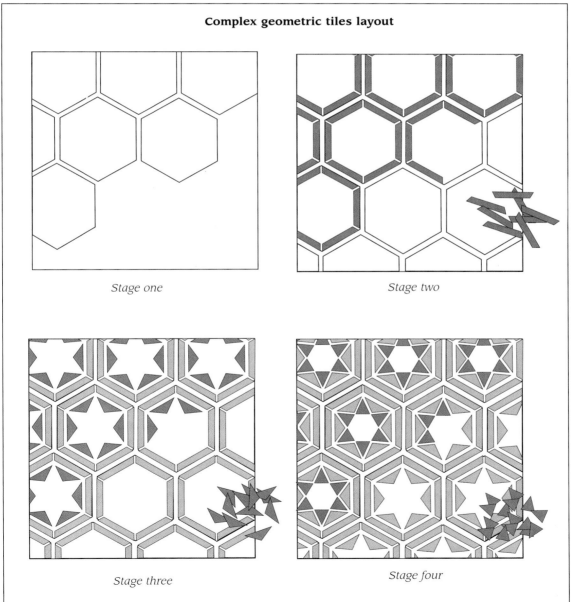

Complex geometric tiles layout

Stage one

Stage two

Stage three

Stage four

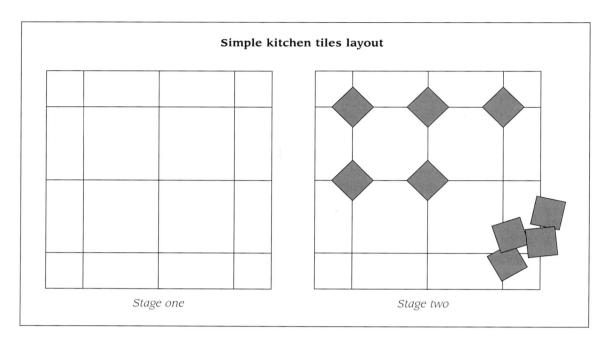

Simple kitchen tiles layout

Stage one

Stage two

Finally, glue the small hexagons in the centre of each panel on the baseboard. You could varnish to finish.

SIMPLE KITCHEN TILES

Using a ruler and fine black pen, draw out a grid of squares on white card (see stage one diagram above), then glue the card to your baseboard.

On a piece of coloured card, draw out a grid of smaller squares. Cut them out and glue a coloured square on each crossover on the grid at a 45-degree angle (see stage two diagram).

BRICK TILED BORDER

This flooring is particularly useful for outdoor patio, driveway or courtyard areas, or for Tudor kitchens. Paint a large piece of paper with brick colours and use a sponge to dab on different tones of browns, ochres and reds. Once dry,

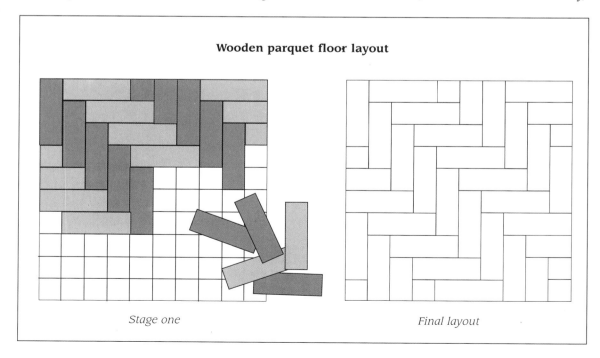

Wooden parquet floor layout

Stage one

Final layout

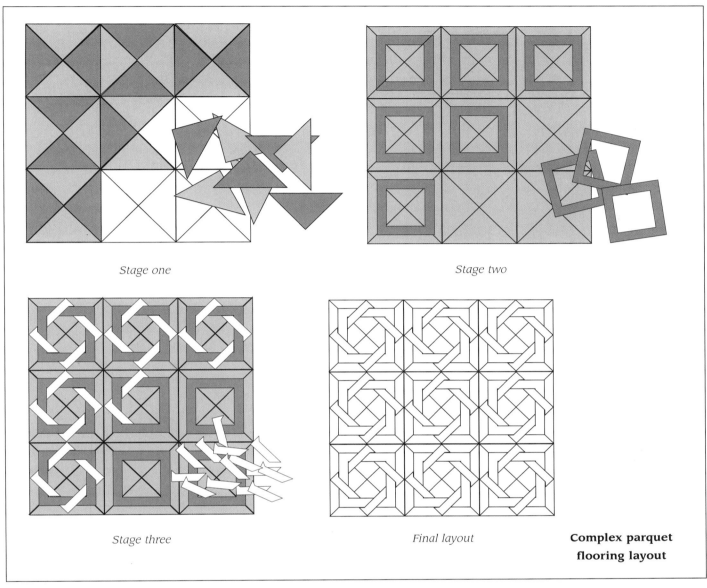

Stage one

Stage two

Stage three

Final layout

Complex parquet flooring layout

cut 3/4in x 1/4in rectangles from the paper to stick as brick tiles to your baseboard. Paint the baseboard brown and build up a parquet design as described below, but leaving a small grouting border around each brick. Sort the rectangles into tones and frame your floor area with dark and light lines of bricks (see photograph on page 93 as a guide).

WOODEN PARQUET FLOOR

This flooring is particularly good for ballrooms and dining rooms from the eighteenth century onwards. The layout stages are on page 96. Cut

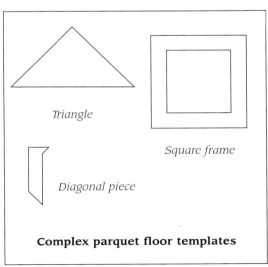

Triangle

Square frame

Diagonal piece

Complex parquet floor templates

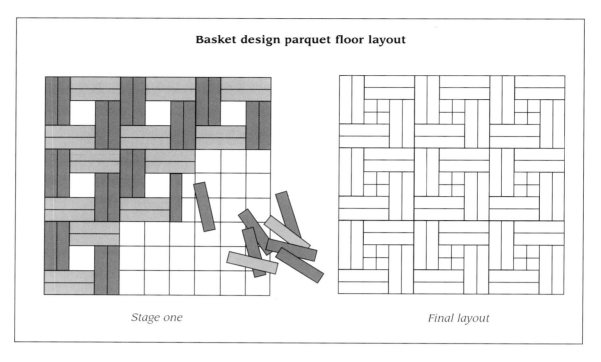

Basket design parquet floor layout

Stage one   *Final layout*

¾in x ¼in tiles from wood-effect paper. Draw out a grid of ¼in squares on your baseboard. Glue the tiles to the baseboard, using the guidelines to help you keep the parquet design accurate (see stage one diagram page 96) and using the final layout diagram as a guide.

COMPLEX PARQUET FLOOR

Draw out a grid of 1¼in squares on your baseboard. Use the triangle template on page 97 to cut triangle pieces from wood-effect paper – half of them in a dark tone, half in a medium tone. Glue them to the baseboard (see stage one diagram page 97), and using the final layout diagram as a guide.

Use the square frame template to cut square frame pieces from wood-effect paper. Glue them to the baseboard (see stage two diagram).

Use the diagonal piece template to cut diagonal frame pieces from a contrasting wood-effect paper. Glue them to the baseboard (see stage three diagram).

BASKET DESIGN PARQUET FLOOR

Cut 1in x ¼in tiles from wood-effect paper – half of them in a medium tone, half in a light tone. Draw out a grid of ¼in squares on your

baseboard. Glue the tiles to the baseboard, using the guidelines to keep your parquet design accurate (see stage one diagram above) and using the final layout diagram as a guide. Glue ½in squares of dark brown wood-effect paper in the centre of each basket panel.

PARQUET BORDER ON WOODEN FLOOR

Using the three templates below, cut parquet corner pieces from wood-effect paper. Glue them directly to a wooden floor. Glue strips of wood-effect paper around the edges of the floor as a border. Varnish the whole floor to finish.

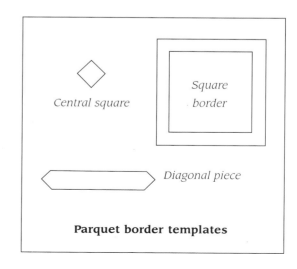

Central square   *Square border*

Diagonal piece

Parquet border templates

Curtains, Blinds and Textiles

*T*extiles are a rich source of texture, colour and style for a room. Dark red velvet curtains drawn across the windows of a Victorian study, with an oil-lamp lit before them, will help give the impression of a cosy interior, shutting out a cold winter's night. Floral or checked curtains in a kitchen setting will bring colour and life to a room, especially if a vase of flowers is set on the windowsill between them. Brocaded curtains, bedecked with golden-tasselled tiebacks could evoke the extravagance and flirtatious intimacy of a lady's boudoir.

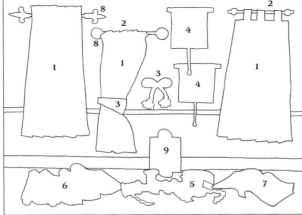

PROJECTS KEY

1 curtains

2 hanging rings and loops

3 fabric and tasselled tiebacks

4 blinds

5 spools of ribbons and braids

6 rolls of fabric

7 fabric swatch

8 curtain poles (see page 87)

9 fabric samples box (see page 81)

WORKING NOTES: Choose your fabric for its thickness as well as for its colour and design. Certain fabrics that look beautiful in full-scale settings will hang oddly in miniature. Thick velvets, for instance, fray badly and are very stiff when used for $1/12$th scale projects. Synthetic knitted velour fabrics drape better and do not fray, but still have a velvety texture. Look out for fabrics with tiny patterns or checks, especially for modern kitchen and bathroom settings. These fabrics will particularly suit the looped hanging arrangement described below. The hooks and eyes used for the curtain pole fittings and tiebacks are available in hardware stores. They can be screwed directly into thick plywood walls.

CURTAINS

Measure the width of your window and cut two pieces of fabric the same width. If you are using a heavy fabric such as velvet, cut them a little narrower to allow for heavy bunching. Cut the curtains as long as you wish them to hang, plus an extra inch to allow for hems. Hem around all of the edges. Run two parallel lines of running stitch along the top of the curtain in a matching thread and pull up to the width of half the window. Secure the ends of the threads with a few stitches.

Curtain edges can be decorated by sewing on lengths of braid, cord, ready-threaded beading, a strip of contrasting fabric, or lace – examples of which are shown in the photograph on page 99. Many different edgings are available from haberdashery (notions) departments. Take a sample of your curtain fabric with you to match up with what is on offer.

HANGING RINGS AND LOOPS

A range of decorative curtain poles is described in Home Improvements on page 87. Fit the curtain pole to the wall, and the curtains to the curtain pole, before gluing the curtain pole end pieces in place.

ATTACHING A CURTAIN POLE TO THE WALL: Screw two screw-eyes (available from hardware shops) into the wall near the top corners of the window. Push the ends of the curtain pole (complete with curtain) through the eyes. Glue the curtain pole end pieces in place.

SIMPLE CURTAIN FITTING: Sew the curtain directly to the pole with big loop stitches. These curtains cannot be drawn, but they can be tied back (see fabric and tasselled tiebacks, opposite).

CURTAIN RINGS: Curtain rings can be made from loop earring fittings, or rings cut from a chain. Sew the rings at regular intervals along the back of the gathered curtain, near the top. Thread the rings onto the curtain pole before fitting it to the wall.

LOOPED CURTAINS: Fabric loops are suitable for curtains that are not very 'full' (i.e., they do not have a lot of fabric gathered up). Make each curtain with fabric only just wider than half of the window width, plus a little extra for hems. Hem the curtain pieces. Cut lots of 1in x 2in rectangles of matching fabric. Fold in half lengthways with right sides together and sew along two edges. Turn right side out, push the raw edges of fabric inside the tube, and sew the open edge closed. Press flat, and make more the same. Fold each loop piece in half and sew

the two short edges together. Sew the loops to the top of the curtain at regular intervals. Thread the loops onto the curtain pole before fitting it to the wall (see above).

FABRIC AND TASSELLED TIEBACKS

FABRIC TIEBACKS: Cut a 2in wide length of fabric, long enough to reach around the gathered curtain, plus 1in for hems. Fold in half lengthways with right sides together and sew along two edges. Turn right side out, push the raw edges of fabric inside the tube, and sew the open edge closed. Press flat, and make another tieback in the same way. Gather each short edge with running stitch and sew it to a small ring or earring fitting. Wrap around the curtain and hang the rings over small hooks screwed into the wall on either side of the curtains, about halfway up.

TASSELLED TIEBACKS: Cut a piece of cord long enough to go round the curtains twice, plus 2in. Tie the ends in knots and fray out the loose cord into tassels. Fold up the cord and bind it together in the centre, as shown in the diagram. Wrap around the curtain and hang the loops over the hooks, as described above.

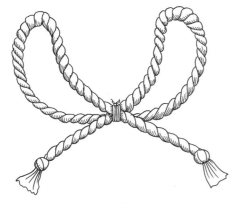

Making a tasselled tieback

BLINDS

Cut a piece of 5mm diameter dowel ³/₄in wider than the window. Cut a strip of fabric as long as the height of the window and apply Fraycheck (or a similar product) to stop the edges from fraying. Glue the end of the fabric to the dowel and wrap it around a few times.

Cut a piece of ¹/₈in square wood strip as wide as the fabric and glue it to the bottom. Roll up the fabric around the strip and glue in position. Screw a tiny screw-eye into the strip, through the fabric, and tie on a pull thread from thin cord. Tie a bead to the end of the pull thread.

Fit the blind to the wall with screw-eyes, as for the curtain poles above. You could leave the blind plain or decorate with a length of lace.

SPOOLS OF RIBBONS AND BRAIDS

From 10mm diameter dowel, cut a length ¹/₁₆in wider than the width of the ribbon or braid to be displayed on the spool. Cut two ⁷/₈in diameter circles of card and glue them to the ends of the dowel. Glue the end of the ribbon to the dowel and wrap it around.

ROLLS OF FABRIC

Cut a 5in length of 10mm diameter dowel. Cut a 4¹/₂in wide length of fabric and glue one end to the dowel, wrapping the rest around into a fabric roll.

FABRIC SWATCH

Make a fabric swatch as for the carpet or wallpaper samples book in Home Improvements on page 87. Choose samples of fabrics of a similar weight or colour and stack them in an attractive colour order. Edges can be trimmed into a tiny zigzag to mimic the anti-fray edge on real fabrics swatches.

THE COLLECTOR

A specialist collection of objects can be a point of interest in a room. In this Victorian hallway, an explorer prepares for an adventure surrounded by artefacts from previous journeys. Also in this chapter, a grandfather fine-tunes his clock collection and a grandmother displays her favourite ornaments. There are ideas for other favourite collectibles, such as stamp and postcard albums, and ways of displaying collections, such as in picture frames and display cabinets.

The Victorian Explorer

This Victorian explorer has a great love of Africa, and his collection reflects this specialist interest. The objects in his hallway are the crafts and tribal artefacts gathered on his travels – masks, drums, a spear and a shield – all come from tribes around the continent. And a collection of rocks reveals the explorer's love of geology. Look out for useful pictures relating to your own collection, which can be framed and stuck to the wall. These might be maps, paintings of wildlife, or postage stamps from the area of your choice. Postage stamps can also be stuck to the travelling trunk as travel labels.

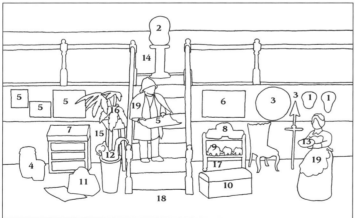

PROJECTS KEY

1 tribal masks
2 Egyptian mask
3 spear and shield
4 African drums
5 framed maps and prints
6 butterfly display
7 display case with shells
8 rock collection
9 'ivory' elephants
10 trunk
11 travel bag with hotel labels
12 walking sticks and umbrella
13 mail on silver tray
14 pedestal (see page 128)
15 plant stand (see page 34)
16 large-leafed palm (see page 135)
17 trolley (see page 34)
18 complex parquet floor (see page 98)
19 dolls (see Suppliers, page 172)

WORKING NOTES: Some of the projects in this section use polymer clay which is baked to harden following the manufacturer's instructions. When making polymer clay models on cardboard or sticks, the models can be baked with the cardboard or sticks in place. When painting models with acrylic paint, add a little PVA glue to the paint to help it stick to the surface. When using metallic paints such as Humbrol enamel, always wash the brush thoroughly after use, following the manufacturer's instructions.

To use templates, trace or photocopy the template onto paper, cut it out, draw around it on the material described and cut it out using an appropriate tool. PVA glue is suitable for all of the projects.

TRIBAL MASKS

On a piece of cardboard, press out a lump of polymer clay into a face shape. Add features and raised markings, smoothing the joins with your finger. Make eye and mouth holes with a pointed stick, then bake to harden. Once cool, paint bold designs on the masks (see photograph on page 103).

EGYPTIAN MASK

Model a mask from polymer clay (as above and see photograph) and bake to harden. Paint the top section gold and the bottom blue. Use black to paint eyebrows. Copy the cartouche template below onto paper, cut it out and glue in position (see photograph on page 103).

 Cartouche template

SPEAR AND SHIELD

SPEAR: Cut a 6in length of kebab stick. With thread, bind on a 1¼in length of kebab stick as a cross piece, using glue to secure the thread ends. Model a spear tip from polymer clay and push it onto the end of the spear. Add a polymer clay ball just above the cross piece. Bake to harden with the sticks in place. Once cool, paint the stick and ball.

SHIELD: Cut a circle of cardboard and model shapes on the surface with polymer clay. Bake to harden with the cardboard in place. When cool, remove the shapes, paint the cardboard, then glue the clay pieces to the shield.

AFRICAN DRUMS

Carve the end of a 1in diameter dowel into a flat-ended cone shape. Saw off the shape and use sandpaper to smooth the cut end, then paint brown. Cut a 1¾in diameter circle of textured paper and glue it to the top of the drum. Fold down the edges and glue them to the side. Wrap thread around the paper and glue the ends in position, or push short dressmaker's pins through the paper into the drum (see photograph, right, as a guide).

FRAMED MAPS AND PRINTS

Refer to page 119 for Picture Framing Suggestions and to page 118 for ideas on Picture Sources. These maps were cut from an antiques catalogue. Alternatively, you could copy the map of Africa template provided onto paper and colour the details with pencil crayons. The small prints are postage stamps; the perforated edging can be trimmed away, or left as an interesting feature.

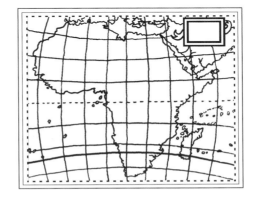

Map of Africa template

BUTTERFLY DISPLAY

Refer to page 119 for Picture Framing Suggestions and to page 118 for ideas on Picture Sources. The butterfly pictures were colour-photocopied from a butterfly book, then covered with sticky-backed plastic.

The paper 'skins' on the drums are attached with thread or short pins

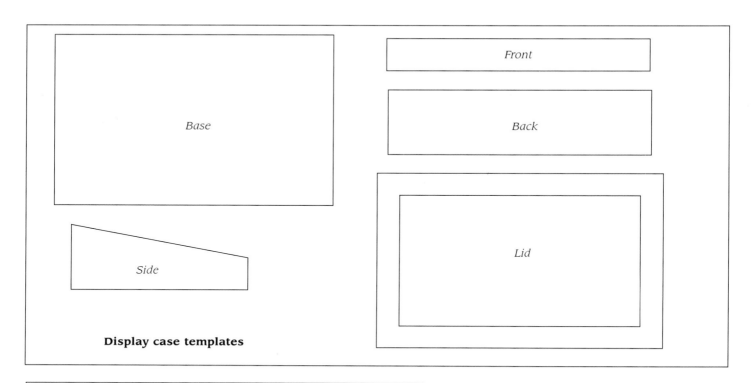

Display case templates

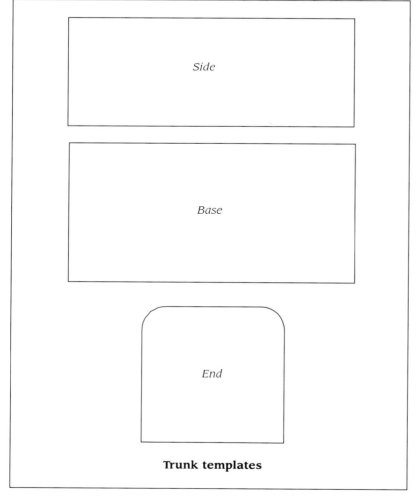

Trunk templates

DISPLAY CASE WITH SHELLS

CASE: Using the templates, cut the following from ⅛in thick wood: two sides; one front; one back and one base. Glue the pieces together into a box shape and then paint brown. Line the base with a rectangle of coloured felt and arrange a collection of small objects in the frame. If preferred, glue pieces in place.

LID: Use the lid template to cut a frame piece from thick card and paint it brown. Cut a rectangle of clear acetate and glue it to the back. The lid can be glued in place, or attached with fabric or metal hinges. Glue a strip of fabric between the lid and the case for a fabric hinge. Metal hinges are available from dolls' house suppliers (see Suppliers page 172).

TRUNK

TRUNK: Using the templates, cut the following from card – one base, two sides and three end pieces (one of these is a lid strengthener). Glue each piece (except the lid strengthener), to leather-effect paper, then cut away excess paper. Alternatively you could paint the pieces dark red. Glue the pieces together into a box shape then glue the lid strengthener inside the box, in the middle.

LID: Cut a 3in x 2¹/₈in piece of card and cover it with leather-effect paper (or paint it dark red). Curve into a domed lid shape and glue on top of the box. Wrap the box with string to hold in shape until dry.

Cut strips of copper-coloured paper and glue them along the edges of the box, around the bottom of the lid, and as bars across the lid (see photograph as a guide). Glue a strip of black paper to each end of the trunk, with copper-coloured paper squares on the handle ends.

ROCK COLLECTION

Press out some dark brown polymer clay. Use a knife to cut an oval base shape, then trim away excess clay. Mark a line around the edge. Bake to harden, then glue a rock sample on top.

'IVORY' ELEPHANTS

Model three elephants from white polymer clay and arrange into a line. Cut a length of fine chain and drape it between the elephants. Use a pointed stick to push the chain into the sides of the elephants at intervals to hold it in shape. Bake to harden with the chain in place.

TRAVEL BAG WITH HOTEL LABELS

Using the templates and instructions for the sports bag on page 67, make a travel bag from dark red or brown felt. Sew a bead to the front. Use the template provided to cut a fastener from felt, and cut a slit in the position marked. Sew the straight end to the back of the bag and push the slit over the bead.

Copy the hotel labels onto paper and colour with felt-tip pens. Cut them out and glue them to the bag or trunk. The names on the tem-

plates are hotels from a Sherlock Holmes story. You could write your own names on coloured paper for alternative labels.

WALKING STICKS AND UMBRELLA

WALKING STICKS: Cut 3¹/₂in lengths of kebab stick. Model a handle and tip on each from cream polymer clay and push onto each stick. Bake to harden with the sticks in place. Once cool, remove the clay and paint the sticks. Clay pieces can be left plain for ivory or painted silver or brown (see photograph below). Glue the pieces to the sticks.

UMBRELLA: Make a 3in long walking stick, as described above, with a brown handle and a pointed end. Paint the stick silver. Cut a 2in diameter semicircle from thin black felt, fold it in half and sew the straight edges together. Push the stick through the middle and hold in place with glue. Wrap black thread around the umbrella to pull the black felt into a closed umbrella shape. Push 1¹/₂in lengths of cocktail sticks into the folds to mimic spokes.

MAIL ON SILVER TRAY

Paint a button with silver metallic paint. Use the templates and instructions on page 118 to make letters and glue them to the tray.

A close-up of the walking sticks and mail on a silver tray, showing the colouring and shape details

Travel bag fastener template

Hotel labels templates

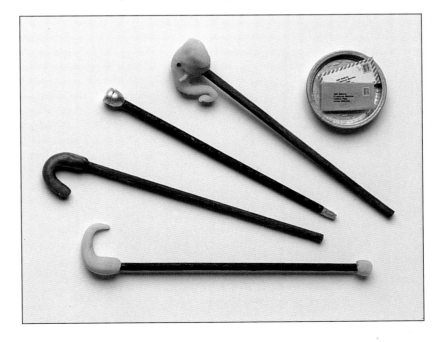

Grandpa's Clock Collection

*F*rom earliest days, people have explored ways to work out what time of day it is. A simple shadow-casting device developed into the formal sundials which grace stately gardens. When mechanical devices began to be refined, more complex clock mechanisms became possible. In this section, designs for different clocks form a collection of family heirlooms, accompanied by more modern clocks, such as a 1960s starburst clock, and an electric clock radio.

WORKING NOTES: The clock faces can be photocopied or copied onto card, with dotted lines showing the position of fold lines. In each case, two faces have been supplied – one set at nearly lunchtime and a blank one. If you want to set your own time, refer to the box, right. The clock shapes can be painted, covered in wood-effect paper or made in brown card. Metallic paint can be applied directly to card shapes to make them look as if made from brass, copper or silver. When using metallic paint, wash the brush thoroughly afterwards, following the manufacturer's instructions.

To use templates, trace or photocopy the template onto paper, cut it out, draw around it on the material described and cut it out using an appropriate tool. PVA wood glue is suitable for all of the projects, unless otherwise stated.

GRANDFATHER CLOCK

BASE: Cut a rectangle 1¼in wide x 1⅛in tall from ¾in thick pine strip.
BODY: Cut a rectangle ⅞in wide x 4in tall from ½in thick pine strip.
TOP: Cut a rectangle 1¼in wide x 1¾in tall from ¾in thick pine strip.

Glue the pieces together, following the photograph. Add decorative edging on the front and sides as follows: use ¼in moulding at the top and bottom of the clock; use ⅛in square pine strip to cover the joins on top of the base and under the top piece. Glue strips of ⅛in square pine strip as a rectangular door moulding on the front of the body (see photograph). Paint or stain

BLANK CLOCK FACES

If you want to make a clock set to a time of your choice, select the correct blank template from the set provided here, copy it and then carefully draw in the hands on the blank face.

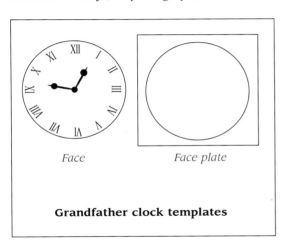

Face   *Face plate*

Grandfather clock templates

the clock dark brown and when dry add brass metallic paint for a key plate, or glue on a key plate from a specialist supplier (see page 172).
FACE: Copy the face and face plate templates onto paper and cut them out. Paint the corners of the face plate with brass metallic paint. Glue the face to the plate, then glue them both to the front of the clock. Cut strips of ⅛in thick pine strip to frame the face, stain them brown and glue them in position.

ART DECO MANTEL CLOCK

BODY: Copy the three clock base and body templates (overleaf) onto thin card and cut them out. Glue each piece to wood-effect paper and allow to dry, then cut away any excess paper. Score along the dotted lines, fold up the shapes, and glue the tabs in position. Glue the base pieces together and the clock body on top.
FACE: Copy the face template onto thin card and cut it out. Glue the clock face to the front of the clock. Add a small strip of wood-effect paper underneath.

TIP

Individual clocks could be displayed in a school, station or kitchen. Or a collection of clocks could contain many examples of these elegant machines, selected from different periods.

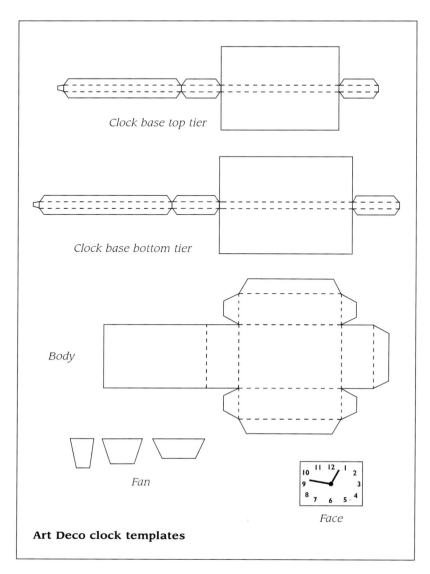

Clock base top tier

Clock base bottom tier

Body

Fan

Face

Art Deco clock templates

FAN: Copy the fan templates onto thin card and cut them out. Glue the pieces into a fan and glue them above the clock face.

1940s MANTEL CLOCKS

DOMED CLOCK: Copy the body and face templates onto thin card and cut them out. Glue the body piece to wood-effect paper and allow to dry, then cut away any excess paper. Score along the dotted lines and fold up the shape. Glue the tabs in position, shaping the top piece into a curve. Glue the clock face in place.

UPRIGHT CLOCK: Copy the body and face templates below onto thin card and cut them out, then follow the instructions for the domed clock above. Once the face is glued in place, copy a decorative front template onto contrasting wood-effect paper, cut it out and glue it to the lower front of the clock.

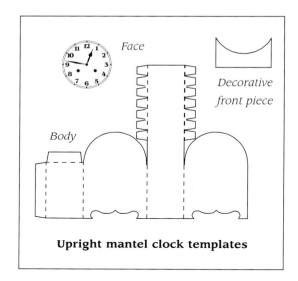

Face

Decorative front piece

Body

Upright mantel clock templates

VICTORIAN CARRIAGE CLOCKS

LARGE CLOCK: Copy the body template from page 111 onto thin card and cut out the face circle. Score along the dotted lines and cut out the shape then colour the shape with brass metallic paint.

Copy the face template onto card, cut it out and glue it inside the clock body piece so that the face shows through the hole. Fold up the body and glue the tabs in position. Cut four $^{15}/_{16}$in lengths of kebab stick, colour with brass

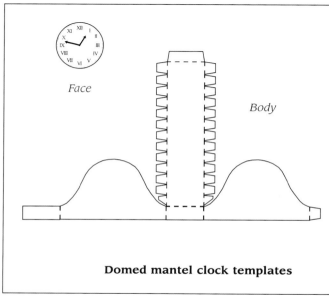

Face

Body

Domed mantel clock templates

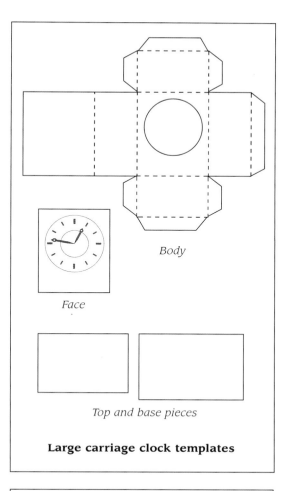

Body

Face

Top and base pieces

Large carriage clock templates

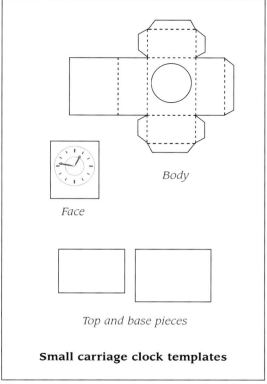

Body

Face

Top and base pieces

Small carriage clock templates

paint then glue to the corners of the body piece (see photograph as a guide).

Using the top and base templates, cut two large and two small rectangles. Glue them in pairs (a large and a small together) and colour with brass metallic paint. Glue to the top and bottom of the clock.

Model a handle from polymer clay and bake to harden. When cool, glue to the top of the clock and colour with brass metallic paint.

SMALL CLOCK: Using the small carriage clock templates, follow the instructions for the large clock, but use 5/8in lengths of cocktail stick instead of kebab sticks.

ROUND SCHOOL CLOCK

Copy the face template onto card and cut it out. Roll out a thin sausage of polymer clay and use it to frame the face, then bake to harden on the card. Once cool, paint the frame silver and glue it to the clock.

OCTAGONAL STATION CLOCK

Copy the face template onto card and cut it out, leaving a 1/4in border. Use the cutting guide template to cut eight lengths of 1/4in wide wooden moulding. Glue them around the clock face. Cut a 1/2in square of 1/8in thick wood and glue it at the base of the clock. Frame with three pieces of moulding.

School clock face template

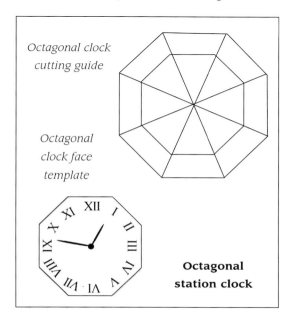

Octagonal clock cutting guide

Octagonal clock face template

Octagonal station clock

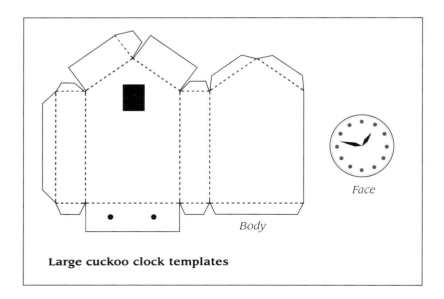

Large cuckoo clock templates

Face

Body

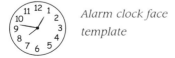

Body

Face

Small cuckoo clock templates

CUCKOO CLOCKS

LARGE CLOCK: Copy the clock body template onto thin card and cut it out. Glue it to wood-effect paper, allow to dry then cut away any excess paper. Score along the dotted lines. Mark a black rectangle and make holes through the two dots marked on the template. Thread a length of chain through the holes, so that the ends dangle below the clock (see photograph below). Fold up the clock shape and glue the tabs in position. Squash blobs of air-drying clay onto the ends of the chain. Model a tiny cuckoo and glue it to the black rectangle.

To make the clock face, copy the clock face template onto paper, cut it out and glue it in place.

To make the roof, cut two rectangles $3/4$in x $7/16$in from $1/16$in thick wood. Bevel one end of each piece. Stain or paint the pieces then glue to the top of the clock with the bevelled edges meeting at the peak.

To make the door, cut a tiny rectangle of wood-effect paper, glue it to a scrap of card and glue it to the edge of the black rectangle.

SMALL CLOCK: Using the small cuckoo clock templates, follow the instructions for the large clock, but for the roof use two $3/8$in x $3/16$in rectangles of $1/16$in thick wood.

ALARM CLOCK

Copy the face template onto thin card. Model the alarm clock shape from polymer clay, pressing the card face into the front of the clay. Add three blobs of clay for feet; two blobs for bells; a handle and a striker. Bake to harden with the face in place.

Once cool, remove the face, paint the clock with metallic paint, then glue the face back in position.

Alarm clock face template

ELECTRIC CLOCK RADIO

BODY: Cut a block of white polymer clay about 1in long, and smooth the edges. Mark button and grill details and make two knobs and attach them to the side. Push a length of plastic-coated wire into the clock. Put a blob of polymer clay on the end. Cut tiny lengths of craft wire and push them into the plug. Bake to harden with the wires in place.

DISPLAY: Copy the display template onto paper. Cut it out, colour the numbers with a red pen and glue it to the clock. Block out sections of the numbers with a black pen to display your chosen time setting.

The fine chain for the cuckoo clocks is available from model shops (see Suppliers, page 172), or you could cut lengths from a broken necklace

Electric clock radio display template

1960s WALL CLOCK

Copy the star template onto thin card. Score along the black dotted lines then turn the star over and score along the lines marked in grey on the template. Fold each star point into a shallow peak. Cut a $3/4$in circle of card and glue it to the back. Paint the star with brass metallic paint. Copy the face template onto card, cut it out and glue it to the front of the clock.

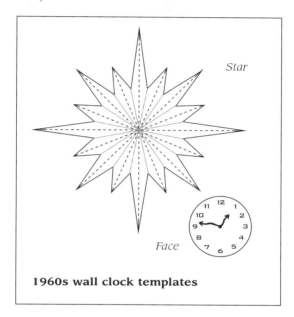

1960s wall clock templates

GARDEN SUNDIAL

Copy the sundial template onto paper, colour with a felt-tip pen and cut it out. For a brass dial, draw out the design on metallic-coloured card with a fine permanent marker. Use the triangle template to cut a shadow-caster from $1/8$in thick wood. Paint it with brass metallic

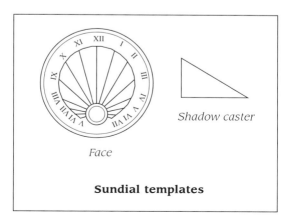

Face

Sundial templates

paint and glue it to the dial.

PEDESTAL: Press out three circles and one thick sausage of polymer clay. Cut the ends of the sausage to make flat faces. Bake the pieces to harden and, once cool, glue them together. Glue the sundial on top of the pedestal.

CLOCK PIECES AND OIL CAN

CLOCK PIECES: Collect cogs and other workings from broken watches and clocks. They can be displayed in a box, or on a table laid out on a newspaper (described on page 29).

OIL CAN: Model an oil can from polymer clay and bake to harden. Paint the can silver.

TEA TRAY

From $1/16$in thick wood, cut a rectangle $1 3/8$in x $2 1/8$in. Frame with $1/4$in thick wooden moulding, then stain or paint the pieces.

Cut pieces of wire from a brass paperclip and bend them into handle shapes (see photograph below). With a sharp nail, make holes in each end of the tray where the handles will be attached. Push the ends of the wire into the sides of the tray and secure with tiny drops of Super Glue.

Grandma's Ornaments

Wherever there is a dull corner, an empty mantelpiece or window ledge, there is an opportunity to display ornaments and bring colour and charm to a scene. In this section are ideas for designs from the Art Nouveau and Art Deco periods, and a pair of Staffordshire dogs from the eighteenth century. Such objects might tell a story of the experiences and background of the collector. Perhaps the wooden doll belonged to the grandmother in the scene, when she was a girl. Perhaps the photographs are of her relatives, and the shells were collected on her honeymoon. Through a collection, you can hint at the life history and interests of your dolls.

PROJECTS KEY

1 Staffordshire dogs
2 wooden doll
3 'doughcraft' heart and ring
4 decorative shells
5 mirrors
6 Art Deco picture frame
7 hinged photograph frame
8 oval photograph frame
9 beads and button displays
10 three-dimensional pictures
11 polished stones
12 flower in vase
13 hand bell
14 cat (see page 166)
15 side table (see page 83)
16 carpet and wallpaper (see page 87)
17 feather duster (see page 62)
18 small fern (see page 135)

WORKING NOTES: Beads and buttons provide useful shapes for many of these projects. Look for shapes that remind you of miniature vases, pots and display stands. With simple additions, such as metallic paint, painted flowers or bead feet, they can be transformed into an ornament. Where shaped buttons or beads have been used in these projects, alternative methods of creating the objects are also included.

To use templates, trace or photocopy the template onto paper, cut it out, draw around it on the material described and cut it out using an appropriate tool. PVA wood glue is suitable for all of the projects, unless otherwise stated.

STAFFORDSHIRE DOGS

Model a dog shape from cream polymer clay. Wrap fine chain around the neck and drape a lead across the chest, pushing the end into the clay at the back. Make a second dog in the same way. Bake to harden with the chain in place.

Add PVA glue to brown paint and paint the ear, face and tail details (see photograph). The dogs can also be painted with floral motifs.

WOODEN DOLL

BODY: Cut a 1in length of 5mm diameter dowel. About 1/4in in from one end, roll the dowel under a sharp knife to form a stop cut, but do not go all the way through. Carve away wood on either side down towards the cut, to form a neck. Use sandpaper to smooth cut edges and to round the head. Paint the dowel white, then use black to add the face and hair details (see photograph on page 114 as a guide).
DRESS: Cut a piece of fine fabric, 2 1/2in x 1in. Hem around the edge, then sew into a tube. Gather the tube around the doll's neck, pull the thread tightly and secure with stitches. Bind the top section of the dress tightly around the body with more thread.
LEGS: Cut two 3/4in lengths of kebab stick and use sandpaper to round the cut edges. Paint the sticks black. Glue the ends of the legs to the base of the body with Super Glue, so that the doll is in a sitting position. Allow to dry thoroughly.

ARMS: Cut two 1/2in lengths of kebab stick and use sandpaper to round the cut edges. Paint the sticks white. Cut a piece of fabric 1/2in x 1 1/2in. Roll the fabric into a long tube and glue the ends around the arms and leave to dry thoroughly. Glue the arm section around the doll and clip together until dry.

'DOUGHCRAFT' HEART AND RING

Roll three thin sausage shapes of light brown polymer clay. Pinch them together at one end, plait the strands together and then pinch together at the other end. Shape into a circle or heart, press the ends together and trim off excess clay. Add a coloured polymer clay bow then bake to harden.

DECORATIVE SHELLS

GLITTER SHELLS: Paint PVA glue along the lines of shells, dust with glitter, shaking off any excess.
SHELL COIL: Using a fine-bladed hacksaw, carefully cut a shell in half to reveal its internal spiral. Smooth the cut edge with fine sandpaper.

FLOWER IN VASE

Using the template, cut a flower piece from coloured crêpe paper. Run a little glue along the long straight edge and roll up the flower, starting at the narrower end. Once dry, push a length of craft wire up into the flower and display it in a bead vase.

Flower template

MIRRORS

If you are making a small mirror, copy one of the stand templates onto card (two sizes are provided with the Art Deco stained-glass picture frame on page 116). Fold along the dotted line and glue the smaller section to the back of the frame.
SMALL ART NOUVEAU MIRROR: Cut a small rectangle of plastic mirror tile (available from dolls' house suppliers – see Suppliers page

TIP

A display of ornaments might be beautifully complemented by a vase of flowers. For lilies, poppies, chrysanthemums, sunflowers and camellias, see the Flower Seller's scene on pages 122–126. Decorative pots and vases in which to display them can be found on page 151.

172). Cut a piece of card the same size and make the frame on the card by rolling out a sausage of polymer clay and framing the card. Roll out a thinner sausage and press it gently on top. Model a face, with hair that reaches out to the corners of the frame (see photograph). Bake to harden with the card in place.

Once cool, remove the cardboard. Colour the frame with silver metallic paint and glue to the mirror tile.

TEDDY BEAR MIRROR: Follow the instructions for the Art Nouveau mirror frame, but make a single line of polymer clay for the frame, and attach a clay teddy bear to the corner.

Larger mirrors, such as handbag mirrors, can also be framed. See picture framing suggestions on page 119.

ART DECO STAINED-GLASS PICTURE FRAME

Copy the picture frame template onto paper and glue it onto the back of black card. Cut out the frame and the triangles then colour the paper black with a felt-tip pen. Glue a rectangle of coloured acetate (a smooth sweet wrapper or a piece of lighting gel) on the back over the triangle cut-outs. Depending on the type of acetate used, PVA glue may let the acetate peel off once dried. If this happens, try a contact adhesive instead. Cut out a photograph or picture from a magazine and glue it in place.

STAND: Using the larger stand template, cut a stand piece from card. Fold along the dotted line and glue the small section to the back of the frame.

OVAL PHOTOGRAPH FRAME

Cut a picture from a magazine and glue it to an oval earring fitting. Alternatively you could glue the picture to a piece of cardboard, cut it out and frame it with a line of polymer clay. Bake to harden with the picture in place.

HINGED PHOTOGRAPH FRAME

Cut three rectangles of cream card the same size (about 1 1/8in tall x 7/8in wide). Glue a small oval photograph in the middle of each rectan-

Picture frame

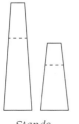

Stands

Art Deco stained-glass picture frame templates

gle then frame each rectangle by gluing on strips of 1/8in square wood coloured with felt-tip pen or wood stain. Place the pictures face down in a line on a flat surface, with 1/8in gaps between them. Glue rectangles of fabric across the joins, as shown in the diagram, and allow to dry thoroughly.

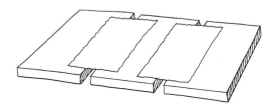

Making hinges on the hinged photograph frame

BEADS AND BUTTON DISPLAYS

BEADS: Pile decorative spherical beads onto a plate. Arrange tube beads as a collection of pots.

BUTTON PLATE OR SHIELD: Push a length of craft wire through the shank of a large decorative button. Bend the wire into a stand and hold in position with a blob of Blu Tack.

THREE-DIMENSIONAL PICTURES

Glue black fabric or felt to a rectangle of cardboard (about 1 1/8in tall x 7/8in wide). Frame with strips of 1/8in square wood coloured with metallic paint. Glue a three-dimensional button or bead in the centre of the frame. If the bead does not match the frame, colour it with metallic paint before gluing it in place.

POLISHED STONES

Glue a polished stone (available as earring fittings) to a black button. Glue four small black beads to the base as feet.

HAND BELL

The bell handle is modelled from brown polymer clay around the shank of a small bell. If you cannot find a small bell, use a bell-shaped earring fitting. Push a dressmaker's pin up through the fitting's hole and shape the polymer clay around the end of the pin. Bake to harden with the metal pieces in place.

Collector's Items

The hobby of collecting came into its own in the nineteenth century. New manufacturing industries of the Industrial Revolution made porcelain, metalware, books, pictures and printed materials widely available and affordable. This section looks at a range of everyday ephemera that people have enjoyed collecting – projects suitable to any period from the nineteenth century onwards. A

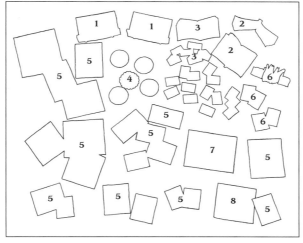

PROJECTS KEY

1 egg collection
2 photograph and postcard albums
3 stamp album and letters
4 decorative plates
5 pictures
6 books and bookends
7 cork pinboard
8 soccer cards

young boy doll might be found with a stamp album, or arranging pictures of sporting heroes on a pinboard in his bedroom. A Victorian traveller might have a collection of eggs displayed in a chest of drawers in his study. Walls all over the dolls' house can be adorned with photographs, paintings and pictures – all framed with the techniques described in this section.

WORKING NOTES: Many of the collector's items in this section feature tiny pictures – for sources of such pictures see box below. Some of the items are displayed in frames – see box on page 119 for framing suggestions.

For projects that use polymer clay, bake to harden following the manufacturer's instructions. To use templates, trace or photocopy the template onto paper, cut it out, draw around it on the material described and cut it out using an appropriate tool. PVA wood glue is suitable for all of the projects.

EGG COLLECTION

Model eggs from polymer clay in a range of colours and sizes. Bake to harden following the manufacturer's instructions. Cut coloured felt to fit inside a drawer from a dolls' house chest of drawers. Glue the eggs in an arrangement on top, adding tiny labels from white card.

PHOTOGRAPH AND POSTCARD ALBUMS

ALBUM: Cut twenty rectangles of grey or beige paper. (The photograph album shown is 1^1/2in x ^{1}/2in and the postcard album is 1^1/4in x 1^1/2in.) Cut two more rectangles of the same size from black card. Hold all the rectangles together in a

clip with the black card pieces on the outside. Use a hammer and a sharp nail to make five or six holes along one edge. Keeping the rectangles in the clip, sew through the holes with strong thread to create a hinge. Tie the thread ends together and remove the clip.

PHOTOGRAPHS AND POSTCARDS: Glue tiny photographs or postcard images into the album – these can be found from many sources (see box left). For black and white postcards, leave a small white border around the edge. For old sepia photographs, cut the picture into an oval and stick it to a rectangle of cream paper.

STAMP ALBUM AND LETTERS

ALBUM: Make an album as described above. (The album shown is 1^1/4in square.)

STAMPS: Cut tiny rectangles of coloured paper and stick them onto white paper. Cut them out leaving a tiny white border. Glue the stamps onto grey paper and then into the album.

LETTERS: Copy the envelope template onto brown or white paper and cut it out. Fold along the lines indicated by the folding markers, and glue the triangular flaps together. Add a stamp (described above) and a postmark, using a fine black pen. For white airmail envelopes, add red and blue marks around the edge.

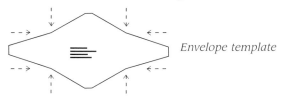

Envelope template

DECORATIVE PLATES

BASIC PLATE: Using the plate templates on page 119, cut two circles from card. Glue the smaller circle in the middle of the larger circle and allow to dry. With the smaller circle facing upwards, press polymer clay on top of the shape. Trim off excess clay around the edge and bake to harden with the card in place. Once cool, prize off the card with a knife. Use fine sandpaper to smooth any rough areas.

FLORAL PLATES: Copy the floral plate rim template or the plain rim template onto paper. Paint designs around the edge of the plain rim,

---

PICTURE SOURCES

• Cut tiny pictures from magazines or catalogues. Christmas-card catalogues and art gallery exhibition catalogues are particularly useful.

• Draw or paint the pictures by hand, or get a child to draw a picture.

• Search the Internet for your chosen subject and print out a computer graphic at an appropriate size.

• Cut small images from your own photographs.

• Take a photograph of an arrangement of your own family photographs, and cut tiny images from the resulting print.

• Ask your photograph developer if they can make tiny reproductions (contact prints) from your negatives.

• Reduce pictures using a photocopier or colour photocopier.

• Create abstract designs within a frame, using scraps of coloured card.

or colour the flowers in the floral rim. Cut out the rim and glue it to the basic plate.

RIMMED PLATE: Make a basic plate as described above. Add PVA glue to coloured paint and use this to make a line around the plate. Once dry, add a rim of gold paint.

DECORATIVE GOLD PLATES: Make a basic plate as described above. Glue tiny earring fittings or beads around the edge of a plate. Once dry, colour with metallic paint.

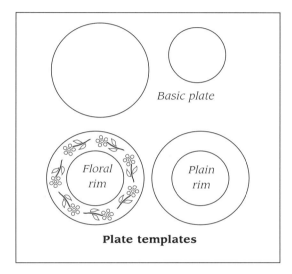

Basic plate

Floral rim

Plain rim

Plate templates

PICTURES

Practically any room in the dolls' house can be enhanced by pictures. See the box far left for ideas on picture sources and the box above for picture framing suggestions.

TO CUT NEAT 45-DEGREE ANGLES: Draw an exact square on a piece of paper. With a ruler, draw a line between two opposite corners of the square, and extend the line slightly at both ends. Tape the paper to a cutting surface and lay a frame piece on top, lining it up with the edge of the square. With a sharp craft knife, cut through the frame piece, using the diagonal line as a guide, as shown in the diagram.

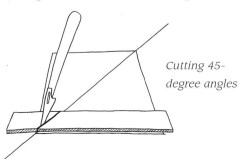

Cutting 45-degree angles

PICTURE FRAMING SUGGESTIONS

• Glue a picture to a piece of coloured card and cut it out leaving a small border. Glue this to a larger rectangle of brown card.
• Glue a picture to a rectangle of coloured card and cut it out leaving a large border. Cut a frame from cardboard then make decorative details on the frame from polymer clay and bake to harden with the cardboard in place. Once cool, colour the frame with metallic paint and glue it to the picture.
• Glue a picture to card and frame with strips of wood. Cut four pieces of wood ($^1/_8$in thick wood strip, or $^1/_4$in thick half-round dowel) the lengths of the outer dimensions of the finished frame. Trim the ends into 45-degree angles (see Pictures below, left) and glue around the picture.

BOOKS AND BOOKENDS

BOOK: Use the book page template and the book cover template to cut a page piece from thick white card and a cover piece from coloured paper or leather-effect paper. Fold the cover along the dotted lines and glue the tabs to the inside of the cover. Fold the cover around the white card and glue in position.

BOOKENDS (MAKE TWO): Cut a $^1/_4$in square and a $^1/_4$in x $^5/_8$in rectangle from $^1/_6$in thick wood. Glue them together in an L shape. Use the bookend templates to cut an elephant body shape from $^1/_{16}$in thick balsa wood. Paint it grey. Use the same templates to cut two ears from grey paper and two tusks from white paper. Glue in place. Draw eyes with a black pen.

CORK PINBOARD

PINBOARD: Cut a $2^3/_8$in x $1^1/_4$in rectangle from a cork table-mat. Split a 5in length of 5mm diameter half-round dowel in half lengthways and use to frame the board (see box above).

PICTURES OF SPORTING HEROES: Cut tiny pictures from a sports magazine and glue them to the cork pinboard.

SOCCER CARDS

On paper, draw out a grid of rectangles (about $^1/_4$in x $^1/_8$in). Draw in faces and coloured shirts with fine pens or pencil crayons. Mount the paper on cardboard.

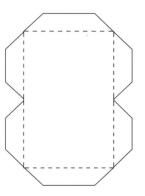

Cover

Page

Elephant bookends

Book and bookends templates

FLOWERS AND PLANTS

This chapter explores the wonderful world of flowers and plants, starting with blooms such as the sunflowers, camellias and poppies in this flower seller's scene. At an autumn wedding, lilies, roses and single-flower hollyhocks are gathered into beautiful arrangements to grace a church or reception. There is greenery and foliage in the sculptured shapes of topiary in a formal Tudor garden, and in the leaves of cheese plants, palms and ferns in a dolls' house conservatory.

The Flower Seller

Flowers are an irresistible addition to any dolls' house. Even if your house doesn't have a garden in which to display the blooms, a vase of flowers will brighten up a dark hallway or bring a splash of summer sunshine to a Welsh dresser in the kitchen. Some of the flowers can also have a special significance – a rose in a gift box is appropriate for a Valentine's Day gift, and lilies and poppies are symbols of remembrance. All of the flowers in this picture are created from very simple patterns, using brightly coloured cards and papers. Take a look in garden catalogues for more flowers to try your hand at.

PROJECTS KEY

 1 camellia
 2 sunflower
 3 white lily
 4 chrysanthemum
 5 gift rose in a box
 6 black-eyed Susan
 7 daisy
 8 petunia
 9 blue auricula
10 poppy
11 dried plants
12 hanging basket and ivy (pictured in detail on page 125)
13 window box
14 tall tubs
15 braid pots
16 baskets
17 clay pots (see page 151)
18 medium tiered trees (see page 131)
19 railings (see page 88)
20 small globe and medium cone trees (see page 132)

WORKING NOTES The flowers in this section are all made from paper and card so it is a good idea to wash your hands frequently when making these projects, as paper quickly picks up grease marks. A good range of colours and weights of paper and card is available from most art shops or take a look in a stationery shop for coloured writing papers.

In most cases enough templates have been provided for several of each flower or leaf type, to save repeated copying. Templates can be photocopied directly onto coloured paper or card but not onto crêpe paper. Alternatively they can be traced onto paper, cut out and drawn round on crêpe paper, paper or card. Cut templates out with a sharp craft knife.

Use gardening books or your garden as reference for plant colours and markings. Display blooms in vases surrounded by pointed strips of green card, curved into leaves. PVA glue is suitable for all the projects.

CAMELLIA

Using the camellia templates, cut two large, two medium and two small petal pieces from pink crêpe paper. Make markings on the small pieces with a red pencil crayon. Glue the petal pieces in a pile – the largest at the bottom, the smallest at the top. Rotate each piece so that all the petals show (see photograph as a guide). Use a needle to make three holes near the centre of the flower then push through three flower-arranger's stamens. Glue the shanks of the stamens together and mould the petals forwards into a shallow cup shape.

Camellia templates (half of one flower)

SUNFLOWER

Copy the petal templates onto thin yellow card and cut them out. Glue the complex petal piece on top of the plainer piece then glue a $5/8$in diameter circle of black felt to the middle. Bend

Sunflower templates (three flowers)

the end of a length of plastic-coated wire into a small flat coil and glue to the back of the flower (see photograph on page 124).

WHITE LILY

Copy the petal templates onto white paper. Glue them together in pairs so the petals form a six-pointed star. Use a needle to make a hole in the centre then push through a single flower-arranger's stamen and glue in position.

Lily templates (three flowers)

CHRYSANTHEMUM

Cut a $5/8$in x 8in strip of yellow crêpe paper. Make lots of parallel cuts along one long edge. Run a little glue along the long uncut edge and roll up the flower. Once dry, push a piece of wire into the back of the flower and secure with glue. Once dry, gently separate the petals.

GIFT ROSE IN A BOX

BOX: Copy the box template onto red card and score along the dotted lines. Cut it out, fold into shape and glue tabs in position. Glue a rectangle of crumpled white tissue paper into the box.

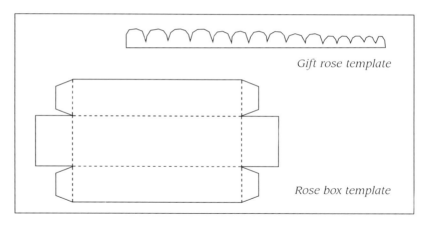

Gift rose template

Rose box template

TIP

To make more flowers to your own design, look for simple shapes, or composite flowers that can be built up from a number of layers.

Details of constructing the sunflower, black-eyed Susan and chrysanthemum. Florist's stamens are shown on the far left

STALK: Cut two leaf shapes from green paper and glue them to a thin twig or pine needle. Glue the stalk on top of the tissue paper in the box.

ROSE: Using the template, cut a rose piece from red crêpe paper. Run a little glue along the long straight edge and roll up the flower, starting at the narrow end. Once dry, gently spread out the petals, then glue the flower into the box.

CARD: Cut a small rectangle of coloured paper, draw on details and glue it into the box.

BLACK-EYED SUSAN

Copy the templates onto yellow paper and cut them out. Push a black-headed pin through the centre of each flower and into your display.

DAISY

Copy the templates onto white paper and cut them out. Glue two petal shapes together, rotating the top one so that all the petals show. Push a yellow-headed pin through the centre of each flower and into your chosen display.

PETUNIA

Copy the petal templates onto white paper and cut them out. Colour the triangle details magenta with a felt-tip pen. Curve each flower and glue into a shallow cone shape. Push a small pin through the centre and into your chosen display. Paint the pin head white.

BLUE AURICULA

Copy the petal templates onto blue paper and cut them out. Push a small pin through the

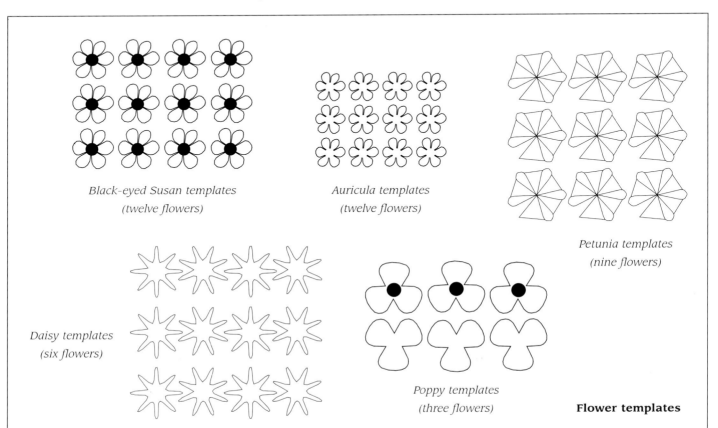

Black-eyed Susan templates
(twelve flowers)

Auricula templates
(twelve flowers)

Daisy templates
(six flowers)

Poppy templates
(three flowers)

Petunia templates
(nine flowers)

Flower templates

centre of each flower and into your chosen display. Paint the pin head white.

POPPY

Copy the petal templates onto red paper and cut them out. Glue two petal shapes together – a plain one underneath and the one with the black marking on top. Push a small pin through the centre of each flower and into your chosen display. Paint the pin head black.

DRIED PLANTS

Grasses, bracken fronds and herbs, once dried, can make attractive displays or useful backgrounds to the paper flowers. Tie fresh leaves and grasses in bunches and hang in a warm, dry place for a few weeks.

HANGING BASKET

BASKET: Bend craft wire into a 1¹/₂in diameter circle. Continuing with the same length of wire, curve it across the circle in an arch. Bind the wire around the edge of the circle, then make another arch, as shown in the diagram. Repeat around the circle until four arches are in place. Leaving 5¹/₂in at the end, cut the wire and bind the remaining wire around the top circle of the basket. At two or three points around the circle, make small loops for hanging the basket.

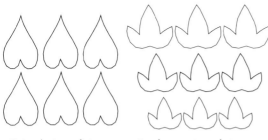

Petunia templates   Ivy leaves templates

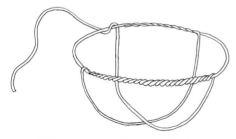

Making the wire hanging baskets

Thread fine chain through the loops for hanging the basket up. Fill the basket with a piece of foam packaging material or a lump of flower-arranger's foam, into which can be pushed a selection of pin flowers (such as the black-eyed Susan, daisies, auricula, petunias and poppies, or the roses from page 128 – see photograph, below).

IVY AND LEAVES: Use the ivy leaf templates and petunia leaf templates to cut leaf shapes from coloured paper. Glue to thin strips of paper and push the ends into the foam in the basket. Using acrylics, paint vein markings on the ivy leaves – see photograph below.

WINDOW BOX

From ¹/₈in thick wood, cut the following: two side pieces ⁷/₈in x 3¹/₄in, and two end pieces ⁷/₈in square. Glue the pieces into a rectangle, then glue the whole box on top of a piece of card, cutting away excess card.

Paint a button gold and glue it to the front of the box (see photograph as a guide). If the button has a shank, cut a hole for it in the front of the box. Use the templates to cut two sets of decorative front pieces from card. Glue these together in pairs, paint gold, then glue one set on either side of the button (see photograph on pages 120 and 121).

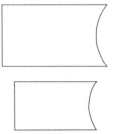

Window box templates

TALL TUBS

Copy the tub base and side templates onto thin card, score along the dotted lines and cut them out. Curve the side piece around and glue into a tube. Glue the base piece to the bottom tabs. Push a little modelling clay in the bottom of the tub and push the flower stalks and grasses into the clay to finish.

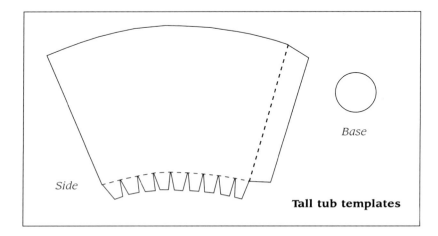

Side

Base

Tall tub templates

BRAID POTS

Small arrangements of pin flowers, such as the black-eyed Susan, daisies, auricula, petunias and poppies, or the roses from page 128, can be made in pieces of foam. Cut a small dome shape of foam packaging material or flower

arranger's foam. Glue a length of braid around the edge and bind with thread to hold in shape until dry. Once dry, remove the thread and push pin flowers into the foam.

BASKETS

Both types of basket shown can be filled with a piece of foam packaging material or a lump of flower-arranger's foam, into which can be pushed a selection of pin flowers.

WHITE CANVAS BASKET: Use the templates to cut a base piece from cardboard and a side piece from thin card. Glue the side piece to fine canvas, trimming away excess. Coil this around the base piece and glue in position.

To make a handle, fray three 6in threads from the canvas and knot them together at one end. Plait, then knot the end. Glue the ends inside the basket. Clip together until dry.

BROWN CANVAS BASKET: Find a small pot or tin (about 1¹/₄in in diameter, a Humbrol enamel paint tin is ideal) and cut a circle of tapestry canvas, about 1in larger all round than the base of the pot. Wet the canvas, then mould it over the end of the pot folding excess fabric into neat tucks around the edge. Bind the wet canvas with thread to hold it in shape. When dry, remove the thread and trim the top of the basket. Make a handle as for the white canvas basket above.

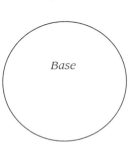

Base

Side

Basket templates

An Autumn Wedding

*F*lower arrangements bring a splash of colour to special occasions. In this scene, a wedding day is made complete by pedestal flower arrangements, a bouquet and floral swags. You could also use the pedestal arrangements to flank a grand stairway in a large town house, or select just a few flowers and leaves to put into a vase on a window ledge or side table in a more simple dwelling. A range of vases and pots is described on page 151.

PROJECTS KEY

1 pedestal flower
   arrangements
2 floral swags
3 bride's bouquet
4 bridesmaid's posy
5 carnation buttonhole
6 wedding cake
   (see page 59)
7 side table (see page 83)

WORKING NOTES: The flowers in this section are all made from paper and card. It is a good idea to wash your hands frequently when making these projects, as paper quickly picks up grease marks. A good range of colours and weights of paper and card is available from most art shops, or look in a stationery shop for coloured writing papers.

Templates can be photocopied directly onto coloured paper or card, but not onto crêpe paper. You can trace the templates onto paper, cut them out and draw round them on the crêpe paper, paper or card. Cut them out with a sharp craft knife or scalpel.

Use gardening books or your own garden as reference for flower colours and markings. The best way to curve fronds and petals is to hold a pencil under the cut paper piece. Pressing your thumb on top of the piece and keeping up a gentle pressure, pull the pencil outwards towards the end of the piece. Repeat until the desired curve is achieved. PVA glue is suitable for all of the projects.

PEDESTAL FLOWER ARRANGEMENTS

PEDESTAL: Press out three circles of polymer clay – two 1¼in in diameter and one 1⅛in in diameter. Roll out one thick sausage of polymer clay and cut the ends of the sausage to make flat faces. Bake all the pieces to harden and, once cool, glue the pieces together (see photograph on page 127).

Carve a block of flower-arranger's foam into a 1½in tall x 1½in wide dome with a flat base and glue this to the top of the pedestal.

Now make up the following flowers and leaves for one pedestal arrangement.

BEECH BRANCHES (MAKE THREE): Cut a 3in length from a thin twig. Use the templates to cut leaves from brown paper and glue these to the twig, using the tem-

Rose template

Beech leaves templates

plate as a guide. Once the glue has dried, push the twigs into the top of the foam.

LILIES (MAKE SIX): Copy the lily templates on page 123 onto white paper. Add pink markings with pencil crayon, using the photograph below as a guide. Glue two pieces together and curve the petals. Make a hole through the centre and thread through a yellow stamen (available from flower arranging shops). Push the stamen into the arrangement.

ROSES (MAKE FOUR): Using the template (left), cut a rose piece from coloured crêpe paper. Run a little glue along the long straight edge and roll up the flower, starting at the narrow end. Once dry, push a length of craft wire up into the flower. Splay out the petals, then push the wire into the arrangement.

SINGLE-FLOWER HOLLYHOCK (MAKE SIX): Using the template, cut a hollyhock piece from coloured crêpe paper. Shape into a cone and glue the straight edges together. Push a short dressmaker's pin through the centre and into the arrangement. Dab a little brown paint onto the pin head.

 Hollyhock template

FERN FRONDS (MAKE SIX): Using the small fern templates on page 135, cut leaf shapes from green paper. Bend into curves and push the ends into the foam.

LONG LEAVES: Cut long strips of green paper. Mark the edges with green felt-tip pen. Push the ends into the arrangement, then curve the free ends downwards. Trim to the desired length.

DARK LEAVES: Cut strips of dark green card with pointed ends. Curve slightly, then push the straight ends into the foam to fill in gaps and frame the arrangement (see photograph).

FLORAL SWAGS

Cut long narrow leaf shapes of coloured crêpe paper. Sew six together down the middle – it's easiest to do this with a sewing machine on a straight-stitch setting. Make lots of parallel cuts along the edges, as shown in the diagram. Separate the fronds. Display swags on a church or reception room wall, with three lilies at each join (see lily instructions above).

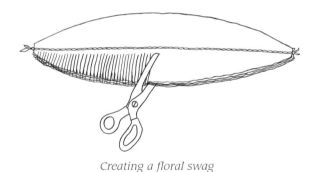

Creating a floral swag

CARNATION BUTTONHOLE

Cut a $^3/_8$in x $2^1/_8$in rectangle of coloured crêpe paper. Make lots of parallel cuts along one of the long edges, run a little glue along the other long edge and roll up the flower. Once dry, push a length of craft wire up into the flower. Splay out the petals, then push the wire into the bridegroom's lapel.

BRIDE'S BOUQUET

Carve a triangle (about 2in x 1in x 1in) from flower-arranger's foam and smooth the edges. Make three lilies, one rose, three fern leaves and seven dark leaves following the instructions above. Push into the foam, using the photograph as a guide.

IVY FRONDS (MAKE THREE): Copy the ivy leaf templates onto green paper, adding details with green felt-tip pens. Cut out the leaves and glue them to thin strips of green paper. Push the ends of the strips into the bottom of the bouquet and secure with a little glue.

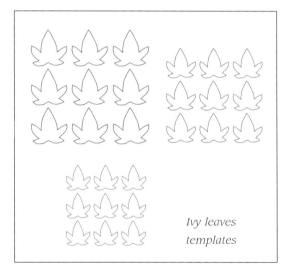

Ivy leaves templates

BRIDESMAID'S POSY

Copy the posy cone template onto white paper and cut it out. Shape into a cone and glue the straight edges together. Make a rose as described above but without the wire. Glue the rose inside the cone. Copy the posy fern templates onto green paper, cut them out and glue them around the rose.

Posy fern template

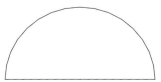

Posy cone template

Topiary

*T*opiary is an ancient art dating back to the time of the Romans. People have always enjoyed crafting their bushes and trees into the shapes of birds and animals, or making more formal geometric designs such as spheres and cubes. In later centuries, this formality led to the development of complex mazes in the gardens of stately homes and mazes became particularly popular in Elizabethan times. If you have the space, you could create a maze for your own dolls' house garden, or you could design a miniature hedge in the shape of a Celtic knot to serve as a knot garden. Small topiary can also be put into pots to grace the steps, hallways and window boxes of grand houses.

PROJECTS KEY
1 hedge
2 archway
3 peacock topiary
4 large tiered tree
5 medium tiered tree
6 medium cone trees
7 small cone trees
8 small globe trees
9 plant pots (see page 151)
10 brick tiled border (see page 96)
11 sundial (see page 113)
12 dolls (see Suppliers, page 172)

WORKING NOTES: The topiary shapes in this section are all constructed using the same technique, the base being a plain shape created from card, clay or polystyrene. For projects that use polymer clay, bake to harden following the manufacturer's instructions. Look out for twigs that can be used for trunks, or use dowel. The height of the trees you make will depend on your type of dolls' house garden and space you have available – the largest shown here are 10in tall. The leaf texture used to coat the topiary shapes is made from clippings trimmed from fur fabric mixed with PVA glue and acrylic paint.

To use templates, trace or photocopy the template onto paper, cut it out, draw around it on the material described and cut it out using an appropriate tool. PVA wood glue is suitable for all of the projects, unless otherwise stated.

LEAF TEXTURE

Choose a medium-toned brown fur fabric with a long pile for the best effect. Trim the pile from the fur fabric and discard the backing cloth. Collect the clippings in a plastic tub, add PVA glue and stir until you have a smooth, sticky texture. Add acrylic paint and keep on stirring. Note that the paint will dry darker than it appears whilst the glue is wet.

When applying the leaf texture to a topiary shape, hold the shape in a vice or clip where it can be left to dry. Put a piece of newspaper underneath, as it can be a messy process. Apply the mixture in small clumps, using a stick or paint brush to spread it on the surface. Once the shape is covered, use a paint brush to smooth out any uneven patches by gently pushing and moulding the surface. Note that the glue in this form will take a very long time to dry, so leave the completed project in a clean, dry place for a couple of days. When dry, use scissors to trim any loose ends.

HEDGE

The base for each hedge is a cardboard cereal box. Cover this with leaf texture (described above). For a curved top, pile the leaf texture into the curved shape on top.

ARCHWAY

Cut two arch shapes (with the centre big enough for a doll) from cardboard. Use fabric tape (gaffer or duck tape) to stick strips of card around the outer and inner sides of the arch to hold them rigid and apart, as shown in the diagram. Cover the archway with leaf texture.

PEACOCK TOPIARY

The base pieces of the peacock are carved from polystyrene packaging. This can be very messy, so carve the pieces over a box or large area of newspaper to catch unwanted bits.

BODY: Take a block of polystyrene and draw the shape of the body on the side with a felt-tip pen, then use a knife to carve away polystyrene to the rough shape. Use the edge of the knife as a scraper for finer shaping. Push a stick up into the body as a trunk and another as a long neck, which will run right up into the crest.

Carve the head, tail and crest from pieces of polystyrene. Push the head and crest onto the neck stick. Use fabric tape (gaffer or duck tape) to stick the tail in place. Cover the polystyrene shapes with leaf texture.

LARGE TIERED TREES

Carve three polystyrene circles for the tiers, and a sphere for the top. Push them onto a stick, then coat all the circles with leaf texture (described above).

MEDIUM TIERED TREES

SQUARE-EDGED TIERS: From thin card and using the three templates on page 132, cut two circles and one edge piece for each tier. Make holes in the centre of each circle in the positions marked on the templates. Score along all the dotted lines and fold the tabs inwards.

For each tier, curl the edge piece into a tube and glue the large tab to the free edge of the tube. Put glue on one set of tabs and glue one of the circles in place. Repeat for the other side. Push a twig trunk through the layers, then cover the shapes with leaf texture. Once dry, glue the base of the twig in a plant pot.

ROUND-EDGED TIERS: Model the tier shapes

Making the arch

*Square-edged
medium tiered tree*

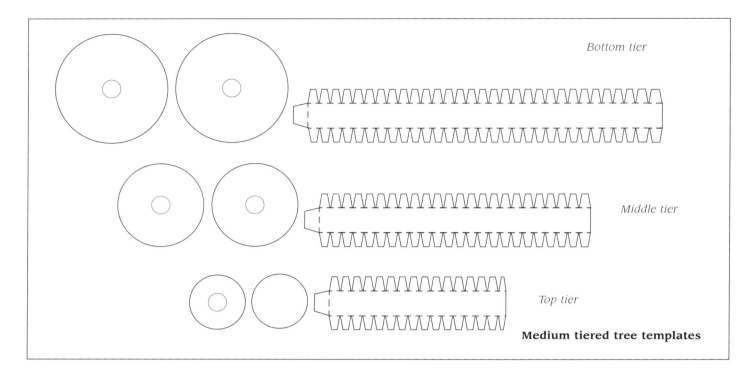

Bottom tier

Middle tier

Top tier

Medium tiered tree templates

from polymer clay (see photograph on pages 120–121 as a guide), push in a twig trunk and bake to harden with the stick in place. Cover the shapes with leaf texture. Once dry, glue the base of the twig in a plant pot.

MEDIUM CONE TREES

Using the templates, cut a top and base piece from card. Coil the top into a cone shape and

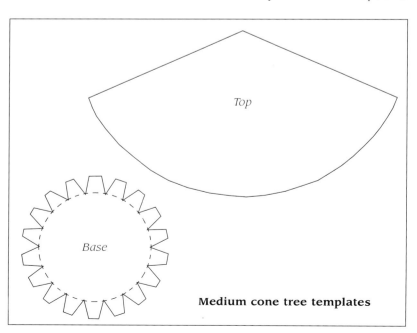

Top

Base

Medium cone tree templates

glue the straight sides together. Make a hole in the centre of the base piece. Fold up the tabs on the base piece along the dotted lines then glue the tabs inside the cone. Cover with leaf texture. Once dry, push a twig up inside the cone and secure the other end in a small plant pot with a lump of air-drying clay.

SMALL CONE TREES

Model small cone shapes from polymer clay (see photograph on page 130 as a guide). Push in a twig trunk and bake to harden with the stick in place. When cool, cover the cone with leaf texture. Once dry, glue the base of the twig in a small plant pot.

SMALL GLOBE TREES

Model the globe shapes from polymer clay, push in a twig for a trunk and bake to harden with the twig in place. When cool, cover the globe with leaf texture. Once dry, glue the base of the twig in a small plant pot.

For a selection of plant pots and vases see the Potter's Studio on pages 150–153. There are also suggestions for decorating the surface of these clay items.

In the Conservatory

A conservatory is a beautiful addition to a dolls' house – a light place to keep a host of plants and seedlings. As transport became easier and more affordable, plant collections became popular throughout the eighteenth and nineteenth centuries – showpieces of the wealth and courage of adventurous men and women.

PROJECTS KEY

1 cheese plant (see page 153)
2 small-leafed palm
3 large-leafed palm
4 small fern
5 'rabbit tracks' plant
6 spider plants
7 seedlings
8 seed packets
9 large garden fork and spade
10 small garden fork and trowel
11 gardening gloves
12 shelving
13 plant pots (see page 151)
14 music stand, bag and recorder (see pages 143–145)
15 toy chest (see page 16)
16 plant stand (see page 34)
17 side table (see page 83)
18 basket design parquet floor (see page 98)

TIP

In the early part of the nineteenth century many houses featured 'ferneries' full of exotic ferns brought back from abroad. You might fill your own conservatory with a range of plants or make just one to brighten up a corner of a hall or dining room.

WORKING NOTES: Writing papers are widely available in a range of different greens and browns. Good quality writing paper is the ideal weight for these paper projects (see page 11 for folding and cutting paper). It is a good idea to wash your hands before making a paper project as grease marks show up clearly on absorbent surfaces. PVA glue is suitable for all the projects in this section.

To use templates, trace or photocopy the template onto paper, cut it out, draw around it on the material described and cut it out using an appropriate tool. Where a template has many parts you may find photocopying easiest. Fold lines have not been included on the leaf shapes as it looks more natural to have slightly varying folds on each leaf.

CHEESE PLANT

Copy the leaf and stem templates onto thin green card – there are enough for one large cheese plant. The largest leaves are for the base of the plant, working up to the smallest at the top. Cut out the leaves using a scalpel.

Make a score line down the centre of each leaf and fold it into a shallow V shape.

Cut out the stem pieces and cut lines along the positions marked. Wrap a stem piece around a 7in length of green pipe cleaner and hold it in place at the base with glue. Curve the stems (the cut lengths) outwards and glue a leaf on the end of each one. Make three more stem-and-leaf sections at intervals up the cheese plant, using smaller leaves each time (see photograph as a guide). Secure the base of

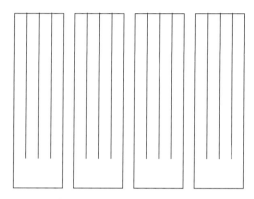

Cheese plant stems templates

Cheese plant leaves templates

the pipe cleaner in a small plant pot with a lump of air-drying clay.

SMALL-LEAFED PALM

Copy the small-leaved palm templates onto thin green card – there are enough for one small palm. Cut out the leaves with a scalpel then glue each leaf to the end of a green pipe cleaner. Twist the pipe cleaners together at the end and glue them into a plant pot (described on page 151).

LARGE-LEAFED PALM

Copy the large-leafed palm templates onto thin green card – there are enough for one large frond. The palm in the photograph has four fronds. Cut out the leaves with a scalpel and then glue the leaves together – the biggest one in the middle. Glue each frond to the end of a green pipe cleaner. Twist the pipe cleaners together at the end and glue them into a plant pot (described on page 151).

SMALL FERN

Copy the fern leaf templates onto thin green card – there are enough for one small fern. Cut out the leaves with a scalpel, then glue them into a small plant pot (described on page 151) with the ends draping over the edge.

Small-leafed palm templates

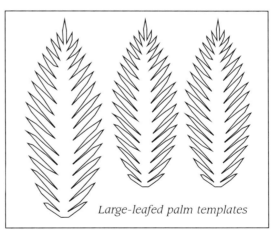

Large-leafed palm templates

Small fern templates

push it down in the centre with a stick, add a drop of glue then push the second leaf group down on top. Leave to dry.

'RABBIT TRACKS' PLANT

Copy the leaf templates onto thin green card – there are enough for one small plant. Cut out the triple leaf groups with a scalpel and curve each leaf slightly downwards. Fill a plant pot (described on page 151) with air-drying clay, place the large leaf group over the pot and

'Rabbit tracks' plant templates

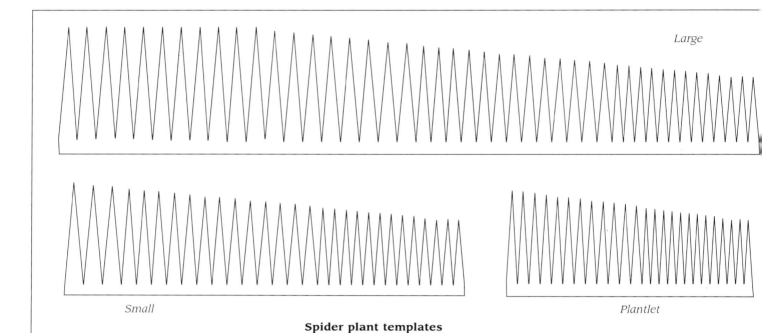

Large

Small

Plantlet

Spider plant templates

SMALL AND LARGE SPIDER PLANTS

SMALL AND LARGE PLANTS: Copy the large and small leaf templates onto green paper – there are enough for one large plant, one small plant and one plantlet. Use a scalpel to cut out the leaf pieces, making each cutting stroke outwards towards the leaf points.

Roll up the large leaf shape, starting at the narrow end and securing the end with a little glue. Gently ease out the leaves so that they spray outwards and place in a pot. Form the small spider plant in the same way.

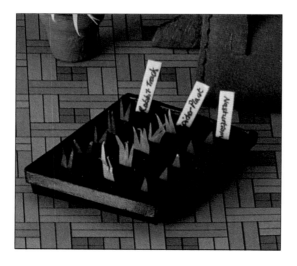

Use a fine pen to write the names of plants on the white seed markers

PLANTLETS: Copy the plantlet template onto green paper. Make a plantlet as described above. Bend a length of craft wire into a hook and hang it from the edge of the plant pot. Glue the plantlet on the other end. Add PVA glue to green paint and then colour the hanging stem.

SEEDLINGS

TRAY: Using the template, cut a seed tray from card. Score and fold along the dotted lines and glue the tabs in position. The top edge folds out and down to form a rim (see photograph, left). Once assembled, paint and varnish.

Fill the tray with brown polymer clay but do not bake. Push in rows of tiny green card

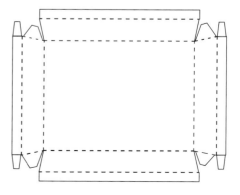

Seed tray template

leaves (see photograph on page 136). Cut strips of white card as seed markers and push into the 'soil'.

SEED PACKETS

Copy the seed packet templates onto paper, then score along the lines indicated by the folding markers. Cut out the shapes, fold along the score lines and glue the tabs in position. Colour the flower designs with felt-tip pens.

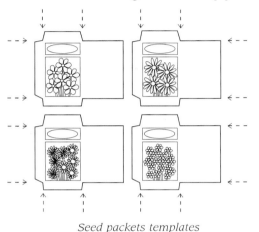

Seed packets templates

LARGE GARDEN FORK AND SPADE

Make each tool in the same way. Use the templates to cut a fork and a spade shape from card. Cut a 3in length of 5mm diameter dowel. Whittle one end into a point and shape the

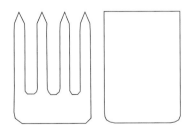

Large fork and spade templates

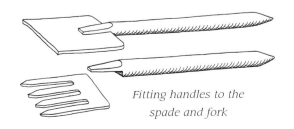

Fitting handles to the spade and fork

other end as shown in the diagram then glue the dowel to the card. Cut a ³/₄in length of 5mm diameter dowel and carve a hole in one side but do not go all the way through. Glue the end of the handle into the hole. Using acrylics, paint the handle red and the lower part silver (see photograph below).

SMALL GARDEN FORK AND TROWEL

Make each tool in the same way. Use the templates to cut a fork and a trowel shape from card. Cut a ³/₄in length of kebab stick and glue it to the card. Using acrylics, paint the handle green and the lower part of the handle and card shape silver.

Small fork and trowel templates

GARDENING GLOVES

Using the template and a fine ballpoint pen, mark four glove shapes on brown felt and cut them out. Use red thread to sew along the cuff edge of each piece and dark grey thread to sew lines on the cuff. Match the glove pieces up in pairs and sew them together around the edge.

Gardening gloves template

THE ARTIST'S WORKSHOP

The tools and materials of creative pursuits are a stylish addition to a dolls' house scene. Striking designs and brightly coloured papers are characteristic of a modern illustrator's studio. In a potter's studio there are pots with classic curves and earthy colours to suit any setting from Roman times on. An eighteenth-century musician prepares for music practice with instruments and manuscripts. And in this Parisian attic, portraits are created with the paints and canvases of a traditional artist.

The Parisian Artist

High up in an attic room in a Paris, an artist is working on a portrait. Around him are strewn the tools of his trade – paints, paint brushes and canvases, and an easel for work to be displayed. There are also the subjects of his paintings – a skull, oranges, wine and musical manuscript – reminiscent of a seventeenth-century Dutch painting. And a canary in a cage waits patiently to be included in some future masterpiece.

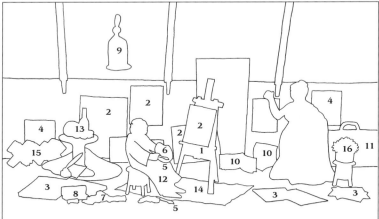

PROJECTS KEY

1 easel
2 plain and painted canvases
3 plain frames
4 ornate frames
5 paint brushes
6 palette
7 paints
8 travelling paint tin
9 canary in a cage
10 scrapbook
11 portfolio and watercolour paper
12 painting smock
13 still-life arrangement
14 paint cloth (see page 90)
15 wine rack and wine bottles
    (see page 56)
16 daisies (see page 124) in braid
    pot (see page 126)

WORKING NOTES: Tiny nails for the easel and canvas projects are available from dolls' house suppliers (see Suppliers, page 172), or you could make holes with a bradawl and then cut off the points of dressmaker's pins and push the shortened pin into the hole. When drilling holes in small or delicate pieces of wood, drill the holes before cutting out the piece. Tape the piece to a larger spare piece of wood to keep it steady and to protect your work surface.

The wire used for the bird cage is thin, flexible craft wire which can be cut with pliers or an old pair of scissors.

To use templates, trace or photocopy the template onto paper, cut it out, draw around it on the material described and cut it out using an appropriate tool.

For more ideas on picture framing and picture sources, see pages 118 and 119. PVA glue is suitable for all of the projects.

PLAIN AND PAINTED CANVASES

CANVAS: Cut a rectangle of white cotton fabric, 1/2in bigger than the frame all round. Fold the fabric around the frame and glue the edges to the back of the frame. Tuck the fabric into a neat fold at each corner and glue in position. When dry, make holes in the sides of the frame with a bradawl and push in tiny nails, or ends cut from dressmaker's pins. Draw the first strokes of a painting on the canvas – either with paint or with felt-tip pens.

FRAME: Follow the instructions for plain frames which are described below.

PLAIN FRAMES

From 1/8in thick x 1/2in wide wood cut the following – two horizontal sides each 2in long and two vertical sides each 1 1/4in long. Glue them together into a frame shape. For a more authentic finish, the ends of each piece of wood can be cut into 45-degree angles before gluing (see page 119 for cutting angles). You can vary the lengths of the pieces to make different sizes of frame. Hang the frames around the studio, or use them to frame tiny paintings and prints (see Pictures Sources on page 118).

ORNATE FRAMES

Cut frames with wide borders from cardboard. Make polymer clay mouldings directly onto the frames (see photograph as a guide) and bake to harden with the cardboard in place. Once cool, glue the clay pieces to the frame, then colour with metallic paint.

PAINT BRUSHES

Take a cocktail stick and roll it under the blade of a knife about 1/4in in from one end to make a small stop cut. Carve away a little wood in towards the stop cut on either side. Leave the brush on the cocktail stick to give you something to hold, then paint in the details – a brown brush, a silver stripe, a black handle and a gold tip on the end of the handle (see photograph as a guide). Once dry, cut the brush from the stick, neaten the end with sandpaper and touch up the paintwork.

EASEL

Cut the following from 3/16in wide, 1/8in thick wood strip: one 3/4in back leg; two 5 3/8in front legs; one 2 1/4in top cross piece; one 2 1/2in bottom cross piece; two 4 1/2in central uprights. Glue them together as shown in the diagram (without the back leg) then hammer a tiny nail into each joint. Glue a tiny strip of fabric to the top of the back leg as a hinge. Glue the other end of the strip to the back of the easel. Cut a 2 3/4in length of 1/4in moulding and glue it to the front. Balance a canvas on this ledge (described above). Cut a 3/4in length of moulding and glue it at the top of the canvas.

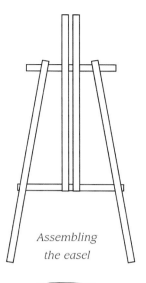

Assembling the easel

PALETTE

Using the template, cut a palette shape from 1/8in thick wood – balsa wood is ideal. Use sandpaper to smooth cut edges. Put blobs of coloured paint around the palette and mix some in the middle. Once this is dry, varnish the paint to make it look wet.

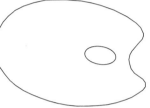

Palette template

PAINTS

Model tiny paint tubes from polymer clay (about 5/8in long). Once hardened, paint them silver. Cut strips of paper for labels. Draw coloured lines at the tops and bottoms, and add tiny black lines for text. Glue the labels around the paint tubes.

TRAVELLING PAINT TIN

Copy the paint-tin palette template onto thin card and cut it out. Model a paint-tin shape from polymer clay slightly larger than the template, then press the card into the top of the clay. Make a separate lid piece from polymer clay. Bake to harden with the palette in place. Once cool, remove the card palette, colour the details with felt-tip pens, then glue back in position. Glue the lid in place, either flat or at a slight angle.

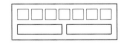

Paint tin palette template

CANARY IN A CAGE

CANARY: Cut a 1in length of kebab stick and carve it into a point at one end. Model a canary from yellow polymer clay and push it onto the top of the point. With more clay, make orange feet that stick out at the front, and a beak. Bake to harden with the stick in place. Once cool, glue the canary to the stick. Cut a ³/₄in length of cocktail stick and glue it under the canary's feet as a perch.

CAGE: Draw out a 1¹/₂in diameter circle on ³/₁₆in thick wood. Drill sixteen tiny holes at regular intervals around the circle about ³/₁₆in in from the edge (If you use very soft wood, such as balsa, you can make the holes with a bradawl.) Cut out the circle and neaten the edge with sandpaper. Make a hole in the centre of the circle and glue the canary on its perch into the hole.

To make the wire frame for the cage, cut eight 7in lengths of craft wire. Bend one in half and push the ends through two adjacent holes. Repeat around the circle. Start to bend each wire end into a cage shape, working around the circle. Make a small hook from a length of thicker wire (such as from a paper-clip) to pull out the bend at the top of the cage (see photograph as a guide). Bring all of the wires together at the top of the cage and thread through a bead. Hold in place with glue and allow to dry. Bend the remaining wire into a loop at the top, then paint the bead silver to finish.

SCRAPBOOK

Cut ten rectangles of cream paper and one of a dark colour. Clip together in a pile with the dark paper on the outside and sew a line of stitches down the centre, then tie the thread ends together. Unclip and fold the scrapbook in half. Cut tiny images from magazines, or draw little sketches to glue into the book. (See also Pictures Sources on page 118.)

PORTFOLIO AND WATERCOLOUR PAPER

PORTFOLIO: Using the templates on page 147, cut a portfolio and a handle piece from card. Glue them to black leather-effect paper and cut away excess paper. Glue leather-effect paper to the reverse of the handle. Construct the portfolio following the instructions on page 147, but

don't add the corner and decorative top pieces.

WATERCOLOUR PAPER: This is made with a deckle (uncut) edge. To mimic this effect, use a pencil and faint marks to draw out rectangles on a large sheet of watercolour paper. Put a metal ruler on one of the pencil lines and press down firmly. Lift up the free edge of the paper and tear it along the pencil line against the ruler. Leave the sheets loose around the portfolio.

PAINTING SMOCK

Lay out a doll on a piece of fabric, with limbs outstretched. Draw a big T-shaped shirt shape, leaving a border around the edge to allow for movement and seam allowance, as shown in the diagram. Cut out two of these T shapes and sew them together at the shoulders, under the arms and up the sides. Sew a hem along the bottom edge. Cut a short line down the centre of the smock from the neck edge, to enlarge the neck hole then turn right side out. Cut strips of coloured felt and sew them around the raw edges of the neck hole. Cut squares of felt to sew onto the front of the smock for pockets. Splash the smock with paint.

Drawing the smock shape

STILL-LIFE ARRANGEMENT

Make fruit and vegetables as described on pages 38 and 49 to appear in your still-life arrangement. Details of the feather quill and manuscript music are on page 144. Model a skull from white polymer clay, and a wine bottle from green clay and bake to harden.

TIP

Other projects in this book also make interesting subjects for a doll's drawing or painting class. For instance a school art lesson might feature toys from pages 13–29, or musical instruments from pages 143–145. And a Victorian lady sketching in her conservatory might choose flowers and plants from pages 122–137.

The Eighteenth-Century Musician

*M*usical instruments are a beautiful addition to any room, whatever the period. Here, a court musician prepares for his daily practice. As instruments tend to become heirlooms, these eighteenth-century pieces would not look out of place in làter periods of dolls' houses.

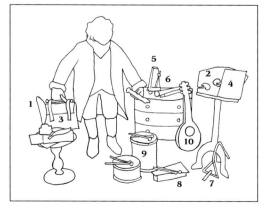

PROJECTS KEY

1 quill and inkwell	6 recorders
2 music stand	7 triangle
3 music bag	8 xylophone
4 music manuscripts	9 drums
5 metronome	10 lute

WORKING NOTES: The musical projects in this section are mostly created simply with scraps of wood, leather and paper, stuck together with PVA glue or contact adhesive. In projects for which templates are provided, trace or photocopy the template onto paper, cut it out, draw around it on the material described and then cut it out using an appropriate tool.

QUILL AND INKWELL

QUILL: Trim the end of a tiny feather into a point, dip it in black ink and leave to dry.

INKWELL: This is made of two wooden beads. Sand the beads to remove any varnish or paint, glue them together and then colour with wood stain or paint. Finish with varnish.

MUSIC MANUSCRIPTS

Photocopy the blank manuscript templates, the half-written manuscript template and the sheet music template onto cream paper and cut them out.

Blank manuscript templates

Half-written manuscript template   *Sheet music template*

MUSIC STAND

The top of the music stand is a full-size violin bridge (available from music shops). Cut off the legs and sand the base flat. Trim a length of pine strip (^{1}/16in thick x ^{3}/8in wide) to the width of the bridge. Glue to the bottom of the bridge

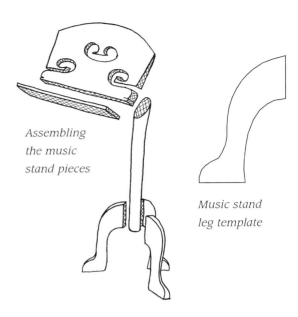

Assembling the music stand pieces

Music stand leg template

with one edge sticking out. Trim one end of a piece of 5mm dowel 2^7/8in long into a wedge and stick it to the back of the bridge (see diagram). Use the music stand leg template to cut three legs from ^{1}/8in thick wood. Clamp the legs together in a vice and sand them at the same time so they match up. Glue the legs to the bottom of the dowel. Colour with wood stain and finish with varnish.

MUSIC BAG

Using a 3in x 1^5/8in rectangle of leather, fold one short edge part of the way up and sew along the sides. Fold the top edge downwards as a flap, dampen and leave under a weight to dry. Glue a glass bead on each end of a ^{13}/16in length of jewellery-maker's wire. Cut two 1^5/16in x ^{3}/16in strips of leather. Fold and glue the ends over the wire then glue the free ends on the front of the bag (see photograph on page 143). Cut a 2in x ^{3}/16in strip of leather and glue it to the back of the bag as a loop handle.

METRONOME

Cut a 1in length of ^{1}/2in square-section pine strip. Carve three sides into a pyramid, leaving a ledge at the bottom. Trim the flat front into a slight recess from the ledge. Glue four wooden beads to the base for feet. Glue a ^{7}/8in long earring fitting to the front at an angle and add a silver-foil 'weight' three-quarters of the way up.

Recorders

Recorders come in different sizes according to their pitch, so use whichever scraps of pine doweling you have (3–8mm diameter). Roll the doweling under the blade of a knife, applying gentle pressure to make the edges of the ridge details. Using a sharp knife or scalpel, shave the recorder thinner between the cut lines and sand smooth. Use wood stain to colour the bottom section brown, leaving the mouthpiece and end section plain. Mark sound and finger holes with a sharp pencil or fine black pen.

Triangle

Bend a paper-clip into a triangle and hang it on a piece of thread. Cut a length of kebab stick for a striker.

Drum

Drum: Paint and varnish a $1^1/_{16}$in diameter cardboard tube. Make pairs of $^1/_{16}$in slits at $^1/_2$in intervals around the ends of the tube. Use these slits to hold silver thread in a zigzag pattern around the drum (see diagram). Cover each end of the tube by gluing on paper. Finish by gluing $^1/_8$in wide strips of leather around the ends of the tube.

Drumsticks: Use pliers to cut off the points of two glass-headed pins.

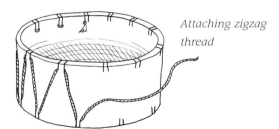

Attaching zigzag thread

Xylophone

Trim a $^7/_{16}$in length of $^1/_2$in square-section pine strip to $^5/_{16}$in thick, then trim it into a wedge shape, $^1/_2$in thick at one end and $^1/_4$in at the other. Cut a kebab stick in half lengthways to make half-round sticks, then cut pieces grading from $1^3/_{16}$in to $^1/_4$in in length. Glue them to the top of the xylophone. For strikers, cut two lengths of kebab stick and glue a tiny wooden bead on the end of each stick.

Lute

Body: Use the lute body template to cut a body piece from $^1/_2$in thick wood. The lute shown is made of walnut. Carve then sand the back of the body piece into a dome. Paint a black circle on the front of the lute in the position marked on the template. Cut a circle of paper and use a craft knife to cut a filigree pattern. Glue it to the lute on top of the sound hole.

Neck: Using the lute neck pieces templates, cut neck pieces from $^5/_{16}$in thick wood. Carve each piece into a half-round shape, leaving the front face flat. Cut away a little from the underside of the fat end of the larger piece to form a ledge to sit the lute body on, and glue in place using Super Glue. Trim the fat end of the smaller neck piece into an angle so that it points downwards and glue it in place. Paint gold stripes on the neck as frets.

Strings: Using a strip of black leather, attach string threads as shown in the diagram. Glue the leather to the lute and allow to dry thoroughly. Gather the threads at the top of the lute and drip Super Glue onto them. Use a pin to spread them out evenly as the glue dries. Trim any excess, then paint the tops of the strings black. Glue silver beads to each side of the top of the neck for pegs.

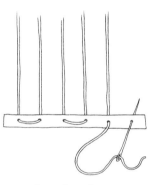

Threading the lute strings

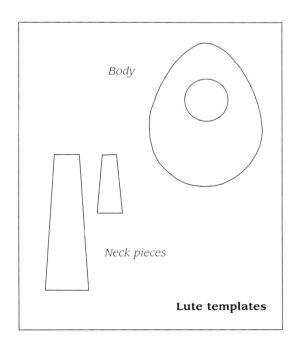

Body

Neck pieces

Lute templates

The Illustrator's Studio

In the modern setting of a city apartment block, the rainbow colours of an illustrator's papers and pencils are shown off to their best advantage. An illustrator's studio is an excellent opportunity to exploit the clean lines and vibrant colours of modern design. Some of the projects here could also make an appearance in older settings, for example, the coloured pencils in late Victorian and twentieth-century houses. And any cultured lady doll would be pleased to sit in a dolls' house garden with pastels and a sketchbook, drawing her prize flowers.

PROJECTS KEY

1 portfolio
2 coloured papers
3 children's colouring pictures
4 pencil crayons and pencil
5 box of pastels
6 sketch pad, book and sketches
7 drawing board
8 stool
9 set square, ruler, protractor
10 pictures
11 wooden parquet floor (see page 97)

WORKING NOTES: Wonderful coloured papers are now widely available in stationery shops and art materials outlets. Choose a selection of papers to complement the decor of your room, or select a rainbow of colours to fan out on the floor. Wood and paper projects can be coloured using paints or felt-tip pens. Pens will give the most satisfactory effect, as they cover well and dry quickly. The pencils, crayons and pastels are made from cocktail sticks.

To use templates, trace or photocopy the template onto paper, cut it out, draw around it on the material described and cut it out using an appropriate tool. Dotted lines on templates show fold lines, which should be scored before folding. PVA glue is suitable for use on all of the projects.

PORTFOLIO

Using the main template, cut a portfolio piece from brown card. Score along the dotted lines, fold up the shape and glue the tabs in position.

Using the templates, cut two corner pieces, one top, one handle, one tab and one lock. Score along all the dotted lines.

CORNERS: Fold each corner piece and glue in the positions marked on the main portfolio template.

TOP: Fold along the dotted line and glue in place on the lid.

HANDLE: Make two holes in the top of the portfolio in the positions marked on the template, through the decorative top piece. Push the handle ends through and secure the ends with glue.

TAB: Glue the tab piece to the front of the lid.

LOCK: Fold the lock piece along the dotted lines and glue it in place on top of the tab so that the tab can slip in and out of the loop.

COLOURED PAPERS

Cut rectangles (about 1¼in x 1in) of rainbow-coloured papers and arrange them around the portfolio.

TIP

For a stylish black leather-effect portfolio, cover your portfolio main piece with leather-effect paper, and omit the decorative corner and top pieces (see photograph on page 139).

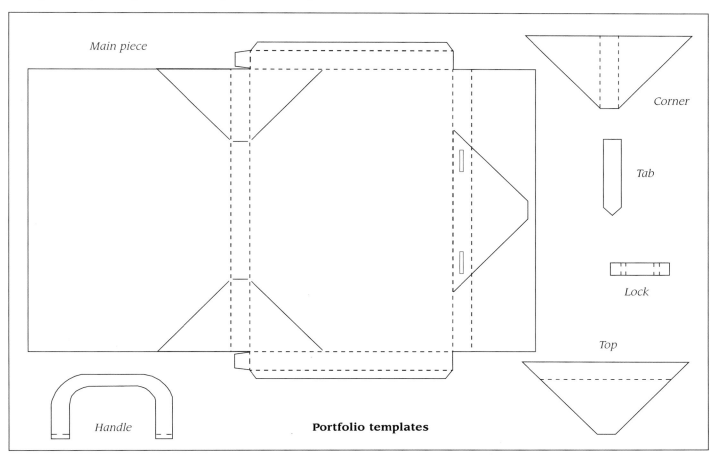

Main piece

Corner

Tab

Lock

Top

Handle

Portfolio templates

CHILDREN'S COLOURING PICTURES

Copy the pictures templates onto paper and cut them out. Colour some with pencil crayons.

PENCIL CRAYONS AND PENCIL

Cut a $7/8$in length of cocktail stick, with one pointed end and one straight end. With a sharp knife, trim the point into a shallow tip. Colour the stick with paint or felt-tip pen and dip the tip into coloured paint. Varnish to finish.

Colouring pictures templates

BOX OF PASTELS

BOX: Copy the pastel box and lid templates onto white card. Score along the lines indicated by the folding markers and then cut out the shapes. Fold up the shapes and glue the tabs in position, using the diagram as a guide for the box. If you photocopy the box base directly

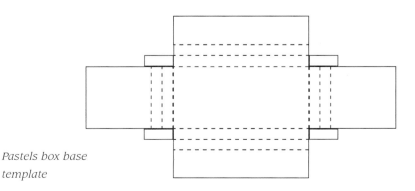

Pastels box base template

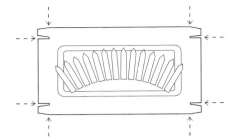

Pastels box lid template

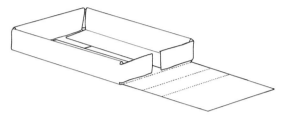

Folding up the pastels box

onto the card, you can fold all the lines inwards which means they will be hidden inside the finished box.

PASTELS: Cut fourteen $5/8$in lengths of cocktail stick, having each pastel with one pointed end and one straight end. Colour the pastels with different-coloured felt-tip pens and arrange them inside the box. Use the same pens to colour the lid design.

SKETCH PAD, SKETCH BOOK AND SKETCHES

SKETCH PAD: Cut ten rectangles of white paper, $1 1/4$in x $1 3/4$in. Do a small drawing on the top piece of paper. Cut a rectangle of coloured paper and a rectangle of card. Stack the card, paper and coloured paper into a pad, then, holding the pieces together in a clip, sew a line of stitches in silver thread along the top. Remove the clip.

SKETCH BOOK: Cut ten rectangles of paper, $2 1/2$in x $1 1/4$in. Fold them in half, then, holding the pieces together in a clip, sew a line of stitches in white thread along the fold line. Glue the book inside a folded rectangle of black paper, slightly larger all round than the pages.

SKETCHES: Tear one of the pieces of paper out of the sketch pad and do a sketch in coloured pencils to mimic a pastel drawing.

DRAWING BOARD AND STOOL

The drawing board and stool are made from 5mm thick mounting board, which has a polystyrene interior sandwiched between outer layers of paper. It is light, easy to cut with a sharp craft knife and glues together neatly.

DRAWING BOARD: Using the four drawing board templates, cut the following from mounting board: two front legs; two back legs; three long joining pieces and four short cross pieces.

Using a back leg, front leg and two short cross pieces assemble a side, gluing the pieces

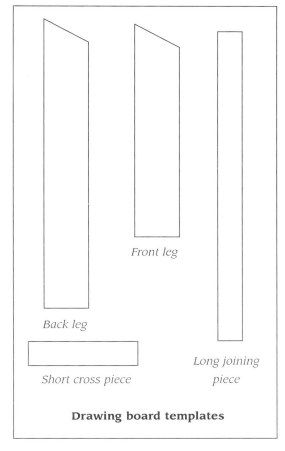

Front leg

Back leg

Short cross piece

Long joining piece

Drawing board templates

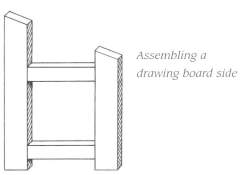

Assembling a drawing board side

together as shown in the diagram. Repeat to make a second side. Join the two sides together with two long joining pieces, using the photograph as a guide. Cut a little off the end of the third joining piece, paint it black and glue it as a foot rest between the side pieces.

Cut a piece 2³/₄in x 3³/₄in and glue it on top. Glue a strip of white card along the front. Glue black pop-fastener 'adjusters' to the back legs (see photograph).

STOOL: Using the three stool templates, cut the following pieces from mounting board: four legs; six struts and one top. Glue the legs to the underside of the top piece then glue the struts in place as shown in the diagram.

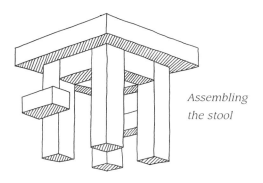

Assembling the stool

SET SQUARE, RULER, AND PROTRACTOR

Photocopy the templates onto acetate (the type designed to be photocopied on for use in overhead projections). Cut them out using a scalpel.

PICTURES

On rectangles of card, make modern designs using offcuts of coloured paper, creating abstract designs of your own. (The largest picture shown is 1³/₄in square, without its border and frame. The smaller pictures are about 1¹/₄in x 1¹/₂in.) Alternatively you could mimic the designs of painters such as Mondrian with black grids and blocks of primary colours. Small photographs or pictures of artworks cut from catalogues can also be used. (See also Picture Sources on page 118 for picture suggestions.) Frame the pictures with strips of wood painted black.

Top

Strut

Leg

Stool templates

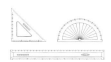

Ruler, set square and protractor templates

The Potter's Studio

Pottery items are useful in any room of the house, and depending on the choice of colour and shape, clay items would not look out of place in any period. This section gives details of the basic techniques for creating a range of shapes of pots, bowls, jugs and teapots. It also has a clay sculpture, for the more creative dolls' house potter. Take a look at Collector's Items on pages 118–119 for ideas on decorating the plain surfaces of plates and bowls to transform them into family heirlooms.

PROJECTS KEY

1 plant pots and vases	tub and window box
2 bowls, plates and saucers	9 clay pots
3 pots with rims and lids	10 clay sculpture
4 jugs and cider bottles	11 coil pot in progress
5 teapots	12 tools
6 mug, cups and plate of biscuits	13 shelving
	14 radio
7 casserole dishes	15 dustbin (trash can) and bucket (see pages 62-63)
8 square garden	16 pictures (see pages 118–119)

WORKING NOTES: All of the clay projects have been made from polymer clay. Bake finished models to harden following the manufacturer's instructions. Air-drying clay can also be used for the simpler projects although it is more difficult to model into fine shapes such as spouts and handles. You could use raw clay colours for your pieces but if you prefer a finished look then choose coloured clay. Finished models can be painted (e.g. the cider bottles and kitchen mixing bowls). Put PVA glue into the paint to help it stick to the surface. To mimic a glaze or to make a piece look wet, finish with a coat of varnish. If creating a potter's studio, lay out extra handles and half-finished pots on a work surface and lumps of clay wrapped in cling film to suggst work in progress. The surface of polymer clay items can be decorated in various ways – see Surface Decoration of Polymer Clay Items, right.

To use templates, trace or photocopy the template onto paper, cut it out, draw around it on the material described and cut it out using an appropriate tool. PVA is suitable for the projects in this section.

PLANT POTS AND VASES

To make plant pots and vases, model polymer clay around the end of a piece of dowel varying the shapes (see photograph as a guide). Draw patterns on the surface of decorative pots by pushing the end of a piece of cardboard into the clay. Bake to harden with the dowel in place. While still warm, remove the dowel.

BOWLS, PLATES AND SAUCERS

BOWLS: Follow the instructions for the plant pots (above) but using large dowel such as a section cut from a broom handle. Use a knife to trim the top of the bowl.

PLATE AND SAUCER: Using the templates, cut two circles from card. Glue the smaller circle in the middle of the larger circle and allow to dry. With the smaller circle facing upwards, press polymer clay on top of the shape. Trim off excess clay around the edge and bake to harden with the card in place. Once cool, prize off

SURFACE DECORATION OF POLYMER CLAY ITEMS

Many items made from polymer clay can be made to look much more like the real thing if a little time is taken to decorate the surface of the clay. Here are some suggestions for creating designs and texture.

• Make geometric surface designs by pressing the edge of a small piece of cardboard into the clay in square and triangular patterns (e.g. the soccer ball on page 69).

• Create stippled surface designs by pressing the point of a cocktail stick into the clay in a random pattern.

• Three-dimensional rope edging can be formed by rolling out two long, thin sausage shapes from polymer clay. Twist them together into a rope, then gently press the rope around the edge of a pot (e.g. the edge of the large square-based pot on the right-hand side of the picture on page 150).

• Create low-relief motifs by press out polymer clay on a flat surface to about $1/8$in thick. Use a craft knife to cut out the shape of a flower, animal or crest. Lift up the motif and press it gently on the side of the pot. Smooth the edges into the pot side using a small piece of cardboard. Press surface details into the clay with a cocktail stick (e.g. the leaf designs on the long window box on page 150). Details such as feet and handles can also be added in this way.

• Make cut-out designs by using a scalpel to cut shapes out of the side of a hollow or pot shape to make a design or filigree pattern. Smooth the edges of the holes with a small piece of cardboard (e.g the pumpkin lantern on page 170).

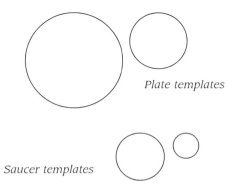

Plate templates

Saucer templates

the card with a knife and use fine sandpaper to smooth any rough areas.

POTS WITH RIMS AND LIDS

Follow the instructions for the plant pots (above) and trim the top of the pot with a knife.

Roll out a sausage of polymer clay and wrap it around the top of the vase. Smooth the join, and pinch into a rim.

To make a lid, press out a blob of polymer clay, then add a smaller blob on the top as a handle.

JUGS AND CIDER BOTTLES

JUGS: Follow the instructions for the plant pots on page 151, using a thin dowel and making the body of the jug thicker in the middle. Before baking, poke a pointed kebab stick into the top of the jug and ease it forward to create a spout. Roll a small sausage of clay and press it to the back of the jug as shown in the diagram. Smooth the join then curl the clay into a handle and smooth the end to the base of the jug.

CIDER BOTTLES: Follow the instructions for the jug above, but omit the spout. Once baked, use acrylics to paint the bottom section pale grey and the top mustard yellow. Once dry add a coat of varnish. With a scalpel cut tiny stoppers from a wine cork.

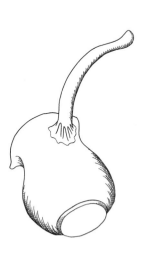

Attaching the jug handle

TEAPOTS

Model the main body of a teapot from polymer clay. Mark the line of the lid by pushing a piece of cardboard into the clay. Add a handle using the instructions and diagram for the jug (above). Model a spout and smooth the end to the front of the teapot. Add a small blob of clay on top for a lid handle.

MUG, CUPS, AND PLATE OF BISCUITS

MUG AND CUPS: Follow the instructions for the jugs (above), without the spout. Once baked, fill the mug with brown polymer clay.

BISCUITS: Model biscuits from polymer clay and bake to harden.

CASSEROLE DISHES

Model the casserole dishes from polymer clay or air-drying clay – refer to the photograph or use your own dishes or pictures from catalogues as a guide to the shapes. These dishes do not have removable lids – the details are

drawn onto the shape with a pointed stick. Add a blob of clay on the top as a handle.

SQUARE GARDEN TUB AND WINDOW BOX

SQUARE TUB: Using the templates, cut four side pieces and one base from cardboard and tape them together into a tub shape. Model polymer clay around the card and add decorations (see photograph and refer to Surface Decoration of Polymer Clay Items on page 151). Bake to harden with the cardboard in place. Once cool, remove the cardboard, or leave it in place (it can be painted matt or be hidden by contents such as soil).

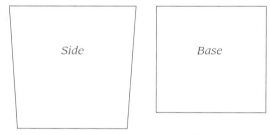

Side   *Base*

Square garden tub templates

WINDOW BOX: Using the templates, cut two long sides, two short sides and one base from cardboard. Make the box following the instructions for the tub (above).

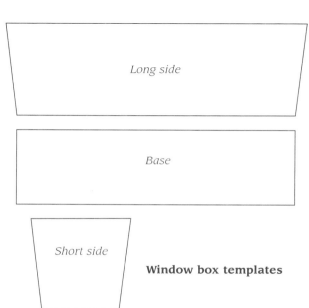

Long side

Base

Short side

Window box templates

CLAY POTS

POT: Make a basic pot by moulding polymer clay around the end of a circular dowel. Make a rim by poking a flat piece of card into the top of the pot and easing it outwards – repeat this around the rim of the pot.

SPOUT: Create a spout by poking a cocktail stick into the top of the front of the pot and easing it forwards.

HANDLE: Make a handle by first drawing a handle shape on card. Roll out a tiny sausage of polymer clay and lay it on top of the drawing, forming it into the handle shape. Stick the handle to the side of the pot and smooth the join. Make decorative marks on the pot with a knife, then bake the pot to harden with the dowel still in place. While still warm, remove the dowel.

CLAY SCULPTURE

Model a head or other subject from polymer clay. Cut a rectangle of $1/8$in thick wood, put the sculpture on it and surround the sculpture with offcuts of clay. Bake to harden on the board.

COIL POT IN PROGRESS

Press out a blob of polymer clay for the base of the pot. Roll out a thin sausage of polymer clay and coil it around the edge of the base. Add more coils, building up the pot. Bake the pot to harden, adding a coat of varnish if you wish it to look wet.

TOOLS

CHEESE WIRE: Cut two $5/8$in lengths of kebab stick and make a hole in the middle of each stick. Cut a $2^1/2$in length of craft wire and glue the ends into the holes.

PALETTE KNIFE: Cut a long, thin rectangle of silver card and round the corners. Glue tiny strips of wood to either side of one end of the card for a handle.

CLAY SCRAPER: Cut a $3/4$in length of kebab stick and make a hole in the end. Bend a triangle of craft wire and glue the ends into the hole.

SHAPER: Model a shaper from polymer clay (see photograph on page 150 as a guide).

SPONGE: Cut a block from a bath sponge.

SHELVING

For each shelf, cut four 6in lengths and two $1^1/2$in crosspieces of $1/4$in wide x $1/8$in thick wood. Cut uprights from the same wood: for a tall shelving unit with three shelves, cut four 6in uprights; for a shorter shelving unit with two shelves, cut four $3^1/4$in uprights. Glue each shelf together as shown in the diagram. Glue the shelves to uprights using the photograph as a guide.

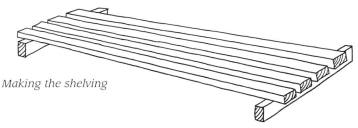

Making the shelving

RADIO

Copy the radio template onto thin card, score along the dotted lines and make a hole in the position marked. Cut out the shape, fold it up and glue the tabs in position. Paint the radio dark red or dark green. Model buttons from polymer clay and, once baked, glue to the top. Copy the grill template onto card, cut it out and glue to the front. Push a small bead onto the top of a cocktail stick. Paint the stick and bead silver and when dry push it through the hole into the top of the radio.

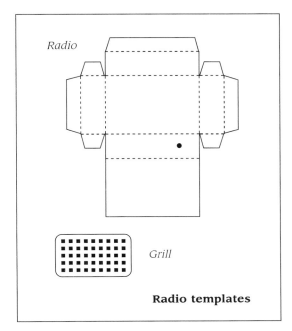

Radio

Grill

Radio templates

CELEBRATIONS

A gathering of dolls for a celebration can be an exciting part of a dolls' house. In this chapter, children enjoy a birthday party surrounded by decorations and party food. In another setting a mother prepares for Christmas, wrapping presents by the tree. A suburban back garden hosts a barbecue, with kebabs, burgers and fireworks. Celebrating another fun occasion, children meet on the street in Hallowe'en costumes, ready for a mischievous evening of trick or treat.

A 1950s Birthday Party

Everyone remembers the thrill of preparations for a birthday party – the mysterious-looking parcels that appear, the colourful decorations, and the wonderful spread of food put out for the guests. The projects in this section help to evoke the excitement felt by a child on their special day, with balloons, streamers, party food, costumes and a party game. Take a look in the Baking Days section on pages 57–60 for more ideas of delicious cakes and biscuits to load down the birthday table. Refer also to the Toys and Games chapter pages 12–29 for further ideas on birthday presents.

PROJECTS KEY

 1 party food
 2 bottles of pop
 3 decorations
 4 pin-the-tail-on-the-donkey game
 5 party costumes
 6 presents and wrapping paper
 7 birthday cards
 8 teddy bear dressing doll
 9 birthday cakes (see page 60)
10 toys (see pages 14–20)
11 tomatoes and fruit (see pages 49 and 38)

WORKING NOTES: It is useful to choose a colour or subject theme for your birthday celebration: in this scene, simple reds, purples and greens have been chosen for the decorations. Ribbons, card and tissue paper can all be chosen to fit in with the theme. The cake, wrapping paper, banners and cards have a teddy bear theme. The food projects in this section are all made with polymer clay – finished models should be baked to harden, following the manufacturer's instructions.

To use templates, trace or photocopy the template onto paper, cut it out, draw around it on the material described and cut it out using an appropriate tool. PVA glue is suitable for all of the projects.

PARTY FOOD

ICED CUP CAKES: Roll a tiny blob of brown polymer clay and press it down onto a 3/8in diameter circle of white tissue paper. Use the side of a pin to push the tissue paper at intervals into the side of the blob, as shown in the diagram. Decorate the top with polymer clay icing – brown for chocolate or white with a red cherry on top.

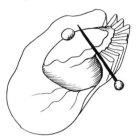

Putting tissue paper round a cup cake

To make simple plates, cut a 1in diameter circle from thin card. With a coloured pen draw a decorative line around the edge, then glue food to the plates.

BATTENBURG CAKE: Model two square-section sausages of polymer clay, each about 1/4in square – one pink, one yellow. Cut in half, then stack them together to give the characteristic chequered pattern (see photograph top right as a guide). Gently press the pieces together, then cover with a thin layer of cream polymer clay. Cut into slices.

SWISS ROLLS: Press out rectangles of coloured polymer clay. Stack them, roll them up then cut into slices.

SANDWICHES: Model a loaf of bread shape from light brown polymer clay, then add a darker crust using dark brown clay. Cut into slices and make into sandwiches with brown, green and red clay fillings.

SAUSAGES ON STICKS: Roll sausage shapes from polymer clay. Push tiny twigs or pine needles into the top and bake to harden with the sticks in place.

BOTTLES OF POP

Model bottle shapes from polymer clay and push a tiny twig or pine needle into the top to act as a straw. Bake to harden and once cool, use acrylics to paint the twig.

DECORATIONS

BALLOONS: Model balloon shapes from polymer clay, with knot sections. Once hardened, tie three balloons together with ribbon around their knot sections then varnish the balloons.

BANNERS: Copy the banner template onto coloured paper and cut it out. Colour it with felt-tip pens.

STREAMERS: Cut narrow strips of tissue paper, or lengths of 1/8in wide ribbon.

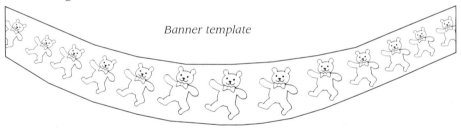

Banner template

PIN-THE-TAIL-ON-THE-DONKEY GAME

Copy the donkey template onto paper, colour it with felt-tip pens and cut it out. Cut a strip of felt for the tail and glue a scrap of fur fabric to the end. Push a short dressmaker's pin through the top.

Donkey template

Party masks templates

PARTY COSTUMES

HATS: Cut a strip of tissue paper to fit around a doll's head. Cut the top into decorative points, then glue into a tube.

MASK: Copy the mask templates onto coloured card. With a needle, make holes in the positions marked. Cut out each mask. Sew thread through each hole and secure with a knot.

BLINDFOLD: Tie a length of ribbon around a doll's eyes.

PRESENTS AND WRAPPING PAPER

Using the parcel templates on page 161, cut box pieces from thin card. Score along the dotted lines then fold up the boxes and glue the tabs in position. Alternatively you could cut offcuts of wood and wrap these up. Wrap presents in small-print paper or plain wrapping paper adding string and bows. For teddy bear wrapping paper, copy the template onto paper and colour the details with a felt-tip pen.

BIRTHDAY CARDS

From a card catalogue, cut out the designs that have been reproduced in miniature. Glue them to little folded cards. (See also Pictures Sources on page 118.)

TEDDY BEAR DRESSING DOLL

Copy the template onto thin card, colour the details with felt-tip pens and cut out the rectangle. The dressing doll can be displayed as a card by folding the rectangle along the fold line indicated. Alternatively you could use a scalpel to cut out the bear and costumes. Fit the stand to the bear as shown in the diagram.

Teddy bear dressing doll template

Teddy bear wrapping paper template

Assembling the teddy bear stand

Christmas Eve

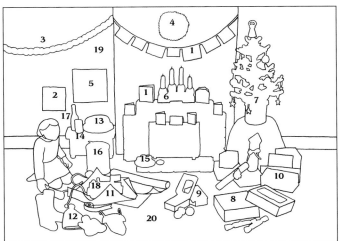

In this scene, a mother is wrapping presents to place under the Christmas tree. The decorations are for a modest Christmas but many of them could be made in more lavish materials for an extravagant Christmas in a grander dwelling (see Tip overleaf).

PROJECTS KEY

1 Christmas cards
2 calendar
3 paper chain
4 tinsel wreath
5 Advent calendar
6 candle holder
7 Christmas tree
8 box of crackers
9 box of baubles
10 parcels
11 wrapping paper, string and ribbon
12 Santa costume
13 Christmas cake (see page 60)
14 tumbler (see page 165)
15 plate of mince pies (see page 60)
16 drum (see page 145)
17 wine bottle (see page 56)
18 pull-along train (see page 15)
19 wallpaper (see page 87)
20 carpet (see page 87)

Calendar template

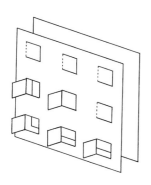

Making the advent calendar

WORKING NOTES: Some of the templates here can be photocopied directly onto thin card, ready for scoring and gluing. For these, the folding lines are marked outside the edge of the template, so they won't show up on the finished piece (see page 11 for scoring card). Other templates can be traced or photocopied onto paper, cut out, and drawn around on the material described. Cut out using an appropriate tool. Dotted lines on templates show fold lines.

PVA wood or paper glue is suitable for all the projects. Clip pieces together with the glue sandwiched between until dry. Clear sheet plastic for box lids can be cut from food packaging.

CALENDAR

Copy the calendar template onto thin card. Cut eleven plain rectangles the same size and clip the rectangles together. With silver thread, sew the pages together along the top. Glue or draw a picture on the front.

PAPER CHAIN

Cut $^3/_4$in x $^1/_8$in rectangles of coloured paper. Roll one into a circle and glue the ends together. Thread a second rectangle of paper through the circle and glue the ends together. Repeat until you have the desired length of chain.

TINSEL WREATH

Coil a length of tinsel into a circle and glue the ends together. Make a tiny bow with ribbon and glue it to the tinsel. Hang a small bell in the centre on a piece of thread.

ADVENT CALENDAR

Cut out a suitable picture for the front of the Advent calendar from a Christmas card catalogue then glue the picture to thin card. Make doors in the card by cutting three sides of little rectangles and folding the doors outwards, as shown in the diagram. Place the picture onto another piece of card and mark the position of the doors on the new piece of card, drawing through the doors. Cut tiny pictures to glue in the positions marked. Put glue on the back of the doors piece, being careful not to get any on the doors themselves, and glue it on top of the second picture piece.

CHRISTMAS CARDS

CARDS: From a Christmas card catalogue, cut out the designs that have been reproduced in miniature and glue them to little folded cards.
STRING DISPLAY: Fold and glue some cards over a piece of string and hang it on the wall.

CANDLE HOLDER

From $^1/_4$in thick pine strip, cut two rectangles, $^1/_2$in x 1$^3/_4$in and $^1/_4$in x 1in. Cut a notch in the larger piece to define two feet, using the photograph as a guide. Glue the pieces together and paint red. Glue tubular beads upright on top and push in birthday-cake candles.

CHRISTMAS TREE

TREE: Using the Christmas tree shapes on page 161 as guides, make three tiers from green pipe cleaners, bending them to follow each shape and twisting the pipe cleaners together where they cross over. Join the tiers together (largest at the bottom) with a pipe cleaner trunk running up the centre, bending it around the centre of each tier on the way up. Secure the base in a small pot with air-drying clay. Glue red felt around the pot, and a border of white felt.
STAR DECORATIONS: Attach hanging threads to sequins and hang them from the branches.
BAUBLES: Add a hanging thread to a tiny star-shaped earring fitting and glue this to a spherical bead. Add a dab of glue to the thread of decorations to keep them in place on the tree.
FAIRY: Using the templates, cut fairy pieces from white paper. Roll the dress into a cone and glue into shape, then glue the arm piece on the front. Glue on a pink bead head and paint on a face, hair and pink hands. Make a tiny circle of tinsel and glue it to the head for a halo.

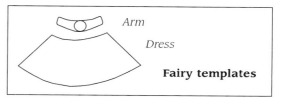

Arm

Dress

Fairy templates

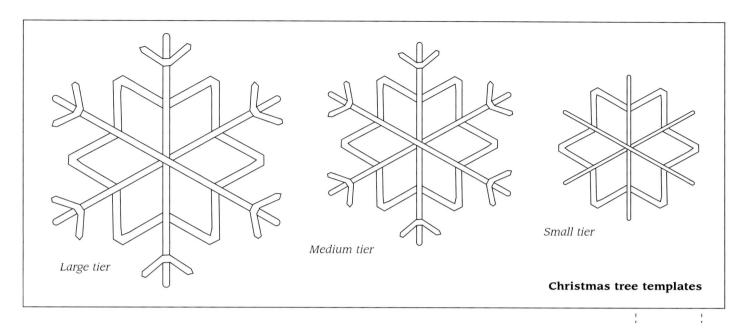

Large tier

Medium tier

Small tier

Christmas tree templates

PARCELS

Using the square or rectangular parcel templates below, cut parcel pieces from thin card. Score along the dotted lines, fold up the boxes and glue the tabs in position. Alternatively you could wrap up offcuts of wood.

Wrap the boxes in small-print or plain wrapping paper, adding string and bows to decorate. Arrange other offcuts of wrapping paper and ribbon around unwrapped gifts. Make little balls of string, holding them together with glue, and a reel of string – string wrapped around an offcut of dowel.

BOX OF BAUBLES

Copy the box and lid templates onto thin card and colour with a felt-tip pen. Score along the lines indicated by the folding markers then cut out the shapes. Using a scalpel, also cut out the rectangle in the lid. Cut a 1in x ⁵⁄₈in piece of clear plastic and glue it to the underside of the lid. Fold up the box and lid and glue the tabs in position. Glue the back flap of the lid inside the box. Fill the box with six baubles (described above), or simply six beads.

BOX OF CRACKERS

BOX: Make the cracker box and lid using the two templates provided overleaf and following the instructions for the bauble box above, but do not glue them together. The box is designed to contain twelve crackers.

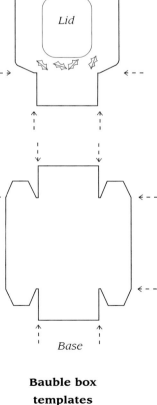

Lid

Base

Bauble box templates

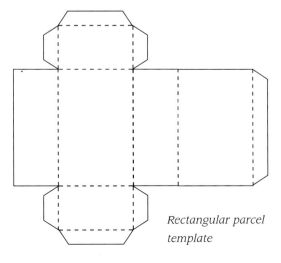

Rectangular parcel template

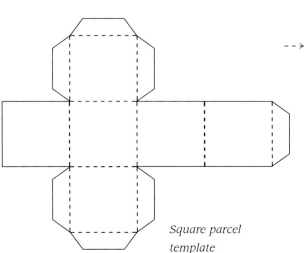

Square parcel template

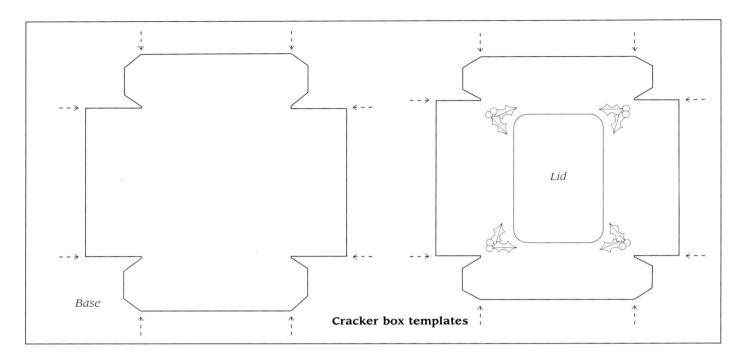

Cracker box templates

Base

Lid

CRACKER: Cut a ³/4in length of 5mm diameter dowel. Cut a 1¹/2in square of tissue paper and wrap it around the dowel, leaving an even amount of tissue paper at each end. Wrap thread around the tissue paper at each end and pull gently to crease the paper, then remove the thread. Glue a diamond of coloured paper and a sequin to the side of each cracker.

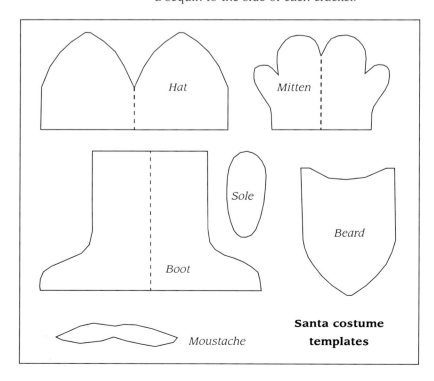

Hat

Mitten

Sole

Boot

Beard

Moustache

Santa costume templates

SANTA COSTUME

BOOTS: Using the templates, cut boot and sole pieces from thin black leather or felt. Fold a boot piece in half and sew it together along the edge, leaving the top and bottom open. Cover the bottom with the sole piece and sew it in place. The boots are not designed to fit a doll – they are for display only.

BEARD: Using the diagram or your own doll as a guide, fold a piece of wire into shape – the hooks are to hang over Santa's ears. Using the beard template, cut two beard pieces and one moustache from white felt. Match up the beard pieces and sew them together around the edge, making stitches at the top corners to hold them to the wire shape. Glue on a white felt moustache to cover the wire.

MITTENS: Using the template, cut two mittens from red felt. Fold a mitten piece in half and sew it together around the curved edge. Glue a strip of white felt around the bottom.

HAT: Using the template, cut a hat from red felt. Fold it in half and sew it together around the curved edge. Glue a strip of white felt around the bottom.

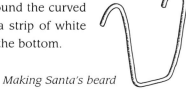

Making Santa's beard

A Garden Party Barbecue

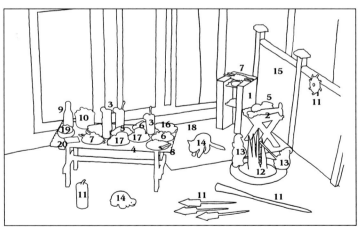

PROJECTS KEY

1 barbecue	15	garden fence
2 tongs		(see page 88)
3 drinks	16	hot-dogs
4 plates		(see page 41)
5 burgers	17	burgers in buns
6 sausages		(see page 41)
7 kebabs	18	crazy paving
8 plastic fork		(see page 94)
9 tomato sauce	19	bowl of
10 salad		strawberries (see
11 fireworks		page 26)
12 garden pond	20	chocolate bar
13 gnomes		(see page 171)
14 cat and tortoise		

A barbecue is an ideal accessory for a small garden or patio, providing a focus for activity. Here, fireworks bring added interest to the occasion. Originating in China, fireworks are a perennial celebration favourite worldwide, particularly for the fire festivals of the winter. The flooring section (page 94) has instructions for crazy paving and other floorings to suit different houses.

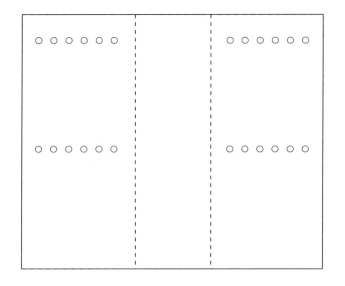

Interior barbecue template

Sewing the racks on the barbecue

WORKING NOTES: Polymer clay is an ideal medium for the food projects in this section (see page 11 for using polymer clay).

To use templates, trace or photocopy the template onto paper, cut it out, draw around it on the material described and cut it out using an appropriate tool. See page 11 for using and scoring card. Labels and firework wrappers can be photocopied or traced onto paper and coloured using felt-tip pens. PVA glue is suitable for all the projects.

BARBECUE

BARBECUE: Using the exterior template, cut an exterior barbecue piece from cardboard. Cover with dolls' house brick paper (available from dolls' house shops and suppliers). Fold along the dotted lines and glue the tabs in position. Using the interior template, cut an interior barbecue piece from cardboard. Cover the inside with dolls' house brick paper and fold along the dotted lines. Sew silver thread backwards and forwards through the holes marked on the template, as in the diagram, to form two racks. Glue the inner piece inside the barbecue.

COALS: Mould red polymer clay into a lump of coal shape. Once hardened, dab black paint on the surface and glue onto the lower rack.

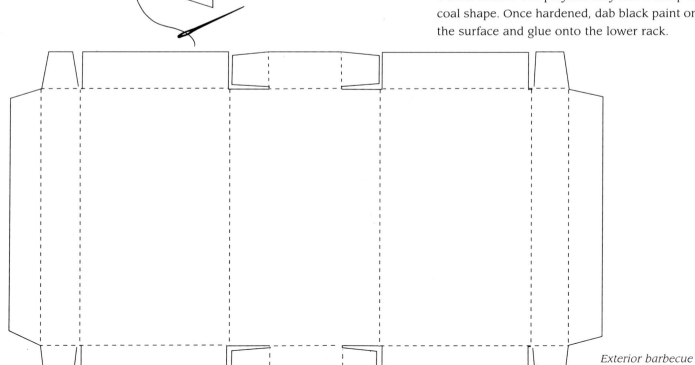

Exterior barbecue template

TONGS

Bend some craft wire into a tongs shape, using the diagram as a guide.

DRINKS

TUMBLERS: Cut 1in lengths of 10mm diameter plastic tube, smoothing the cut edges with fine sandpaper. Glue the base of each tube to a circle cut from a sheet of clear plastic. Fill the tumblers with tiny lumps of coloured polymer clay.

CUCUMBER: Press out a blob of pale green polymer clay, then edge it with a thin layer of dark green clay. Cut a slot in the edge and bake to harden. A slice of lemon could be made in the same way, using yellow polymer clay.

STIRRER: Roll out a very thin sausage of polymer clay and bake to harden.

Forming the tongs

PLATES

The plates are 1in diameter circles cut from card. Draw a decorative line around the edge with a felt-tip pen.

BURGERS

Press out blobs of pink polymer clay and bake to harden. For cooked burgers, add char lines with black paint.

SAUSAGES

Roll out sausage shapes of pink polymer clay and pile onto a plate (described above). Bake to harden on the plate. For cooked sausages, add char marks with black paint.

KEBABS

Roll balls of red, green and brown polymer clay and push them onto a thin stick – a pine needle or a splinter trimmed from the side of a full-sized kebab stick are suitable. Bake to harden with the stick in place.

PLASTIC FORK

With a pencil, draw out a fork shape on card (about 1/2in long). Press out a piece of white polymer clay on top of the shape. Use a knife to cut away the clay to the fork shape. Bake to harden with the card in place.

TOMATO SAUCE

Model a tomato sauce bottle shape from red polymer clay, with a white clay lid. Bake to harden. Photocopy the label template onto paper and colour with felt-tip pens. Cut out the label and glue it to the bottle, wrapping thread around the label to keep it in shape whilst the glue dries.

Tomato sauce label template

SALAD

SALAD: Press out pieces of green polymer clay and pinch them slightly to form lettuce leaf shapes. Roll red polymer clay into tomatoes. Bake the lettuce and tomatoes to harden.

BOWL: Pile the baked polymer clay salad into a small plastic lid. The one in the photograph below is from a pump-action hairspray bottle.

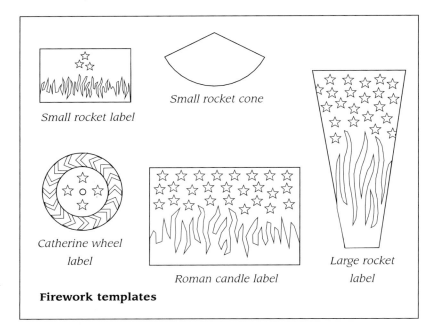

Small rocket label

Small rocket cone

Catherine wheel label

Roman candle label

Large rocket label

Firework templates

Forming the rocket

FIREWORKS

CATHERINE WHEEL: Photocopy the template onto thin card and colour the details with felt-tip pens. Glue the Catherine wheel piece onto card then glue fuses, made from tiny narrow rectangles of red paper, at intervals around the edge. Push a pin through the centre of the wheel and then into a fence or post.

SMALL ROCKETS: Photocopy the top cone and label templates onto thin card and colour the details with felt-tip pens. Cut a 7in x ½in piece of paper. Glue one short edge to the end of a cocktail stick. Wrap the piece round and round the cocktail stick, as shown in the diagram, and secure the end with glue. Cover the rocket head with the rocket label and add a fuse made from a tiny rectangle of red paper. Coil the rocket top into a cone shape and glue the straight edges together then glue the cone on top of the rocket.

LARGE ROCKET: Photocopy the template onto thin card and colour the details with felt-tip pens. Coil the rocket piece into a cone shape with a hole at the narrow end. Glue the straight edges together, push the cone onto a kebab stick and glue in position. Glue on a fuse made from a tiny rectangle of red paper.

ROMAN CANDLE: Photocopy the template onto thin card and colour the details with felt-tip pens. Cut a 1in length of 12mm diameter dowel. Smooth the cut edges with sandpaper and paint the piece red. Glue the label around the rocket and then glue a fuse on top made from a tiny rectangle of red paper.

GARDEN POND

The pond is the base of a circular plastic box set into a circular hole cut into the lawn.

BORDER: Cut a circle of thick card slightly larger than the top of the plastic box. Cut a hole in the centre leaving a ³/8in border. Score the card to make brick shapes then paint in brick colours.

FISH: Model goldfish from orange polymer clay. Once hardened, glue into the base.

REEDS: Cut reed shapes from green card, score each leaf down the middle and fold it in half. Finish with varnish, then glue into the pond.

WATER: Fill the pond with plastic water (available from craft shops and catalogues) or cover the top with a clear plastic sheet before gluing the circular brick piece in place.

CAT AND TORTOISE

The pets are modelled from polymer clay. Mix PVA glue with paint to add features such as the fur markings and tortoise shell details.

GNOMES

GNOMES: Model gnomes from polymer clay (see photograph below as a guide).

FISHING ROD: Cut a short length of cocktail stick and push it into the gnome before baking. Bend a hook from craft wire and tie it to the end of a piece of thread. Glue the other end of the thread to the rod.

Hallowe'en Trick or Treat

Many cultures have a special day when people dress up and let out the impish sides of their nature, with carnivals, music, tricks and costumes. Ancient winter festivals and religions were often associated with people donning masks and costumes to cavort around their

villages. In modern times, the festival of Hallowe'en has taken on the same role – children dress up in supernatural costumes of witches, wizards and ghosts to go around their neighbourhood to ask for sweets. And unfortunate neighbours who can't pay up may have impish tricks played upon them.

PROJECTS KEY

 1 witch costume
 2 wizard costume
 3 devil costume
 4 ghost costume
 5 cat costume
 6 pumpkin lanterns
 7 box of chocolates
 8 chocolate bar
 9 boiled sweets
10 candy twists
11 paper bags
12 window boxes (see page 125)
13 door furniture (see page 87)
14 railings (see page 88)

WORKING NOTES: The patterns in this section are for the details to bring a costume to life. Instructions are not provided for the larger items of clothing, as dolls will vary in size and shape (see Making Simple Dolls' Clothes, right). Felt is the best fabric for costumes – it won't fray so you don't need to sew hems, however a seam allowance is provided on the templates if you are using a fabric that frays.

To use templates, trace or photocopy the template onto paper, cut it out, draw around it on the material described and cut it out using an appropriate tool. Black dotted lines on templates mark fold lines while grey dotted lines show lines of sewing. PVA paper glue is suitable for all the card and paper projects.

WITCH COSTUME

HAT: Using the templates, cut a hat and brim piece from black card. Roll the hat into a cone and glue the straight edges together. Cut the circle from the centre of the brim and cut the lines radiating out to the circular dotted line. Fold the brim tabs along the dotted line and glue them inside the hat.

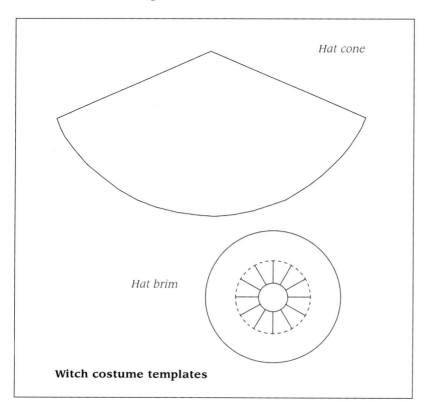

Hat cone

Hat brim

Witch costume templates

MAKING SIMPLE DOLLS' CLOTHES

• To make simple clothes for a doll, lay out the doll on a piece of felt with arms outstretched.
• Draw a T-shaped shirt, leaving a border around the edge to allow for movement.
• Cut out two T shapes and sew them together, enclosing the doll.
• You can make trousers in the same way. The devil and cat clothing in the photograph was also made in this way. The witch's cloak too was made using this technique, with a slightly extended T shape to make the skirt.

BROOM: Cut a 3½in length of 5mm diameter dowel, smoothing both ends with sandpaper. Glue thin twigs or dry pine needles to one end and bind them in place with thread.

HAIR: Cut a strip of green felt to fit around the doll's head. Glue the edge around the inside of the hat and when it is thoroughly dry, snip the free edge into hair strips.

WIZARD COSTUME

CLOAK: The cloak will fit a 3½in to 4½in doll. Using the template on page 169, cut a cloak piece from black fabric. (If you use felt, cut out the template along the grey dotted lines. Sew the felt pieces together with small stitches around the edge, and ignore instructions for hems.) Sew the shoulder sections together along the grey dotted lines. With the right side of the cloak facing outwards, fold under 3/16in of fabric around all the edges and sew in place. The grey line shows the finished shape and size of the cloak. Sew on a thread loop and a black bead fastener. Glue gold star sequins around the hem of the cloak.

HAT: Follow the instructions for the witch's hat above, but do not make a brim. Glue on star sequins.

WAND: Glue a star sequin to the end of a length of gold pipe cleaner.

Wizard cloak template

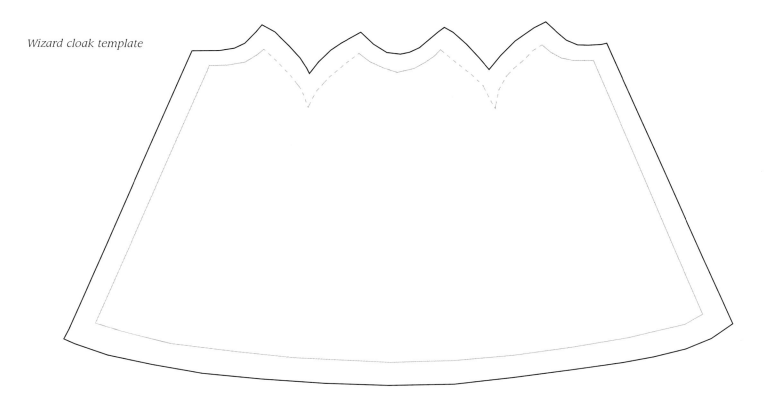

Fork

Mask

**Devil costume
templates**

DEVIL COSTUME

MASK: Photocopy the mask template onto red card. With a needle, make holes in the two positions marked. Cut out the mask then sew lengths of red thread through each hole to tie the mask on with, and secure with a knot.

FORKED STICK: Copy the fork template onto red card. Wrap the rectangular strip around the top of a kebab stick, holding it in place with glue. Paint the stick red.

TAIL: Twist two red pipe cleaners together. Cut two triangles from red felt and sew them together around the edge, trapping the end of the pipe cleaners inside. Sew the other end of the pipe cleaner to the back of the doll's clothes.

GHOST COSTUME

The costume is designed for a 4in doll. Using the template on page 170, cut two ghost costume pieces from white fabric. If you use felt, cut out the template along the grey dotted lines. Sew the felt pieces together with small stitches around the edge, and ignore instructions for hems. Draw eye and mouth shapes with a black ballpoint pen and cut them out.

With right sides of the fabric together, sew up the side seams and across the head seam along the grey dotted line. Snip into the seams in the positions marked on the template, taking care not to cut the stitching. Fold up a little

Ghost costume template

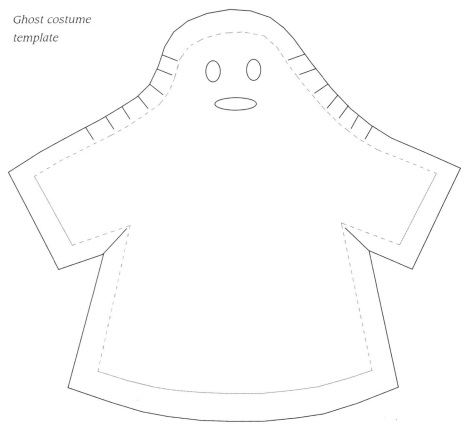

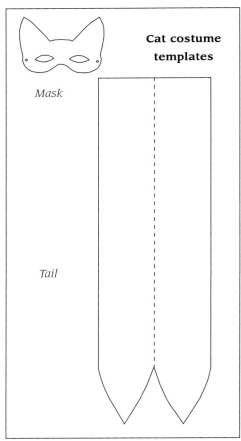

Cat costume templates

Mask

Tail

fabric at the cuffs and bottom of the skirt and hold in place with a few stitches. The grey line shows the finished size and shape of the costume. Turn the costume right side out.

CAT COSTUME

TAIL: Using the template, cut two tail pieces from black felt. Enclosing a 3¹/₂in length of pipe cleaner, sew the felt pieces together around the edge. Sew the end of the tail to the back of the doll's clothes and bend into shape.

MASK: Using the template, cut a cat mask from black card. With a needle, make holes in the positions marked, then cut out the mask. Sew black thread through each hole and secure with a knot.

PUMPKIN LANTERNS

UNLIT LANTERN: Model a pumpkin from orange polymer clay with a green stem. Use a knife to cut eyes, nose and mouth. Bake to harden following the manufacturer's instructions.

LIT LANTERN: Model a hollow lantern as above, with no lid. Once hardened, make a hole in each side with a needle and run a thread handle through the holes. Use a scalpel to cut the lantern in half (see diagram), then cut a hole in the base to fit a small dolls' house light fitting. Glue the pumpkin pieces back together around the light fitting. Model a lid from orange polymer clay.

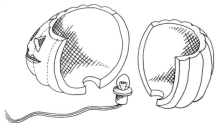

Cutting the pumpkin and fitting the light

BOX OF CHOCOLATES

BOX: Photocopy the box templates onto thin card and colour with felt-tip pens. Score along the lines indicated by the folding markers. Cut out the box, fold along the scored lines and glue tabs in position. Cut out the inner liner, fold down the sides and glue inside the box.

CHOCOLATES: Make chocolates from screwed up pieces of coloured foil and tiny lumps of brown polymer clay and glue in the positions marked on the lining.

CHOCOLATE BAR

Cut a $^5/_8$in x $^3/_8$in piece of cardboard and score deep lines to mark the chocolate segments. Paint the cardboard brown and when dry wrap in silver foil. Photocopy the wrapper template onto paper, colour with felt-tip pens and cut it out. Glue a wrapper around the chocolate bar.

BOILED SWEETS

Screw up small pieces of silver foil. Place one in the middle of a rectangle of coloured cellophane cut from a life-size sweet wrapper. Twist the ends together, enclosing the foil then trim to shape.

CANDY TWISTS

Roll out two thin sausages of pink and white polymer clay. Twist them together and cut into candy lengths. Bend into hooks and bake.

PAPER BAGS

Using the template, cut a bag from a brown paper bag. Fold along the dotted lines and glue the tabs in position. Fill with sweets and chocolates (described above).

Chocolate wrapper templates

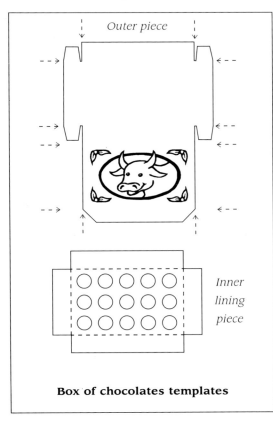

Box of chocolates templates

Outer piece

Inner lining piece

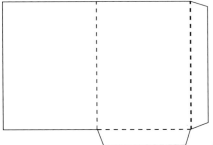

Paper bag template

Suppliers

There are so many suppliers of dolls' houses, accessories and specialist craft supplies that it is impossible to list them all here. Take a look at the advertisements and features in dolls' house magazines for more contacts, or look in your local press for shops and fairs in your area. A big dolls' house fair called Miniatura takes place twice a year at the Birmingham NEC, and features dolls' house makers, accessory makers, doll makers and materials suppliers. For details, contact: Miniatura, 41 Eastbourne Avenue, Birmingham B34 6AR, UK. Tel: (0121) 749 7330; Website: www.miniatura.co.uk.

NOTE: If you are calling any UK telephone numbers from outside the UK, replace the first '0' by the appropriate international dialling code.

MAGAZINES
(all take international subscriptions)

International Dolls' House News
Nexus Special Interests, Nexus House, Azalea Drive, Swanley, Kent BR8 8HU, UK. Tel: (01322) 660070

Dolls' House and Miniature Scene
EMF House, 5–7 Elm Park, Ferring, West Sussex BN12 5RN, UK. Tel: 01903 244900;
E-mail: dolltedemf@aol.com
Website: www.emfpublishing.co.uk

Dolls' House World
Avalon Court, Star Road, Partridge Green, West Sussex RH13 8RY, UK. Tel: (01403) 711511;
E-mail: ashdown@ashdown.co.uk
Website: www.dollshouseworld.com
Also publish Craft Club – a mail-order catalogue for craft supplies and dolls' house materials.

Dolls' House World
3150 State Line Road, North Road, OH 45052, USA.

Dollhouse Miniatures (formerly *Nutshell News*)
Kalmbach Miniatures Inc, 21027 Crossroads Circle, PO Box 1612, Waukesha WI 53187, USA. Tel: (414) 796 8776
Website:
www.kalmbach.com/dhm/miniatures.html

The Australian Miniaturist Magazine
PO Box 467, Carlingford, New South Wales 2118, Australia. Tel: (02) 9873 2442.

INDIVIDUAL MAKERS AND SUPPLIERS

When contacting the following suppliers, please enclose a stamped addressed envelope or IRC (International Reply Coupon, available from post offices).

Dolls
The two little boy dolls (pages 64–65 and back cover) are from: Margaret Davies,

Dandelion Dolls and Miniatures, 14 North East Terrace, Tewkesbury, Gloucestershire GL20 5NT, UK.

The servant dolls (pages 47 and 103), the cook (page 46), Henry VIII and Ann Boleyn (page 130), and the Georgian lady and gentleman (pages 30–31) are all available by mail order (catalogue on request) from: The Heritage Doll Company, 100c New Street, Brightlingsea, Essex CO7 0DJ, UK. Tel: (01206) 306201. For a catalogue send a SAE or IRC.

The girl and woman dolls (pages 6, 57 and front cover), the cricketer boy (front cover), and the Victorian gentleman (page 102), were all made by Katy Sue Dolls, with exclusive knitwear by Joyce Davison. Contact: Katy Sue Dolls, 1 Page Avenue, South Shields, Tyne and Wear NE34 0SY. Website: www.katy-sue-dolls.com

All other dolls appearing in this book are from the author's own collection.

Trees and Foliage
The oak tree and leaves (page 35) were made by Diane Harfield, who also runs workshops and supplies specialist leaf-cutting tools. For details, contact: Diane Harfield, Crickhollow, Berrington Drive, Bodenham, Hereford, UK.

The grass-effect paper (pages 24, 35, 130, 163), and the bushy lichen (pages 24, 35) are from 4D Model Shop (address below).

Furniture
The kitchen table and Welsh dresser (pages 7, 46–47, 57 and front cover) are from: Jane Newman miniatures, Linco Cottage, High Street, Horningsea, Cambridge CB5 9JG, UK.

The benches and barrel tables (page 27) are from: Carole Hilbert, The Miniature Pub, 47 Chapel Road, Bexleyheath, Kent DA7 4HW, UK.

The park bench (page 35) is a kit available from: Martin and Tricia Dare, 10 Mill Street, Puddletown, Dorchester DT2 8SH, UK.

Other Furniture and Accessory Suppliers
Dolls' House Emporium (shop and free mail-order catalogue): Victoria Road, Ripley, Derbyshire, DE5 3YD, UK. Tel: (01773) 514 424
E-mail: enquiries@dollshouse.co.uk

Bodo Hennig Puppenmobel (basic colourful wooden items; send four IRCs for catalogue): Bodo Hennig Puppenmobel GmbH, D-87499 Wildpoldsried, Germany.
Website: www.bodo-hennig.com

Motts Miniatures & Dollhouse Shop (website and mail-order catalogue, for which there is a charge): 7900 La Palma Avenue, Buena Park, CA 90620-1912, USA.
E-mail: info@mottsminis.com
Website: www.mottsminis.com

Acorn Crafts (mail-order catalogue, for which there is a charge), 139b High Street, Hythe, Kent CT21 5JL, UK. Tel: (01303) 265401
E-mail: info@acorn-crafts.demon.co.uk
Website: www.acorn-crafts.demon.co.uk

Craft Materials Suppliers (many are happy to do overseas mail order – check in advance)

Wood and Tools
Craft Supplies (shop and mail order for wood, tools and microtools): The Mill, Millers Dale, Nr. Buxton, Derbyshire SK17 8SN, UK.
Tel: (0800) 146417
E-mail: sales@craft-supplies.co.uk

Tiranti (specialist tools, knives, art materials and carving chisels, shops and mail order): 27 Warren Street, London W1P 5DG, UK; tel: (020) 7636 8565; or 70 High Street, Theale, Reading, Berkshire RG7 5AR, UK; tel: (01734) 302775.

Model Craft Woods (mail-order hardwoods for model-makers): 42 Wetlands Lane, Portishead, Bristol BS20 6RF, UK; tel: (01275) 818451.

Art and Craft Materials and Papers
Paperchase (two central shops stock a wide range of craft papers, including wood-effect, leather-effect and dolls' house brick papers; mail-order catalogue available for coloured writing paper): Paperchase (London branch), 213 Tottenham Court Road, London, UK. Tel: (020) 7467 6200. Paperchase (Manchester branch), St Mary's Gate, Manchester. Tel: (0161) 839 1500.

For art and craft supplies, glues, paints, brushes, etc, try local art and craft shops.

Fabrics, Beads, Threads and Notions
The Dollshouse Draper (mail-order fabrics, ribbons, lace and trimmings, buttons, beads, eyelets and buckles): PO Box 128, Lightcliffe, Halifax, West Yorkshire, HX3 8RN, UK. Tel: (01422) 201275.

Dainty Supplies Ltd (pipe cleaners, fur fabric, toy stuffing, felt, ribbons, beads and sequins; free mail-order catalogue): Dainty Supplies Ltd, 35 Phoenix Road, Crowther Industrial Estate (District 3), Washington NE38 0AD, UK. Tel: (0191) 416 7886.

The Bead Shop (bead specialists; shop and mail-order catalogue, for which there is a charge): 21a Tower Street, London WC2H 9NS, UK. Tel: (020) 8553 3240.

Beadworks Inc (bead specialists), 149 Water Street, Norwalk CT 06854, USA.

Beads (mail-order beads in wood, metal, glass and ceramic): Janet Cole, Perdiswell Cottage, Bilford Road, Worcestershire WR3 8QA, UK.

For beads and buttons, also take a look in department stores and local haberdashery outlets.

Specialist Miniature Components and Materials
Jojay Crafts (specialist dolls' house brass fixtures and fittings - shop and mail order); 17 Geneva Crescent, Darlington Co. Durham DL1 4JU, UK. Tel: (01451) 810081.

Borcraft Miniatures (wood, woodstrip, mouldings, turned legs and spindles by mail order): 8 Fairfax View, Scotland Lane, Horsforth, Leeds LS18 5SZ, UK.
Website: www.borcraft-miniatures.co.uk

4D Modelshop (specialist tools and materials for architectural and miniature modelling. Shop and mail order; catalogue available in print or on CD, for a charge): 151 City Road, London EC1V 1JH, UK. Tel: (020) 7253 1996;
E-mail: info@modelshop.demon.co.uk
Website: www.modelshop.co.uk

Index

Projects are listed in alphabetical order under bold categories. Page numbers in *italic* indicate photographs.

Books, magazines and albums
Book, exercise 65, 69
Book, leather bound 65, *117, 119*
Book, song 70, 72
Bookends *117*, 119
Catalogue, interiors 85, 88
Magazine, baseball 65, 69
Photograph album *117*, 118
Picture sources 118
Postcard album *117*, 118
Scrapbook *139*, 142
Sketch book *146*, 148
Sketch pad *146*, 148
Stamp album *117*, 118

Carpentry tools
Chisel 75, 77
Component box 74-75, 78
Electric drill 74-75, 77
Electric socket 74, 77
Glue 75, 78
Hammer 75, 77
Hand drill 74, 77
Knife 74, 77
Plane 75, 77
Protractor *146*, 149
Right angle, large 'L' 74, 77
Right angle, small 74, 77
Ruler, long 74-75, 77
Ruler, plastic 79, *146*, 149
Ruler, wooden 75, 77
Saw, coping 74, 76-77
Saw, tenon 74, 76
Saw, wood 74, 76
Sawdust 78
Set square, plastic *146*, 149
Spanner 75, 78
Tool board 74, 78
Tool box 74, 76

Clocks
1940s mantel clocks *108*, 110, *112*
1960s starburst clock *108*, 113
Alarm clock, wind-up *108*, 112, *113*

Art Deco clock *108*, 109
Clock pieces *108*, 113
Cuckoo clock, large *108*, 112, *112*
Cuckoo clock, small *108*, 112, *112*
Electric clock radio *108*, 112
Garden sundial *108*, 113, *130*
Grandfather clock *108*, 109
Octagonal station clock *108*, 111
School clock *108*, 111
Victorian carriage clock *108*, 110-111

Craft materials
See suppliers list 172

Decorating and DIY
Brush, paint 75, 89, 90, *90, 91, 138,* 141
Brush, stencil stippling 89, 92
Bucket 47, 61, 62, 89, *150*
Door handle 84-85, 87
Door keyplate 84-85, 87
Door knob 84-85, 87, *120, 167*
Door knocker 84-85, 87, *120, 167*
Paint chart 85, 88, *88*
Paint cloth 89, 90, *138-139*
Paint roller 89, 91, *91*
Paint spill 89, 90
Paint tin 74, 75, 85, 88, 89, 90, *90, 91*
Paint tray 89, 91, *91*
Plaster hod 89, *90*, 91
Plaster trowel 89, *90*, 91
Poster, interiors 85, 88
Sponge 89, 90
Stencil 89, 92
Stencil edging 89, 92
Stencil palette 89, 92
Stencilled chair 70, 89, *92, 92*
Step ladder 51, 89, 91, *91*
Tile box 85, 87-88
Tile chart 85, 87-88
Tiles 46-47, 85, 88
Wallpaper roll 89, 91, 92
Wallpaper, floral 84-85, 87, *114, 127*
Wallpaper, large floral 84, 87
Wallpaper, two-colour 70, 84-85, 87, *156, 159*

Dolls
See suppliers list 172

Dolls' clothes
Simple dolls' clothes 168

Floors and flooring
Bamboo matting 93, 94
Basket design parquet floor 30-31, 93, *98, 99, 133*
Brick tiled border 93, 96, *130*
Carpet 12-13, 27, 70, 84, 87, *108, 114, 156, 159*
Carpet samples book 84, 87
Complex geometric tiles 93, 94-95
Complex parquet floor 93, 98, *102-103, 127*
Cork tiles 93, 94
Crazy paving 93, 94, *163*
Embroidered canvas border 93, 94
Hessian squares 93, 94
Parquet border 93, 98
Simple kitchen tiles 46-47, 93, 96
Vinyl, patterned 84, 87
Wooden parquet floor 93, 97, *146*
Beech leaves *127*, 128, *128*

Flowers and plants
Black-eyed Susan *120, 124, 124, 126*
Blue auricula *121*, 124
Bouquet, bride's *127*, 129
Camellia *120*, 123
Carnation buttonhole *127*, 129
Cheese plant *133*, 134
Christmas tree *159*, 160-161
Chrysanthemum *121*, 123
Daisy 120, 124, *139*
Dried plants 27, 46, *120*, 125
Fern, small *114, 133*, 135
Floral swag *127*, 129
Flower arrangement *127*, 128, *128*
Flower in vase *108, 113, 114*, 115
Gift rose in a box *120*, 123
Ivy, green *127*, 129
Ivy, red *121*, 125
Palm, large-leafed *30, 102, 133*, 135

Palm, small-leafed *133*, 135
Petunia *120-121, 124, 125, 167*
Poppy *121, 125, 126*
Posy, bridesmaid's *127*, 129
Rabbit tracks plant *133*, 135
Reeds *163*, 166
Seedlings *133*, 136
Spider plant 30-31, *133*, 136
Sunflower *120*, 123
Topiary archway *130*, 131
Topiary cone tree, medium *120, 130*, 132
Topiary cone tree, small *120, 130*, 132
Topiary globe tree, small *121, 130*, 132
Topiary hedge *130*, 131
Topiary leaf texture *130*, 131
Topiary peacock *130*, 131
Topiary tiered tree, large *130*, 131
Topiary tiered tree, medium *121, 130*, 131, *131*
Vase, clay or bead 27, 44, *108, 113, 114, 115, 120, 150*, 151
White lily *120*, 123

Food and drink
Bread and pastry
Bread board 46, 49, *51*
Bread bun 39, 41, 43, 45
Bread knife 46, 51, 61, 63
Bread plait 57, 58
Loaf, brown 57, 58
Loaf, burnt 57, 58
Loaf, white 57, 58
Meat pie 35, 37, 38, 57
Sandwich 24, 26, 35, 38, *38, 108, 113, 154*, 157, *157*
Sliced loaf 46, 49, *51*

Cakes, biscuits and sweets
Battenburg cake *154*, 157, *157*
Birthday cake 57, 60, *154*
Biscuit (cookie) 35, 38, *38*, 57, 58, *150*
Biscuit tin *51*, 52
Boiled sweets (candy) *167*, 171
Bun, iced 35, 38, *38*, 57
Cake display board 57, 59, *127, 154, 159*
Candy (boiled sweets) *167*, 171

Candy twists *167*, 171
Chocolate bar *163*, 171, *167*
Chocolates, boxed *167*, 171
Christmas cake 57, 60, *159*
Cookie (biscuit) *35, 38*, 38,
    57, 58, *150*
Cookies on baking trays 57,
    58
Cookies on pastry board 57,
    58
Cracker tin *51*, 52
Cup cake, iced *154*, 157
Flour bag *51*, 57, 60, *60*
Flour shaker 57, 60, *60*
Jam tarts 57, 60
Macaroons in box *51*, 53-54
Mince pies 57, 60, *159*
Mincemeat 57, 60
Pastry 57, 60
Shortbread *35, 38*, 38, 57
Swiss roll *154*, 157, *157*
Wedding cake 57, 59, *127*

Cheese
Brie *31*, 34, *46*
Cheddar *31*, 34, 43, 44, 45, 46
Cheese wire *150*, 153
Edam *31*, 34, *46*
Goat's cheese *31*, 34, *46*
Red Leicester *31*, 34, *46*

Drinks
Bottles of pop *154*, 157
Champagne *24, 26, 51, 56, 56*
Cider bottle *42-43*, 44, 45, *51*,
    150, 152
Fruit punch *163*, 165, *165*
Ginger beer *35, 38*, 38
Milk bottles *51*, 54, *54*
Mug of tea *150*, 152
Stirrer *163*, 165, *165*
Tumbler *24, 26, 163*, 165,
    165, 159
Wine bottle *51, 56, 56, 138*,
    159
Wine rack *51, 56, 56, 138*

Fast food
Barbecue *163*, 164
Barbecue tongs *163*, 165
Burger, barbecued *163*, 165,
    165
Burger, in bun *39*, 41, *163*,
    165
Burger, uncooked *163*, 165

Chinese take-away *39*, 41
Fish and chips *39*, 41
Hot-dog *39*, 41, *163, 165*
Indian take-away *39*, 40
Kebab *163*, 165, *165*
Pie and chips *39*, 41
Pizza *39*, 40
Sausage *39*, 41, 43, 44, 45, 47,
    50, *154*, 157, *157, 163*, 165,
    165
Tomato sauce *39*, 41, *163*,
    165, *165*

Fruit
Apple *31, 35, 38*, 38, 43, 44,
    45, 46, *51*, 154
Banana *35, 38*, 38, *154*
Cucumber *163*, 165, *165*
Grapes *31, 46, 35, 38*, 38
Orange *31, 35, 38*, 38, *46*, 138
Pumpkin *46*, 49, *167, 169*,
    170, 170, *171*
Strawberries *24, 26, 26, 163*
Tomato *35, 38, 46*, 49, *154*,
    163, 165, *165*
Water melon *35, 38*, 38

Meat
Beef *47*, 50
Ham *47*, 50
Meat cleaver *47, 61*, 63
Pasty *35, 37, 38*, 57
Pie *35, 37, 38*, 57
Roast turkey *31, 47*, 50, *51*
Roasting tin *47*, 50, *51*
Sausage on stick *154*, 157,
    157
Sausage roll *35, 37, 38*, 57
Sausage, barbecued *163*, 165,
    165
Sausage, uncooked *47*, 50,
    163, 165, *165*

Vegetables
Aubergine (egg plant) *47*, 49
Cabbage *46*, 49, *51*, 54
Carrot, cooked *31*, 34
Carrot, raw *46*, 43, 44, 45, 49,
    51
Cauliflower *46*, 49
Cucumber *163*, 165, *165*
Garlic *46*, 49, *51*
Mushroom *46-47*, 49
Parsnip *43*, 44, 45, *47*, 49
Peas *31*, 34

Pepper (capsicum) *39, 40, 47*,
    49, *51*
Potato *31*, 43, 44, 45, 46, 49,
    51, 53
Pumpkin *46*, 49, *167, 169*,
    170, 170, *171*
Snow peas *30*, 34
Sprouts *31*, 34
Tinned *51*, 52
Tomato *35, 38, 46*, 49, *154*,
    163, 165, *165*
Vegetable knife *46, 61*, 63

Other
Butter 57, 59, *60*
Dried herbs *46, 51*, 53
Egg rack *46*, 49
Egg, fried *47*, 49
Egg, whole *46*, 49, 57, *60*
Herb jar *46*, 49, *51*
Picnic blanket *35, 37*, 38
Picnic hamper *35, 36-37*, 38
Salad *163*, 165, *165*
Saucepan *47*, 50
Seeds *51, 56*, 57, 60, *60*
Spaghetti *51*, 53
Spaghetti jar *51*, 53
Spice jar *46*, 49, *51*, 57, 60
Toasting fork *43*, 45

Furniture
See suppliers list *172*

Gardening
Braid flower pot *120*, 126,
    126, 139
Fence, garden *85*, 88, *163*
Fence, picket *85*, 88
Flower basket *121, 126*, 126
Flower basket, hanging *122*,
    125, *125*
Garden fork, large *133*, 137
Garden fork, small *133*, 137
Garden gnome *163*, 166, *166*
Garden pond *163*, 166
Garden spade *133*, 137
Garden tub, clay *150*, 152
Gardening gloves *133*, 137
Plant pot *30-31, 102, 114*,
    120-121, 130, 133, 150, 151
Plant stand *30*, 34, *133*
Seed packet *133*, 137
Seed tray *133*, 136
Sundial *108*, 113, *130*
Tall tub, card *120-121*, 126

Trowel *133*, 137
Trug *46*, 50, *51*
Window box, clay *150*, 152
Window box, wooden *120-*
    121, 125, *126, 167*

Kitchen utensils
Chopping board *46-47*, 57,
    61, 63
Cork mat *47, 61*, 63
Knife, bread *46, 51, 61*, 63
Knife, kitchen *46, 61*, 63
Knife, meat cleaver *47, 61*, 63
Knife, vegetable *46, 61*, 63
Pastry board 57, 58, *60*
Rolling pin 57, *61*, 63
Spatula *46*, 57, *61*, 63
Spoon, wooden *46-47*, 57, *61*,
    63
Tiled pot stand *47, 61*, 63
Wire whisk *46*, 57, *61*, 63

Miscellaneous
Ashtray *27, 29, 150*
Canary in cage *138*, 141
Cat *46, 114, 163*, 166
Cigar *27*, 29
Envelope *103, 107, 117*, 118
Fire grate *27, 42*, 44-45
Flowered headband *70*, 73
Glowing coals *42*, 45, *163*,
    164
Hotel labels *102*, 107
Letters (mail) *103, 107, 117*,
    118
Newspaper 9, *27, 29, 108*
Oil can *108*, 113, *113*
Pedestal *102, 108*, 113, *127*,
    128, *130*
Pestle and mortar *51*, 53
Pigeon *24, 35, 38*, 38
Radio *150*, 153
Railings *35, 85*, 88, *120-121*,
    167
Serving trolley *31*, 34, *103*
Side table, circular *79, 83, 83*,
    114, 127, 133, 138
Silver tray *103*, 107, *107*
Skull *138*, 142
Tapers *42*, 45
Tea tray *108*, 113, *113*
Tobacco pouch *43*, 45
Tortoise *163*, 165, 166
Travel bag *102*, 107
Travel trunk *102*, 106

TV remote-control unit *39*, 41
Umbrella *102*, 107
Walking stick *102*, 107, *107*

Music
Blank manuscript music *143*, 144
Drum, African tribal *102*, 105, *105*
Drum, toy or army *143*, 145, *159*
Guitar *70*, 73
Lute *143*, 145
Metronome *133*, *143*, 144
Music bag *133*, *143*, 144
Music stand *133*, *143*, 144
Poster, music *70*, 73
Record *70*, 71
Record player *70*, 71
Recorder *133*, *143*, 145
Sheet music *143*, 144, *133*, *138*
Song book *70*, 72
Triangle *143*, 145
Xylophone *143*, 145

Painting and drawing
Canvas, painted *138-139*, 141
Canvas, plain *138-139*, 141
Children's colouring pictures *146*, 148
Drawing board *146*, 149
Drawing board stool *146*, 149
Easel *138-139*, 141
Inkwell *143*, 144, *138*
Paint brush *75*, *89*, 90, *90*, *91*, *138*, 141
Paint cloth *89*, 90, *138-139*
Paint tin *74*, *75*, *85*, *88*, *89*, 90, *90*, *91*
Paint tin, artist's travelling set *138*, 141
Paint tubes *138*, 141
Painting smock *138-139*, 142
Palette *138*, 141, *89*, *92*
Paper, coloured *146*, 147
Paper, watercolour *139*, 142
Pastel *79*, *146*, 148
Pencil *64-65*, *75*, *79*, 82, *146*, 148
Pencil crayon *146*, 148
Picture framing suggestions 119
Picture sources 118

Portfolio, decorative *146*, 147
Portfolio, plain *139*, 142
Protractor *146*, 149
Quill pen *143*, 144, *138*
Ruler, long *74-75*, 77
Ruler, plastic *79*, *146*, 149
Ruler, wooden *75*, 77
Set square, plastic *146*, 149
Sketch book *146*, 148
Sketch pad *146*, 148
Sketches *138*, *146*, 148
Still-life arrangement *138*, 142

Pictures, ornaments and displays
Bead display *114*, 116
Butterfly display *103*, 105
Button display *114*, 116
Certificate *65*, 68
Display case *102*, 106
Doughcraft heart and ring *54*, *114*, 115
Egg collection *117*, 118
Egyptian mask *102*, 105
Flower in bead vase *108*, *113*, *114*, 115
Garden gnome *163*, *166*, *166*
Hand bell *114*, 116
Ivory elephants *103*, 107
Map *102*, 105
Mask, African tribal *103*, 105
Mask, animal *154*, 158, *167*, 170
Medals *65*, 68
Mirror, Art Nouveau *114*, 115
Mirror, teddy bear *114*, 116
Photograph album *117*, 118
Photograph frame, hinged *114*, 116
Photograph frame, oval *114*, 116
Picture *12-13*, *27*, *30*, *46*, *57*, *64*, *70*, *102-103*, *114*, *117*, *118-119*, *138-139*, *146*, *150*, *154*
Picture frame, Art Deco *114*, 116
Picture frame, ornate *27*, *30*, *119*, *138-139*
Picture frame, plain *12-13*, *46*, *57*, *64*, *70*, *102-103*, *114*, *117*, *118-119*, *146*, *150*, *154*
Picture framing suggestions 119
Picture sources 118

Picture, three-dimensional *114*, 116
Pinboard *64-65*, 117, 119
Postcard album *117*, 118
Rock collection *103*, 106
Scrapbook *139*, 142
Shell collection *102*, 106
Shell, decorative coil *114*, 115
Shell, glitter *114*, 115
Shield, African tribal *103*, 105
Soccer cards *64*, *117*, 119
Spear, African tribal *103*, 105
Staffordshire dogs *114*, 115
Stone, polished *114*, 116
Wooden doll *114*, 115

Pottery projects
Ashtray *27*, 29, *150*
Bowl *24*, *30-31*, *46*, *57*, *60*, *150*, 151
Casserole dish *46*, *57*, *150*, 152
Cider bottle *42-43*, 44, 45, *51*, *150*, 152
Clay pipe *42-43*, 45
Clay tools *150*, 153
Cup *35*, 38, *46*, *108*, *113*, *150*, 152
Garden tub, clay *150*, 152
Jug, milk *57*, 59, *60*, *150*, 152
Jug, plain *35*, 38, *43*, *51*, *150*, 152
Mixing bowl *46*, 50, *57*, *150*, 151
Mug *150*, 152
Plate, decorative gold *117*, 119
Plate, floral *117*, 118-119
Plate, rimmed *46*, *117*, 119, *150*, 151
Pot, coil *150*, 153
Pot, decorative *46*, *51*, *57*, *120*, *133*, *150*, 151
Pot, lidded *51*, *150*, 151
Pot, plant *30-31*, *102*, *114*, *120-121*, *130*, *133*, *150*, 151
Pot, rimmed *27*, *30*, *46-47*, *57*, *120*, *150*, 151
Saucer *108*, *113*, *150*, 151
Sculpture, clay *150*, 153
Surface decorations 151
Teapot *108*, *113*, *150*, 152
Vase, clay *27*, *44*, *108*, *113*, *114*, 115, *120*, *150*, *151*
Window box, clay *150*, 152

Sewing, knitting and textiles
Bedspread *70*, 73
Blind *99*, 101
Cards of buttons *79*, *83*, 83
Curtain hanging loops *99*, 100
Curtain hanging rings *99*, 100
Curtain pole, curled *84*, 87
Curtain pole, fleur-de-lis *84*, 87, *99*
Curtain pole, wooden *84*, 87, *99*
Curtain poles, attaching 87, 100
Curtain tieback, fabric *99*, *100*, 101
Curtain tieback, tasselled *99*, *100*, 101
Curtains *99*, 100
Embroidery frame *79*, 82
Fabric roll *99*, 101, *101*
Fabric samples box *79*, *81*, 81, *99*
Fabric swatch *99*, 101
Knitting bag *79*, 82
Knitting pattern *79*, 82
Knitting yarn *79*, 82
Needle book *79*, *83*, 83
Patchwork bed cover *13*, *79*, 81
Patchwork cushion *79*, 80, *80*
Patchwork templates *79*, 81
Sewing basket *79*, *83*, *83*
Spools of ribbon and braid *99*, 101

Special occasions
Birthday
Balloons *154*, 157
Birthday cards *155*, 158
Parcels and presents *155*, 158
Streamers 157
Wrapping paper *155*, 158

Christmas
Advent calendar *159*, 160
Baubles *159*, 161
Calendar *159*, 160
Candle holder *159*, 160
Christmas cake *57*, 60, *159*
Christmas cards *159*, 160
Christmas tree *159*, 160-161
Christmas tree fairy *159*, 160
Crackers *159*, 161-162
Mince pies *57*, 60, *159*

Mincemeat *57, 60*
Paper chain *159, 160*
Parcels and presents *159, 161*
Santa beard *159, 162*
Santa boots *159, 162*
Santa hat *159, 162*
Santa mittens *159, 162*
Tinsel wreath *159, 160*
Wrapping paper *159, 161*

Fireworks
Catherine wheel *163, 166*
Rocket, large *163, 166*
Rocket, small *163, 166*
Roman candle *163, 166*

Hallowe'en
Cat costume *167, 170*
Devil costume *167, 169*
Devil's forked stick *167, 169*
Ghost costume *167, 169-170, 170*
Pumpkin lantern *167, 169, 170, 170-171, 171*
Witch costume *167, 168*
Witch's broom *167, 168*
Wizard costume *167, 168*
Wizard's wand *167, 168*

Sports equipment
Baseball *65, 68*
Baseball bat *65, 68*
Certificate *65, 68*
Cricket bails *64, 67*
Cricket ball *64, 67*
Cricket bat *64, 68*
Cricket pads *64, 68*
Cricket stumps *64, 67*
Hockey stick and ball *65, 68*
Medals *65, 68*
Rugby ball *64, 68*
Soccer ball *65, 69*
Soccer hat *65, 69*
Soccer scarf *65, 69*
Sports bag *64, 67*
Tennis racket *64, 67*
Trophy *65, 68*

Storage
Bread bin *51, 54*
Cardboard box (carton) *51, 55, 75, 89*
Cardboard tray *46-47, 51, 55*
Carton (cardboard box) *51, 55, 75, 89*

Cereal packet *51, 53*
Fabric sack *51, 56*
Fabric samples box *79, 81, 81, 99*
Glass jar *51, 53*
Milk crate *51, 54, 54*
Overhead hanging rack *46, 49*
Paper bag *167, 171*
Paper sack *46, 51, 56*
Shelves *133, 150, 153*
Tool board *74, 78*
Toy chest *13, 16, 133*
Trug *46, 50, 51*
Trunk *102, 106*
Wooden crate *51, 54, 54*

Tableware
Bowl *24, 30-31, 46, 57, 60, 150, 151*
Candle snuffer *30-31, 33*
Candlestick *30-31, 33, 42-43, 44, 159, 160*
Cutlery *30-31, 33*
Fork, plastic *163, 165, 165*
Fork, table *30-31, 33*
Fruit stand *31, 34*
Goblet *30-31, 33, 46*
Knife, bread *46, 51, 61, 63*
Knife, table *30-31, 33*
Knife, Tudor *43, 45, 45*
Leather tankard *27, 42-43, 44, 45*
Napkins *30-31, 33*
Place mats *30-31, 33*
Place names *30-31, 33*
Plate, decorative gold *117, 119*
Plate, floral *117, 118-119*
Plate, paper *24, 35, 36, 108, 154-155, 163, 165, 165*
Plate, rimmed *46, 117, 119, 150, 151*
Plate, silver *30-31, 33*
Plate, wooden *42-43, 44*
Serving dish, covered *31, 33*
Serving dish, oval *30-31, 34*
Spoon, serving *30-31, 33*
Spoon, table *30-31, 33*
Spoon, wooden *46-47, 57, 61, 63*
Wooden platter *42-43, 44*

Techniques and materials
Beads and buttons 11
Card, cardboard and paper 10-11

Cutting tools 10
Glues and gluing 10
Paints and painting 10
Photocopying 8-9
Polymer clay 11
Safety 8
Scaling 8-9
Suppliers 172
Templates 9
Wire 11
Wood 10

Toys and games
Backgammon *21, 22, 27*
Boomerang *65, 69*
Boule *24, 26*
Building blocks *12, 15*
Card table *27, 28*
Catapult *64, 68*
Checkers (draughts) *21, 23*
Chess *21, 23, 23, 27*
Costumes *154-155, 157, 158, 159, 162, 167, 168-170*
Croquet *24, 25, 25*
Croquet box *24, 25, 25*
Darts *27, 28*
Darts board *27, 28*
Doll, rag doll *13, 19, 155*
Doll, rag doll rabbit *13, 20, 155*
Doll, teddy bear dressing *155, 158*
Doll, wooden *114, 115*
Dolls' house *12, 18, 155*
Dominoes *27, 29*
Draughts (checkers) *21, 23*
Elephant on wheels *12, 20, 154*
Hobby horse *13, 17, 154*
Jigsaw *21, 23*
Kite *35, 36*
Lorry *12, 15*
Mobile *12, 20*
Model biplane *64, 69*
Pin the tail on the donkey *155, 157*
Playing cards *27, 28*
Pool balls *27, 29*
Pool chalk *27, 29*
Pool cue *27, 28*
Pool cue stand *27, 28-29*
Pool triangle *27, 29*
Pull-along building blocks box *12, 15*
Pull-along train *12, 15, 159*

Quoits *24, 25, 26*
Rocking horse *12, 16-17*
Rocking horse plans *75, 78*
Rocking horse project pieces *75, 78*
Sailing Boat *12, 16*
Scrabble *21, 22, 22*
Skipping rope *13, 16*
Skittles *24, 26, 26*
Snakes & ladders *21, 23*
Solitaire *27, 29*
Teddy bear, modern *70, 72*
Teddy bear, old-fashioned *13, 19, 64, 155*
Tiny houses *12, 16*
Tiny road pieces *12, 16*
Tiny trees *12, 16*
Toy chest *13, 16, 133*

Washing and cleaning
Broom, besom *51, 167, 168*
Broom, yard *47, 61, 62*
Bucket *47, 61, 62, 89, 150*
Carpet beater *47, 61, 63*
Dustbin (trash can) *47, 51, 61, 63, 150*
Dustpan and brush *61, 62, 108*
Feather duster *61, 62, 114*
Floor cloth *47, 61, 62*
Mop *47, 61, 62*
Pegs *47, 61, 62*
Soap *47, 61, 62*
Sponge *89, 90*
Tea towel *47, 57, 61, 62*
Tea towel rack *47, 50*
Washboard *47, 61, 62*
Washing line *47, 61, 62*